THE MEANING OF
TEA

For Brenda Knight,
in tea, poetry,
and friendship,

Phil Cousineau

North Beach, USA
July 2009

THE MEANING OF
TEA

A TEA INSPIRED JOURNEY

Scott Chamberlin Hoyt

Edited with Commentary by
Phil Cousineau

TALKING LEAVES PRESS
NEW YORK CITY
2009

Talking Leaves Press
A Division of Tea Dragon Films
70-A Greenwich Avenue
New York, NY 10011
www.teadragonfilms.com
info@teadragonfilms.com

"Top 20 Tea Definitions" reprinted with permission from: *James Norwood Pratt's Tea Dictionary* (Preliminary Edition) Produced & Published by: Devan Shah & Ravi Sutodiya for Tea Society.

Cover design by Deborah Dutton
Photography by Gordon Arkenberg and Scott Chamberlin Hoyt
Frontispiece by Kathryn B. Kerr
Typeset in Sabon text and Uppsala display

ISBN: 978-0-615-20442-0

Library of Congress Control Number: 2009926986

First Printing: Spring 2009

Printed in Canada

Environmental Benefits Statement
Talking Leaves Press saved the following resources by printing the pages of this book on chlorine free paper made with 100% post-consumer waste.

Trees	Water	Energy	Solid Waste	Greenhouse Gases
19 Fully Grown	6,991 Gallons	13 Million BTUs	898 Pounds	1,684 Pounds

Calculations based on research by Environmental Defense and the Paper Task Force. Manufactured at Friesens Corporation.

THIS BOOK IS DEDICATED TO THE
GREAT TEA MASTERS WHO MADE
POSSIBLE TODAY'S CUP OF TEA.

To see a world in a grain of sand
And a heaven in a wild flower,
Hold infinity in the palm of your hand
And eternity in an hour.

—WILLIAM BLAKE

CONTENTS

THE THIRD CUP · AMERICA

THE FOURTH CUP · JAPAN

THE FIFTH CUP · FRANCE

THE SIXTH CUP · ENGLAND AND IRELAND

SONG OF TEA

LU TONG

—►—►—◄—◄—

The first drink sleekly moistened my lips and throat;
the second banished my loneliness;
the third expelled the dourness from my mind;
the fourth broke me out in a light perspiration;
the fifth bathed every atom of my being;
the sixth lifted me higher to kinship with the immortals;
the seventh is the utmost I can drink.

—LU TONG, TANG DYNASTY
TRANSLATED BY JOHN BLOFELD,
The Chinese Art of Tea

—►—►—◄—◄—

The Infinite Moment

Phil Cousineau

The eminent scholar John Blofeld's translation of Lu Tong's beloved poem about seven cups of tea provides this book with a glorious metaphor. On the wings of that mythic number, this book proceeds in seven cups, or parts: India, Morocco, USA, Japan, France, Ireland and England, and Taiwan. This structure reflects and honors the seven locations where the interviews took place, and together they suggest stages in an exhilarating journey in the discovery of the elusive meaning of tea.

Naturally, it is edifying to learn about the history of tea, which has been told and retold in terms of botany, sociology, psychology, metaphysics, politics, and business. Some modern scholars, such as Liu Tong, have even argued that the tea business has been so powerful that it actually changed the course of history, as evidenced by the Tea-Opium Wars in China and the Boston Tea Party.

In fact, the world's bookshelves groan under the weight of hundreds of books that present myriad facts about the famous *Camellia sinensis* plant that has blessed history. For instance, historians believe tea was discovered in China more than 5,000 years ago. The first historical record of tea appeared in *Erh Ya*, a Chinese dictionary dating back to 350 BCE. Four billion cups a day are sipped around the world, and there are over 5,000 varietals grown in more than a dozen countries. Tea contains over 400 chemical compounds, and the caffeine in plants such as tea may very well be nature's own insecticide.

In the realm of venerable legend it was said in ancient China that there were 62,000 known benefits in the plant world, but over time, 40,000 of them were lost. That left 22,000 benefits that could be attributed to a single plant, which happens to be tea. The raft of remaining benefits included the elimination of fatigue, the alleviation of stress, the lifting of energy, the warding off of disease, the gifts of harmony and tranquility, fraternity and focus, and countless more attributes, giving rise to one of its most popular epithets, "the lusty leaf."

Still, numbers only tell the outer story. The inner story is always where meaning dwells, and is best told personally, through the reflections of people whose lives have been devoted to tea. Thus, one question threads this book together: "What does tea mean to you?" What does it mean to grow it, sell it, drink it, cut business deals, or arrange marriages and funerals over it? What is it that *moves* people to bare their souls over a cup of tea? By *meaning,* I mean its value, its virtue, its inner significance, its intent, and its purpose.

Exploring this mystery dimension of tea has been a daunting task. Tea does not easily surrender its secrets. But, as Lu Tong subtly suggested, the more tea you drink, the more relaxed, serene, companionable, healthy, patient, and wise (if the gods allow) you become.

Similarly, over the course of more than fifty interviews from Taiwan to India, Ireland to Tea, South Dakota, the meaning of tea unfolds in these pages one sip, one cup, one person, at a time. The more you read here, the more you will come to appreciate the "22,000 benefits" of tea.

A favorite Chinese proverb says, "A tree has its roots, a stream its source." So it is with this book. Its roots and its source lie in the curiosity of Scott Chamberlin Hoyt, whose film, *The Meaning of Tea,* sparked the creation of this book. For most of his life, he has been a devoted tea drinker. When traveling widely abroad, he heard scores of tributes to the world's most popular beverage, and began to wonder if there was anything universal about tea and what ultimate value and purpose it might serve. So, in 2006, he embarked on a quest with a documentary film crew to explore the idea of tea as a potentially underutilized salve for the modern world. Along the way he interviewed a wide variety of people about what tea meant to them in their personal, business, social, and spiritual lives.

On the long and winding road of making the film, the crew gathered one hundred and twenty hours of footage. From this treasure trove they created an inspiring and informative seventy-four-minute film, which left a wealth of wonderful material "in the vault." This book is the result of sifting through more than two thousand pages of transcripts and gleaning from them the most meaningful passages from that hard-won footage to form a book that contains an unprecedented range of voices from tea pickers and plantation owners to street sellers, teapot makers, tea tasters, plus a few eloquent tea scholars.

The choir of voices here chimes in on some other familiar aspects of tea discussed above, and its uncanny ability to strengthen one's spirituality and even gladden the heart.

Beyond these valuable reminders of tea's remarkable powers, this collection of interviews lends new perspectives on the way we regard and drink tea. Questions during the filming opened up rarely discussed aspects of the tea world, such as the notion that it is a gift of the gods, a friend of the muses, infused with spiritual energy, and that it smoothes the path of conversation.

Tea is all of these things and more—or less? This delicious ambiguity was voiced best by the great seventeenth-century Japanese tea master Sen no Rikyu, who described his way of performing tea ceremony as *Wabicha*, or "the tea of simplicity." He wrote:

Tea is nothing but this:
First you heat the water.
Then you make the tea.
Then you drink it properly.
That is all you need to know.

More recently, San Francisco tea entrepreneur Roy Fong said, in one of the finest interviews here, that the wisdom of tea is inexhaustible. "The beauty of it," he says, "is that it allows you to directly communicate with nature." He adds that if you take the time and trouble to learn about the long journey that the tea made to reach you—the soil, the growing, the shipping, the refining—then you will better experience its complexity, perhaps even appreciate what he calls "the spirits of tea." This depth dimension of respect for tea, he promises, repays us with infinite dividends. "Then you will understand a little bit more about the true meaning of life."

Since the mid-1990s, tea has played a vital role in what might be called the "Slow Life" movement in Europe and the United States, where the cult of speed has driven many to the edge of exhaustion. Untold millions of people are realizing that more is not always more; sometimes *less is more*, if it means we are able to savor rather than gorge on life. In this spirit, tea offers more than mere liquid refreshment. It provides a daily opportunity to enrich our lives by relishing our time, which can lead to more energy, efficiency, and even happiness.

Perhaps that is what Thich Nhat Hanh, the Cambodian Buddhist monk, meant when he said, "We are most real when we are drinking tea."

The suggestion of the deeper meaning of tea is beautifully revealed by the following passage from the worldwide bestseller, *Three Cups of Tea*. A Balti tribesman, in Pakistan, is addressing the author, Greg Mortenson, who has returned there to build schools for the people who helped save his life:

> The first time you share tea with a Balti, you are a stranger. The second time you take tea, you are an honored guest. The third time you share a cup of tea, you become family, and for our family, we are prepared to do anything, even die. Doctor Greg, you must take time to share three cups of tea. We may be uneducated. But we are not stupid. We have lived and survived here for a long time.

And now it is time to have a cup of tea and enjoy the following interviews, which are offered to the reader in that spirit of celebration. Together, they serve as a reminder that it is possible for each of us to find the tea that speaks to us, the tea that makes us calmer, more compassionate, more observant, and more respectful of the natural world from which we came.

If we do, we may come to understand what was meant by Ogata Ihachi's eighteenth mysterious inscription on the side of his tea bowl: "In tranquility, the universe is great." For many, the meaning of tea and the meaning of peace in our own lives converge there at the bottom of the teacup as one.

Or as the Beatles sang, so simply, in "All Too Much":

"Show me that I'm everywhere
And get me home for tea"

—PHIL COUSINEAU
SAN FRANCISCO, MAY 2008

INTRODUCTION
My Tea Journey

Scott Chamberlin Hoyt

*I was but a meager presence high up near the heavens
on this earth
I was plucked away from my roots
Carried by winds of trade on a journey through time.
An uncertain journey to the lands of strange people
and customs*

*I belong to the mountains where I share peace with the heavens
The land of the people, who have given my presence meaning,
With the gifts of their real, adventurous, magnificent
lives and stories*

*I long for this meaning, everywhere.
I bring with me the joy of the present
So sit down for a conversation
Let peace be upon you
Let it accentuate the meaning of life
Let it etch the meaning of life in your mind.
If your heart warms and races,
Your mind recites words, conjures up fond memories
You have discovered me,
We are of the earth
This is the meaning of tea.*

—"The Meaning of Tea" by E. Razzaghi

L ooking back on the pages of this book, I find myself relearning and remembering the myriad essentials of tea in all its wonder. It occurs to me now that while my experience with tea was the catalyst that moved me to learn more about its historical and medical facts, as found in books and online, I realize more and more that the essential meaning of tea resides in the life of tea.

Here is how my life took a turn toward tea. I wanted to create something that would help shift the world's consciousness, as tea has shifted mine. Tea brings me to a place and time where my heart and mind are evenly balanced. In this spirit, I write these words while drinking tea, to initiate this conversation once again, at the start of this companion book to the film *The Meaning of Tea.*

In making a film about tea, the simple truth is that I wished to generate a stronger interest in tea in a modern world that is losing its connection to the earth. I wished for more people to take more time to experience a gentle film that would cause them to thirst for a cup of tea. By giving a little something to our tiny planet, I hope to find a way for the conversation to flow in a more local, intercultural direction: *person-to-person* versus the *global-mass-cultural*, which, paradoxically, may dilute our truer connections.

Before you read further, I invite you to skip around the different countries and interviews in this book. Feel free to choose your own path in what I hope will be an inspiring journey. Being of a curious mind, fueled by tea, I often find myself reading books from the inside out, or by hopping around the pages—such is the joy of the tea life. This companion book to *The Meaning of Tea* is meant to be read as though we were in conversation. I invite you to allow your mind to wander. Please do return later to where you are now, and read on.

THE OLD MAN PULLING RADISHES POINTED THE WAY WITH A RADISH

You might think of *The Meaning of Tea* as a directional offering—an antidote to our "brave new [and increasingly overdeveloped] world," caught up in the newest technologies. I suppose the seven cups of tea presented in this book are granted just as the rare and the precious life we humans have received was given by simply being born. The wisest among us have conveyed in many great teachings that the divine is within each of us—that which may be realized, if we see and listen reverently—from time to time. There is wisdom reborn in each and every moment: birth, death, and rebirth again. Tea brings nature to society in the withering and agony of the leaves. We return to this inherent truth in nature from which we originate. Tea experience is shared in innumerable ways, in the immeasurable life of tea.

Without actually realizing it, I started following the path of tea in April of 1953, when I was born. I never had much of a sweet tooth even when toothless: I enjoyed the bitter and sour tastes more, much as my mother preferred. We savored sparkling water with lemon over soda pop and simple tea, sometimes hot, and usually cold in summertime. Meaningful conversations began in the earliest years of my life with my younger sister, my parents, and my mother's parents.

This earlier, more gentle, more harmonious period of my life changed dramatically and suddenly on July 9, 1958. Now that it is fifty years later, I can see more clearly how walking the path of tea often requires that even while walking forward, one sometimes must walk backward. Staying on that path can sometimes be quite challenging and disquieting.

MY FIRST DAY AT "WORK": JULY 9, 1958

I was perched on top of the weathered wooden stairs that led down to a quiet lane, waiting patiently, dressed in my navy blue sailor suit. The ocean behind the house was calm, but I could still hear the waves at low tide whispering along the sand. My crisp navy uniform felt stiff compared to the bright green bathing suit I was accustomed to wearing in those cozy weeks of summer. But now I was on the brink of an oceanic journey—an experience unlike anything my five-year-old self could have dreamed. That day's events would abruptly change the quiet reality of my beautiful life in a single afternoon.

Grandfather's limo pulled up. The man behind the wheel told me that he had come to take me to see my father. Nothing seemed to match the reality of that moment. My awareness was floating in the hazy salt air of morning, waiting for the sun to shine. Soon, I was sitting in the springy leather seat of a black Cadillac sedan, wondering if I was going to become carsick. But my apprehension then melded into a vague sensation of wonder and acceptance after an easy conversation with Lloyd, the driver.

When we arrived, Father invited me to have some vanilla ice cream. I was happy to please him and glad to enjoy dessert without the meal. I was placed at the head of a table with twenty old men, a good forty years older than my baby-faced twenty-something-year-old father. They were all quite serious, quite somber. My grandfather was not smiling. I could sense him from a distance at the far end of the table. As for me and the creamy ice cream, its vanilla flavor seemed to taste better when I closed my eyes. Then I learned why I had been brought there that day.

This was to be, unofficially, my first day at "work." I was to participate in a ground-breaking ceremony for a manufacturing plant hosted by my grandfather and Governor Meyner of New Jersey. This was the "promised land." Here, a plant would be built for the first "non-addicting" tranquilizing pharmaceutical drug. The generic drug called

meprobamate was going to be known by a name that people could remember: Miltown, named after a small nearby New Jersey town. To "miltown" meant to *relax*. Doctors could prescribe a drug that alleviated the anxiety of modern life by enabling their patients to pass through life's harsh realities in 1950s America by "miltowning it."

There I was, family icon, grandson of the granddaddy of tranquility. Hours before this momentous event, all I had known about shovels was that they were something I could use for building sand castles and unearthing buried treasure. But I soon felt the wonderment of digging turn to sadness. The shovel in my hands would fill my body with fatigue; to dig earth in a muddy field where perhaps an ancient grove of trees once stood would not wash in my five-year-old imagination, for inwardly I somehow sensed the disappearance of nature. The impending lack of leaf and vine seemed to check my spirit at the gate.

But the main event seemed so straightforward to everyone else standing in the field that afternoon. I asked my father why I was helping to dig the earth for a new "plant" when there wasn't a single plant in sight? Why this blank expanse and this all-so-important ritual-in-the-muck being performed alongside a mammoth yellow bulldozer?

With help from Governor Meyner, I dug the shovel in, and as I lifted it from the ground, the earth seemed to groan beneath my white leather saddle shoes. My body shivered in unison with the earth's deep discontent. The gravity of the whole experience slowly crept into my awareness.

There was no plant to see, no earth to touch. Rather than feeling pride or exhilaration, I felt a dull fear and a physical isolation from my own body. I was cast out into the darkness of a modern world that might soon have a pill for everything. Earth had been attempting to send a message. But the world I entered now was lost, disconnected from the clay. While following the cragged path of my

own destiny, conversations with elders and mentors helped regain an earthly connection: Abide in nature. Endure in the silence of the sacred of ALL—this oneness.

Just now the wind has turned this page as if to say, "Keep traveling—to stop is not to stand still, but to let the flame recede to a faint glow. Breathe in my spirit, breathe in," sayeth the wind. "The oceans below are neither mine nor yours to claim, deep beneath your gaze. That which you can feel coursing beneath every breath—the rocks and birds, daylight and darkness, masculine and feminine, your truth, your quinta essentia—you may know when sipping tea."

A New Path

Forty years later, having joined the family business as a young man, I was relocated from the company offices in Manhattan to a fifties-style modern complex that one could reach from the city by driving an hour south through the oil refineries, tract homes, and global pharmaceutical giants on the New Jersey Turnpike. The company that my great-great grandfather acquired from its founder was based in its origin on the eclectic plant-based medicine of the mid-nineteenth century—medicine that was already quite removed in spirit from the world inhabited by prayerful people. (Those "first people" devoutly performed their rituals to the great world-soul that knew their wisdom tradition. The Lenni Lenape Indians were quite a distance from the early presecular, modern era of our time.) Today's culture, taking so much, has forgotten to give back. The old religion is lost to empirical science: electronically distilled, 99-proof rational thought, lacking gratefulness.

It was during the final years of my family's five-generation company that I was fortunate to learn something about the "new industry" of dietary supplements. Botanicals, or herbal remedies, could be marketed once again in America under a change in the law that regulated their availability to many who were seeking a gentler alternative to the overprescribed and often abused "single entity" drugs.

During this time, tea was primarily found hobnobbing with a few players and gate keepers in the natural or "organic" products industry. Had it not been for my return to the "plant" in New Jersey after many years earning my reputation in the pharmaceutical company, I would never have had met my friend Paul Shu. He had left his career as a petroleum chemist to start a tea shop adjacent to Princeton University. He was selling and teaching about high quality loose leaf teas from China and India. It was this experience of savoring Holsome Teas in Princeton that led me in pursuit of tea again.

A MEETING OF MINDS AND HEARTS

Thus began a journey to find a limited selection of the finest quality teas, with a detour through the medium of film to speak with people from many different cultures about what tea might mean for them in their own lives. If I had not been relocated to New Jersey during that time in my life, I might have missed that rare experience of tasting, savoring, and experiencing "fullness contained in the everything" in high mountain "Black Dragon" or Oolong "char", as tea is sometimes referred to across the pond, in the British Isles.

Over tea, a conversation begins—a meeting of minds that touches the hearts of all who gather. In each place I visited, people whom I chanced upon appeared to search for meaning in their lives, in many ways. Some served their tea ardently, while others reflected on the preparation of tea in ritual. While the ways of making tea were outwardly quite different, the pause in the day and the convivial coming together was the common thread. On each occasion, tea had its own story to tell.

Over the course of ten years, my work shifted from corporate executive to the creative person I had always hoped to become. My library grew to scores of tea books. Friends knowing of my passion helped to fill up the shelves with gifts of books related to tea. There are books filled with brilliant images of tea, history books telling tea tales, and dramatic ancient texts that show how tea has been a cultural force long before we westerners charted the globe. But curiously absent from my vast library was a book that shared the transportative or transcendental meaning of tea—a book devoted to the "inside" of tea, as told from the everyday experiences of ordinary people.

Today, we are living in a postindustrial age characterized by rapid advances in technology. We wear ear buds in our ears and communicate instantly via text message, but we are becoming more and more disconnected from the plant world. Even as I struck the hard earth with that silver-plated shovel in 1958, I somehow understood that building a "plant" to manufacture single-entity drugs was a journey farther away from actual plants. Tea was my journey back to the plant world—to the herbs and tinctures native healers had used since time began.

The Meaning of Tea is my attempt to complete the circle—not to critique or condone one practice or another, but to appreciate tea as a potentially underutilized salve for the modern world. The common threads linking people from Japan to Morocco through India and Taiwan; New Grange, Ireland; and Tea, South Dakota, is altogether one of wonder.

AND NOW, READ ON

Upon meeting Phil Cousineau in Greece on a trip there in the spring of 2005, I knew that he would become one of my many companions on this journey. I saw in him someone who reveled in human mystery, but embraced with wonder what lay around each bend in the road. Upon returning from the final film production, I presented him with transcripts galore to wade through and to create this volume, so that you too might share in the conversation with a sampling of people who have a heartfelt relationship to tea.

Whether you stumbled upon this book on a friend's bookshelf or came to a screening of the film—whether you are a devoted tea drinker or simply curious as to how tea could inspire yet another book—if you are reading this, you might just be seeking meaning.

So take up your cup or glass, open these pages, and sip. Together, each one of us can take time to experience healing. When we take time out to pause, review our lives, and "make haste slowly," we find a wonderful gift to share. We live life with an active role—in a positive way.

—SCOTT CHAMBERLIN HOYT,
NEW YORK CITY, JULY 2008

FOREWORD
SOMETHING WONDERFUL

DEBORAH KOONS GARCIA

I didn't come face to face with a tea plant until I was in my thirties, on a hillside in China in 1988. As I walked through the rounded shrubs, I picked a few leaves and felt subtly thrilled that I held in my hand actual tea, the herb, which could have been growing in that place for thousands of years. I thought of the leaves of tea, the idea of tea spreading out into the world, affecting trade, politics, taste, culture. I marveled that humans had managed to select that particular plant from all that nature offers and cultivate it through millenniums. On the same trip, I was told by our Chinese guide that when she was a girl, she had been pulled away from her parents during the Cultural Revolution, because they were professors and intellectuals in Beijing, and sent to a remote region and forced to work in the tea fields where she almost died from exposure.

After our visit to these tea fields, we went to a tea garden where we drank the tea they grew there, Green Dragon Tea. It was delicious, fresh, green, alive, tasting of the plant itself. I bought a tin and took it with me back to California. I began to enjoy that tea, the fruit of my travels, and soon my morning ritual involved sitting down first thing with a cup of green tea and meditating. I found the green tea did calm and focus my mind. It's said that Buddha became enlightened then had a cup of tea. For me, that cup of tea starts my day and encourages me to try to move towards a more enlightened existence.

I had not really had much of a relationship with tea before I stood in those fields in China. In the 50s when I was very young, we had tea parties with imaginary tea, our teacups set out on a cloth on the grass in Ohio, and I remember the neighborhood boys, brothers included, riding their bikes through our tea party, attacking it with peashooters. We had other tea parties sans tea, sitting cross-legged at the bottom of a pool, shooting up for air between sips. I'd had hot tea in the Caribbean one time when a friend and I developed a wicked sunburn for which the local remedy was drinking hot tea while we were basted with vinegar. In high school and college I'd gone to various ladies teas where I'd taken the perfunctory cup of tea. When I visited England the first time, I'd been amazed to see everything stop in the late afternoon while everyone sat down to tea and cakes. As a filmmaker, I had tea-dyed clothing to cut the dreaded white glare. My friends moved from soda pop to iced tea, while I eventually took to sparkling water and cappuccino.

I had appreciated the power of tea—the economics of tea, the way tea shaped international trade for centuries, tea and technology, ships designed to get tea to market faster, the role of tea in the triangle trade route. I knew about the Boston Tea Party, the classic just-say-no of the activists of that time. I understood the importance to so many people, across cultures, of the ritual of taking tea as a civilizing act. I had a Zen friend who studied the Japanese Tea Ceremony every week for years. But until I stood in a field and felt the leaves in my hand, and drank tea in the place it was grown, the whole tea thing was just theoretical. Somehow for me, it took connecting plant and place and excellent tea, before I appreciated tea itself.

But now that I have my own personal relationship with my favorite cup of my favorite tea, it's a different story. I take my tea with me when I travel, and make it myself on planes, in hotels, my reminder to myself to connect into a calm, focused place. I feel the health benefits of tea, all those anti-oxidants fighting back. I know I can get really wired on cappuccino but I can probably prevail more effectively on tea.

Was tea the first truly globalized product? Tea as connective tissue, as a spur to get bigger and faster and more? Reading Scott Chamberlin Hoyt's wonderful book and watching his beautiful film, I learn much that sets me pondering the amazing substance called tea. How remarkable that more tea is consumed every day than all the other prepared drinks put together! I was raised Catholic and back in the 60s, I felt very strongly that the elimination of the Latin Mass was the beginning of the end of the mojo of the Catholic Church. Did they not realize how powerful having the same ritual performed on the same day in the same language all over the world was? They watered the whole thing down—they took the mystery out and mystical started slipping away.

Tea has maintained its sense of mystery and the mystical. We humans like and need our rituals, and sharing tea involves some of the best, from the imaginary tea party of young girls, to the cultivated exactness of the Japanese tea ceremony to the social ritual required out of politeness, to offer and say yes to a cup of tea, enjoyed by host and guest, in almost any country around the globe. It's a comfort, it's refreshing, and it's real.

In the future, what will we be doing with and to our tea? Will they try to genetically engineer it so a pumped up version of tea can grow anywhere using machines? The corporate food industry wants to turn tea into yet another grab, gulp and go consumer item, stuff we drink in our car between cell phone calls. As we power down our world and use less because we have less, I have a feeling old-fashioned tea and the rituals surrounding it will survive. It may get from field to distant shores by a new kind of clipper ship, driven by wind, a slow boat from China. Tea may seem to the aficionados of the future ever more precious, ever more valued. Right now we can appreciate that tea is hand cultivated and hand picked, that it is being enjoyed everywhere, a kind of global connective tissue.

Sometimes it seems to me that this planet is turning into one big Mad Hatters Tea Party and we are like Alice, just wanting to get up and leave, proclaiming 'It's the stupidest tea-party I ever was at in all my life!' Or things may progress in a different direction. With care and conviviality we could reshape our world, and be free to enjoy in peace a cup of tea that sustains and heartens us. I hope so.

—Deborah Koons Garcia
August, 2008

THE MEANING OF
TEA

THE MEANING OF
TEA

THE First Cup

INDIA

The first drink sleekly moistened my lips and throat . . .

—Lu Tong

In the very first line of Lu Tong's famous poem we find an important clue to the mystery of the meaning of tea. According to the poet, the first drink of tea satisfies the most basic of human desires, that of thirst. He reminds us that the first drink of tea is the most elemental. We drink because we drink; we drink because we are thirsty. His sleek opening line is the essence of the Taoist approach to tea. It is also subtle and poetic, as revealed by the use of the verb "moisten," a hint that one should sip, preferably in small cups; one shouldn't be greedy or indiscreet. Instead, tea should be savored, as should the conversation and the precious moments that are at the heart of a gathering of friends. In other words, tea deserves our respect, and even our reverence.

In the first cup or part one of this book, "India," we begin our exploration of the worldwide phenomenon of tea in the spirit of reverence for this modest plant that has had such a profound influence on human history. As one of the ancient and nearly forgotten virtues, reverence is rooted in awe and wonder and veneration for something that is believed to be sacred or held in the highest esteem.

"Always and in everything, let there be reverence," wrote Confucius. Author Paul Woodruff writes in his book on reverence that if we do not exercise our "capacity to be awestruck at the sight of the majestic of nature [we] are missing part of the usual human endowment."

And so it is with the following interviews. These tea growers, tea tasters, entrepreneurs, shopkeepers, and scholars reveal a remarkable reverence for the plant, the ceremony, the manufacturing, the distribution of tea, as well as its ability to bring peace and calm, health, friendship, and often wisdom into their lives.

In chapter 1, Shiv Saria, of the Tea Auction Committee, in Darjeeling, uses the arresting phrase "God-gifted" to describe what he feels is the transcendent property of tea. He admits that he "eats, drinks and sleeps" tea, and goes on to declare that tea rejuvenates him, encourages him to be reflective, and appreciate his life far more than if he lived without it. His fellow tea field owner, Anil Bansal, reveals a grateful attitude towards nature through his decision to become an organic tea grower. For him, every guest is served tea as if he or she is a "guest of God." His devotion toward tea and friendship infuses his life, he says, with a sense of wellbeing and happiness.

In chapter 2, Indian plantation owner Gopal Somani shares his life-long admiration for tea as a remedy for ailments ranging from diabetes to indigestion, cardiac arrest to modern unrest. While discussing the manufacturing of tea he points out that the custom of serving it is considered an invaluable part of hospitality because it helps relax social tensions. Tea is a "remedy for modern life," he concludes, because it helps reduce physical and mental fatigue and helps people cope with the tremendous amount of energy needed in the modern workplace.

In chapter 3, four different tea growers from India provide a land-based commentary on what is required to grow tea. For B. C. Tiwari, one must begin with a firm conviction that the life of tea and the life of a human being are one and the same. A devoted tea grower, he says, must begin by recognizing the vital force that infuses all life. What we share in common is the propensity to *give life*. What grounds Shiv Saria, in a follow-up interview, is the constant reminder of responsibility he feels for his tea fields, the 18 kinds of tea he produces, the hundreds of workers he employs, and the legacy of his life's work. For him, the land itself provides both physical and spiritual grounding, and so the spirit of the tea and the spirit of the land are one and the same.

Tea plantation owner J. P. Gurung describes, in chapter 4, the daily challenge he faces to remember that he is a custodian of one of the greatest teas in the world. To live up to those standards, he says, he must remember every day "what to look for" in terms of quality in the teas that are sold to his customers not only in India, but in Europe and America. Beyond the physical qualities lies a mystery. "By drinking tea," he says with poetic flare, "whatever is hidden in your heart comes out." By offering a cup of tea to someone, you are serving up "a world of goodness." For Mridul Tiwari, memory is a bittersweet practice. Whenever she visits her ancestral tea farm she is overwhelmed by nostalgia. "Every moment is a memory for me," she recounts. Every walk through the tea fields connects her to her youth growing up on the farm and the lost world of her grandparents who founded the business. Veteran tea-taster and auctioneer Nimish Parikh describes his job like the poet who once suggested we should taste life the way we bite into an apple—by savoring it slowly. By his estimate, he has tasted over two million cups of tea—2000 cups a week for twenty years—and he is still enthusiastic, dedicated, and focused on selecting the utmost quality of tea for his clients.

The erudite tea plantation owner, Ronen Dutta, acts as a contrarian voice in chapter 5 to the rhapsodic reflections elsewhere in this book. His interview reveals a roguish affection for tea, measured by an insistence that there is no overarching meaning to the beverage. To him, tea is but a word and the drinking of tea a simple act.

The final chapter of our opening section features two colorful brother merchants from Darjeeeling, Harkay and Jitendra Agarwal, who have the charming habit of *repeating* each other's words. Together, they playfully describe the ebb and flow of their energy during the course of a normal workday. They admit that they can't imagine a day without tea because it so thoroughly refreshes them and allows them to be alert enough to work well.

What these commentators from the tea world of India share in common is the deep conviction that human beings need an antidote for our dangerous tendency towards hubris in our relationship with nature. If reverence is an attitude that allows us to remember how deeply connected we are to the natural world, tea is one of nature's noblest ways of reminding us of how close are our two thirsts, the physical and spiritual, as hinted at in Lu Tong's poem.

The combination has proved to be revolutionary.

So potent is this complex thirst for tea, it has sparked more than one revolution. In the eighteenth-century, the American passion for tea was such that when the English levied a punitive tax on it, tea became a bitter symbol of oppression—and the rejection of it, an emblem of patriotism. This animus led to the famous announcement of December 16, 1773: "Boston Harbor Tea Party tonight," which, in turn, helped spark the American Revolution. Over a hundred and fifty years later, in India, an echo was heard of this cry for tea and freedom. In 1930, after leading a Salt March in protest of a cruel salt tax, Mahatma Gandhi met with the English viceroy. Smiling, Gandhi showed him a handful "duty-free salt" and said that he carried it with him on his pilgrimage to the sea "to remind us of the famous Boston Tea Party."

The reverence for tea and the reverence for freedom are indistinguishable.

—P. C.

CHAPTER ONE
THE TEA GUEST AS A GOD

WITH
SHIV SARIA & ANIL BANSAL

SHIV SARIA

What divine drink would you have, my God, from this
overflowing cup of my life?

—Rabandranath Tagore, translated by W. B. Yeats

Shiv Saria was born in 1955 in Pokhariabong, a small village in Darjeeling surrounded by tea gardens, including Gopaldhara. He graduated with honors from St. Xavier's College, Kolkata, in 1976. Since that time, Saria has been actively engaged in the management of tea estates in Darjeeling and the Dooars, instrumental in developing the consumer-pack business at Soongachi Tea Estate, which now produces over 2.3-million kgs of tea annually and is growing at a rate of 22 percent. He is also keenly involved in developing special varieties of teas at the Gopaldhara and Rohini Tea Estates. Presently, he is Chairman of Siliguri Tea Auction Committee, which handles about 90-million kgs of tea annually. He is also Chairman of the Engineering and Manufacturing Committee of Tea Research Association.

SHIV SARIA: For me, tea is a passion. I was born in a tea garden. Since graduating from college, I have been managing five tea estates in Darjeeling, India. So I dream tea. I eat tea. I sleep tea. I meditate on tea. Tea makes me happy.

Tea is a way of life in India. I am lucky that I have a deep association with Darjeeling teas, which are good for one's health. They elate your mood and keep you happy. Tea rejuvenates the body and rejuvenates the mind. Tea is creative. Drinking tea gets you thinking. Tea encourages dialogue, it encourages company, it encourages discussion—whereas a cola is encouraged to be drunk in solitude. Even the color is black. It is dull; it is dreary.

By and large, humans are habit oriented. You need to have a habit, whether it is a smoke or chewing tobacco or *paan* (betel leaf) or liquor. I think I've got a good habit—I drink tea. I don't smoke, I don't chew paan, and I don't lose my temper. I drink tea.

Mainly, I drink Darjeeling teas. My favorite is from the Rohini Tea Estate, which we call "Enigma." It's got a sweet honeydew flavor. It's made from an AV2 clone, which is a mid-elevation planting section. I make my own cold brew and sometimes have iced tea. When I drink it, I feel rejuvenated.

Generally, when you sit alone you tend to reflect, and at times you may reflect on past bad experiences while sipping tea. I spend time with myself. I have learned to spend quality time alone. I think I enjoy my own tea company because sometimes I've noticed that when I become conscious of bad reflections about my life, I suddenly smile. It's because I realize it's not worthwhile to think of those things, and those thoughts seem to disappear. Other times, I think about manufacturing processes while sitting alone. So new ideas definitely dawn on me while drinking tea.

Besides tea, something else that I enjoy is reading Sufi ghazals. These poems are very creative and get the thinking mind into gear. I find Sufi ghazals synergistic with Darjeeling Oolong teas and meditation; all three of these passions go hand in hand. They have helped me weather the storm that we have experienced in India since the opening of the World Trade Organization in 1995.

THE SPIRITUAL DIMENSION

Basically, in India, we serve tea to the gods. In Sanskrit, we say, *"Athithi devo bhava,"* which means "The first thing to do for the gods is to serve them a cup of tea." The incredible campaign for India tea revolves around this ancient belief. So whenever we have guests in our house the very first thing that we do is serve them a cup of tea.

Tea is a well-being product. Americans love to be happy and tea goes hand in hand with happiness. It elates your mood; it soothes your nerves; it frays rising tempers; it's good for the digestive system. But the biggest gift that I have from tea is that as soon as I put my head on the pillow, I go right to sleep. I don't need aspirin. I don't need sleeping tablets. Within two minutes I am off to sleep and I never wake up in the middle of the night—never—until five in the morning, when it is time to meditate.

When you meditate, what is happening? You are slowing down the thought process. The number of thoughts per minute that enter your mind is considerably slowed down. Every good book on meditation is based on Tilopa and Nilopa, two great monks, who talk of satori, the experience between two thoughts. A thought comes in and it goes away and before the next thought arises, there is a gap, which is called satori. When there are no thoughts, there is timelessness. Time stands still. The seconds stop ticking. This is the connection between tea and time. Thus, tea time is timeless. If you want to enjoy tea, you need time, and if you have the time then time will stand still.

Remember, when the Buddha attained enlightenment, the first thing he did was laugh and the second thing he did was ask for a cup of tea.

THE TEA BRAKE

Tea has a soothing effect. When you drive a vehicle, an accelerator is there, but along with the accelerator a brake is also provided. Tea is a brake, but it is still a traditional industry; the same machines that were being used over a hundred years ago are in use today. I don't see tea fitting in with a fast-paced life. If you want to have tea and really enjoy it, you will have to take time to prepare it properly. The tea way of life acts like a brake on the fast life that we are now witnessing.

A tea-time moment is when you relax and sip your tea casually. While you sip tea you talk, you enjoy, you reflect on past moments, you discuss, you have a laugh, and you enjoy yourself.

But I am a connoisseur. I love stand-alone teas, tea without milk, without sugar. And I love meditation and music—that's my milk and sugar.

Tea bags are like fast food. With the fast-food counters of today, you can't experience a dinner, the enjoyment of having a dinner it's just all about convenience. Many people have tea straight after the meal, especially the British. Some like to have their tea served with the meal, while we Indians generally like to have our tea after the meal.

I have never tried reducing the caffeine element in tea; it does not stress me out. Even if a little bit of stress enhances performance I never feel stressed and seldom get angry. At times in certain meetings I am required to get angry, but I have to put on an act. It's very difficult for me to lose my temper. I like to pass subtle jokes, even in serious meetings, to keep the atmosphere jovial. That is the way I tackle life's real problems.

At present, I am chairman of the Siliguri Tea auction committee [shown below] and I have represented that committee for many years as an ordinary governing-body member. I have seen meetings start at four and continue till eight at night. But after I took over as chairman, we would generally start meetings at four and finish by five-thirty. Shorter meetings are the result of making light of distressing situations and using good humor throughout—and remembering that tea is a great gift from God.

THE GOD-GIIFTED FLAVOR
TESTIMONIALS FROM THE SILIGURI TEA COMMITTEE

A. K. BANSIL: Twenty-five cups of tea a day makes a man perfect—healthy, wealthy, and wise. In ancient times, they said, *"Sanjeevini Boti."* Nowadays, here in India, we say it again. It means: "Tea makes life long, long, long."

> ✍
>
> *I drink tea to face the morning, for morning strength.*
>
> —SUBHASH RAM PRAJAPATI, NEPALESE ARTIST

PUNEET PODDAR: Of course, all my friends drink tea. If we start off with a good thing in the morning, our whole day goes very bright. We are told that tea can be drunk in every mood. If I am feeling very warm, I opt for a cola, but when we are all sitting together, even if we are sad or even if we are happy, we go for a cup of tea. Tea can also be drunk in other modes, like iced tea, but a cola can't be drunk warm. Slowly and steadily, I am coming to understand the benefits of tea. I am gaining more knowledge about tea, and about cola drinks, which have many harmful effects. I believe that the importance of tea will increase in coming years. It is most rejuvenating.

RISHI SARIA: If you look at the Indian economic scenario, the Indian railways are the largest employer in India. After that it is the tea industry. That tells you the importance of tea throughout India.

MANIKCHAND LOHIA: Tea is a natural drink, whereas other drinks are artificial. It has its own properties, such as antioxidation, and it has flavinoids. It has real flavor, not artificially made flavors. Tea is God-gifted. It has God-gifted flavor. You get God-gifted aroma; you get God-gifted freshness. If you take a cup of tea when you are tired, exhausted, it will freshen your mind.

BANSANT AGARWAL: Tea is not just bread and butter for us, not only a means of doing business. When we deal with tea, we feel proud that we are giving something back to society. In other commodities we are *not* giving anything back to society; we are only providing goods in return for cash. But in this case, we are giving society knowledge, wisdom, energy.

SHIV SARIA: I have seen many people who work in tea gardens leave their jobs for the glitz and the glitter of the cities. But after some time, they return in search of their old job in the gardens. The reason is that in the field of tea there is a certain tradition, a different type of pleasure and a different lifestyle. We have a very good saying that we incorporate in our logo: "Earth, Fire, Water, Air, and Sky: Their combined strengths are all with us." We are saying that the strength of those five basic elements of nature all exist in tea. Their combined strengths are with us in Golden Tea.

If the mind is happy, not only the body but the whole world will be happy. So you must find out how to become happy yourself.
—RAMANA MAHARISHI
(1879–1850)
INDIAN SAGE

THE SOCIAL LIFE OF TEA

RISHI SARIA: One fact of life about tea is its social life. In India, at least 70–80 percent of our marriages are still arranged. When the bride is first seen by the groom's side of the family, she is holding a tray, which probably has on it only tea. Tea is woven so deeply into our social structure that it is not possible to do without it. Let's say in business you are in conflict with a buyer and your client is having trouble and you are all shouting. Ultimately, if you sit back and drink tea, you will all cool down.

IDI AGARWAL: And in cricket there is a "tea drink" time.

PAWAN PODDAR: Any time is tea time; every time is tea time.

MANIKCHAND LOHIA: Tea has value everywhere, in every sphere of life. Today, it is the only commodity where there is something to learn. In any other commodity, you can't learn anything. If you are selling iron, you are selling an object; you know nothing more. The product is iron; iron is the basic product. But in tea, you must learn everything. You can manufacture tea in different ways; you can drink tea in different ways; you can market tea in different ways; and you can offer tea in different ways. It is unique, because it is the only commodity where you earn while you learn.

ANIL BANSAL

I drink my tea in a cup and I enjoy it. It is very relaxing. I have four, five cups of tea in a day. I enjoy it because it keeps me refreshed. It is a social event whenever anyone comes to our home. It's a sign of respect when people come over and you offer them a cup of Darjeeling tea that they can enjoy.

One instant is eternity; eternity is in the now. When you see through this one instant, you see through the one who sees.

—WU-MEN (1183–1260)
CHINESE ZEN MASTER

We are proud to offer our Darjeeling tea because it has got a unique quality, a unique flavor, a unique aroma, that you will never find anywhere else in the world. Its uniqueness is a result of the tea plant being utterly different. The soil is a factor; the plant is a factor; the weather is a factor; and also the factory and the way you process it is a factor. Every step is very important.

For example, the ladybug is a predator and you'll find it in organic gardens. Ladybugs are very sensitive to any pesticides, so here at Ambootia, you'll find them in abundance because we don't use pesticides. They're here in abundance eating harmful insects, like aphids and others. It's a feast for them.

We make our herbal brew in the garden. We chop off the top portion of the herbs, soak them in the water for seventy-two hours, and spray the bushes with our herbal brew. It does not actually harm the pests. We use it as a repellent and it really helps. The proof of the wisdom of not using pesticides at our Ambootia Tea Estates is that people are very happy and healthy around here. The sickness rate has been

reduced because of our producing organic teas, which do not have any pesticides. Our medical costs have also come down. People were frequently having common colds and fevers and stomach disorders, but no more now. They are also not as fatigued after work.

A TEA-TIME MOMENT

🌿

Pattram, puspam phalam toyam yo me bhaktya
prayacchati tad aham bhaktyupahrtam asnami prayatatmanah

Whosoever offers to me with devotion a leaf, a flower, a fruit or
water, that offering of love, of the pure of heart I accept.

—*Bhagvad Gita* CHAPTER IX, VERSE 26

I feel very great going through these lines of the *Bhagvad Gita*. Yes. It is a fact that in this part of India, we accept anything anyone offers. The same thing when our guests come; we treat them as a god and we offer them our tea. When you go to church or you worship you pray to god. When any guest or some special person comes, he should be treated like a god. He should be given the same respect that you give to a god.

A tea-time moment is a very refreshing moment and it brings life to your life. If it is with another person, you share your day's experience when you sit down, and also you can plan for the next day or for the future. It's within reach for everyone. I have to save a great deal of money to buy a bottle of Black Label whiskey. I can't go and pick one off the shelf. But if I want a packet of tea, I can go into any tea stall and choose from an affordable and wide variety.

When you have a cup of tea after a whole day's work is finished, you are tired. The evening tea makes you completely refreshed and relaxed; you are not tired anymore. And if you have a cup of tea with your family, it is really enjoyable, really very refreshing.

*Tea is a divine herb; profits are ample if one plants it. The spirits are
purified if one drinks it; it is something esteemed by the well-born
and the well-to-do, which the plebeians and social dregs also cannot
do without. Truly it is a necessity in the daily life of a man. And an
asset for the fiscal prosperity of the commonwealth.*
— MING DYNASTY

ANIL BANSAL: This says it all. Beautiful, beautiful.

MR. SARKAR: I mean, I think this sums it all up.

ANIL BANSAL: Very well written and very well said—beautiful. Very
nice. It's the truth. This was said four hundred years ago. It's still the
reality today.

MR. SARKAR: It holds good even till today—

ANIL BANSAL: So we've taken tea and we are laughing and the sun is
also laughing because it is shining and bringing its energy to us.

A FUNNY TEA-TIME STORY WITH MR. SARKAR

I remember one particular incident when we had a bungalow servant and needed an errand done. There is a grocery shop within the vicinity of the tea gardens, because we are so remotely located. One day we had some unannounced guests. We had to ask this youngster named Nakul, who worked for us, to go quickly to the grocers and bring back two packets of biscuits for afternoon tea. "Don't delay!" we said. "Take the bicycle along with you. Go on the bike." So we were there entertaining our guests for the next fifteen or twenty minutes when we suddenly looked out and we saw Nakul coming back with the biscuits, but *pushing the bicycle*. I asked him, "What happened to you? Why did you take so long?" His answer was, "I don't know how to ride a bicycle but since you told me to take the bike, I took it along."

Chapter Two
The Tea Remedy for Modern Stress

with
Gopal Somani

GOPAL SOMANI

"The heart at rest sees a feast in everything."

—INDIAN PROVERB

Gopal Somani started his professional tea career in 1981 when he joined Tukvar Tea Estate, Darjeeling. Since then he has been closely associated with Jayshree Tea & Industries Ltd., and as President of the Darjeeling Tea Association he has been instrumental in shaping the tea industry in India. His artistic touch as a planter has been acknowledged by various organizations, including the Tea Research Association (TRA), which has used his services as a taster for evaluating its experimental teas, and as a member of the Area Scientific Committee of TRA. He has planted more than three hundred and fifty hectares of new tea in traditional and nontraditional areas, and has also been very active on the social-welfare front by presenting a series of educational lectures on environment protection, afforestation, health, hygiene, and schemes for social upliftment.

GOPAL SOMANI: Once upon a time, there was a king. One day, he went out hunting with his entourage. As they entered the forest, they were attacked by wild beasts. They lost everything and they forgot their way home. Wandering here and there, they became very tired. But of course, the king always travels with emergency provisions. One of his servants prepared some hot water because they realized the jungle water was not safe. It was windy, and some leaves from a nearby tree fell into the water. When the king drank the hot water with leaves, he felt a new energy flowing in his body. That is how tea was first recognized. Later, they inquired what type of tree the leaves came from. When they discovered that it was a tea tree, they made great use of it.

There is another old reference to tea, in the Indian epic called the Ramayana. In that story, Hanuman, the monkey god brought some *sanjeevani buti* and gave it to Lakshamana to revive him. Probably sanjeevani buti was nothing but the tea that was given to Lakshamana. This story is similar to the king story because it describes how tea can be a motivator in day-to-day life.

Historically, tea was established in China in the eighteenth century. There are earlier references to tea from the sixteenth century, where it was used as a beverage and a health drink. Now, in our time, scientists are finally coming to the rescue and saying that in many ways tea is helpful both in one's personal life and for general public health. Tea helps keep the skin glowing, helps relieve diabetes, helps the digestion system, and even helps against cardiac arrest. But tea cannot help in all these ways in one day. Tea is good for you, but you have to adjust your lifestyle and habits. *Tea is toning:* that is my slogan.

Initially, scientists were of the opinion that a China tea bush lasts for seventy-five years and that the Assam variety lasts for fifty. But I can say this garden, Puttabong Tea Estate, is one hundred and fifty years old and is still economically viable, still giving very good-flavor tea. In this way, tea bushes are like people. Two persons may be of the same age, but one may look younger and the other will look older. It depends on how they have maintained their health. The same applies to how we treat tea bushes.

Tea has other unique features. After about thirty years, we prune the tea bush almost to ground level, up to eight or nine inches, to allow it to grow again. Scientists have a theory about this; they call it the leaf/shoot ratio. When we prune tea branches, the plant pushes out roots. Then it begins a new journey and becomes a new bush. Of course, in our calculation the bush may be a hundred and fifty years old. But if we have maintained it properly you can say it is around thirty years old. That is why tea bushes are a mystery and why we still have very good tea bushes that are over a century old.

Of course, in the production stage we are utilizing a kind of bonsai technique so the bush remains small; otherwise, it is of no real use to us commercially. This is a mystery, even to scientists.

This plantation, Puttabong, is the oldest garden in all of Darjeeling. It was planted in 1852. At that time, it was the first commercial plantation. Simultaneously they started two other plantations, but not as big as this garden. The Williamson Mager garden was then in between owners. The Jay Shree company took it over in 1967 and is now the present management. This is the oldest, and in many ways the first, tea garden. We are the first plantation along with the factory to be certified by ISO for its systematic working, the first to plant a nursery of grafted plants at its nursery stage, which was the biggest nursery in northeast India. We are the first to use the pruning machine in the hills, and the first to start family-planning camps to better the worker's life. If you look at the lives of the workers, tea is the inseparable part of their day–to-day lives. Even in their marriages, even in their death, even in other of life's events, tea songs play a part.

In regard to ecology, we educate our workers about the environment. We have conducted many seminars. I have been one of the speakers, along with many renowned persons who come to educate the workers on how to preserve tea trees, increase their number, and keep our environment clean and green. Our mantra is: Conserve Environmental Operations.

THE TENDER WAY OF TEA

In India, tea is a way of life, a way of hospitality. On every social occasion tea is served. Any time is tea time. Tea gives a great feeling. It gives great satisfaction. It satisfies thirst.

My wife drinks tea, but not Darjeeling. She still enjoys CTC. Crush, tear, and chew; though some say curl. There is also a special process of making tea here in Darjeeling that gives a feeling of tenderness, right from the plucking till the manufacturing. At every stage we take care and we treat the tea tree tenderly, which is not possible in CTC. When the word *tender* comes to mind, it means treating the tea bushes with soft hands, as with roses. Actually, right from the plucking stage there is a certain tenderness.

Manufacturing is of second importance. Our leaves are mostly plucked by the tender hands of women; plucking is done at a very tender stage. "Two leaves and a bud," those are the very famous words for tea. It is why we don't allow tea to grow more than two leaves, which is also a very tender size. At our factory, you will see at the withering stage that our leaves are gently and tenderly handled. Then comes the rolling stage, and there also we avoid hard pressure. The leaves are very

gently twisted, then they are manually carried to the fermentation tray and manually to the dryers. Tasting follows.

In the tea industry, especially in Darjeeling, the use of machines is limited. As such, tea making in Darjeeling is more of an art than a technique. The difference is similar to how you can give the same recipe and the same ingredients to two different cooks and one can spoil the dish and one can give you a lovely dish. That is where the art of tea making comes in.

TEA BAGS

I don't say using a tea bag is bad or good. In English, there are three terms: good, better, best. If you want to taste the *best* tea, it will not be in a tea bag. Although I don't want to undermine the use of tea bags, I feel the best taste and aroma can be enjoyed only from the leaf. That is the primary grade, whereas in tea bags it is generally secondary grade; that is the difference. Of course, in today's lifestyle, many people prefer tea bags.

In India, we can't think of life without tea. Tea is here in our day-to-day life. But even in India, people feel they have no time anymore to boil the water, brew the leaves, wait, and then enjoy their cup of tea. So many people just use tea bags.

Tea helps in releasing stress, of course. A worker who does work physically is not thinking about food, but after heavy work if he gets one cup of tea he's fresh again. There is not only physical stress but also mental stress. Whenever you are bothered, heavily taxed with your workload, try and enjoy a cup of tea.

Tea could be a remedy for modern life. Why not? Whatever work you are doing, the problem will not be only physical fatigue but mental fatigue, which is the toughest thing to cope with. Just take a break. For instance, while you are on the computer, you can sip a cup of tea using your free hand. With one hand you are operating computer and at the same time you can sip a cup of tea, which will give you as good or better a boost of energy than those other beverages, and also with health benefits.

Today, time is an important ingredient. We see it in the planning of everything we do. We feel we are wasting time in having tea, but we may be wasting time doing others things that do not offer beneficial results. Whereas with tea you are assured of them. If you spend time with tea your effort will be rewarded, I can assure you, 100 percent. I have no doubt that you will become an ambassador and advocate for the use of tea.

During exam times in India, students naturally have to put in extra hours for their studies. In this, I feel tea has a role to play. It helps in between studies, it breaks monotony, it gives energy to the body, and helps concentration. There are many benefits. As far as quality of mind is concerned, there is an old saying: "A healthy mind in a healthy body."

Evidence now supports the vision of poet and philosopher that plants are living, breathing, communicating creatures, endowed with personality and the attributes of the soul.
—PETER TOMPKINS & CHRISTOPHER BIRD, *The Secret Life of Plants*

PLANT PSYCHOLOGY

There is a peculiar similarity between human psychology and plant psychology. Of course, a plant doesn't have human wisdom, but certain reflexes are in every living organism. If you throw a stone to a bird, it will fly away, although it doesn't have what we call wisdom. And if you thump your feet on the ground, a snake will go away. That is not wisdom; it is the reflex that nature has given it.

Likewise, there is a similarity between tea plant "thinking" and human thinking, or human psychology. In the work of every human being there is one desire in general. That is, whenever one leaves this world, someone should be there to represent him, to carry on his clan, his heritage.

Similarly, the tea plant also "wishes" to carry on whenever it is in stress. That is why they "throw" their seed. The theory behind this is that the plant wishes that their "clan" should continue. It is a very peculiar similarity.

Another interesting aspect of the tea plant is how it grows from the seedling. It is not like any other seeds that you put it in the ground and then the sapling will come out. You have to cure it for up to three months until the upper skin becomes brownish. After forty-eight hours, you dip the seed into a vessel of water. The seeds that are floating or are not mature enough to reproduce the plant are "thrown away" by the tree—to live again.

For me, tea is very, very important. Apart from the fact that it is bread and butter for me, I can't think of a life beyond tea. In the twenty-five years that I have been working in tea, I always think that it is in the background, even in my personal life. So tea is a way of life for me, it is my way of life.

CHAPTER THREE

THE ART OF GROWING TEA

WITH

B.C. TIWARI, BASANTI & PHULMAYA RAI, & SHIV SARIA

B. C. TIWARI

For the friendship of two, the patience of one is required.

—INDIAN PROVERB

Tiwari started his career in tea by becoming a planter in Assam. He went from being a planter to joining the association where his role was largely advisory to the member gardens on every issue that related to tea planting. "It wasn't my job to tell any planter how to plant his tea, how to manufacture his tea," he says, "but after I came to Darjeeling, I did get involved in the marketing to a peripheral extent." He retired from his association work in 2002 and continued to be consultant advisor to various tea companies that are functioning in the Darjeeling hills, which is an administrative district in West Bengal.

B. C. Tiwari: When we drink tea or coffee when we eat eggs, butter, fruit, jam, or anything else, we don't analyze which drink or food has a good effect on our body and which has not. When you have an empty stomach, you have to eat. But it is not necessary that you drink tea. Drinking tea is not a must, but we do it for many good reasons.

If I drink a cup of tea in the morning I immediately feel very fresh. I can drink as many as two or three cups at a time. There are two reasons. One is because I like it. Two is because it's healthful. I drink Darjeeling tea and sometimes I take good Assam tea with sugar and milk and ginger.

Tea has a special meaning in my life. Gradually, being a tea man, I came to know the benefits of tea. When you start taking too much of anything you become habituated. So you have to take tea knowingly. People ask me if I drink my tea, with music or poetry or meditation. But there's no special occasion. *I drink tea because I drink tea.*

I am habituated to tea, as I suppose anyone would be when taking tea in the morning, noon, and evening. I have heard many people say that if they didn't take tea, they would get a headache. Since I am habituated, I might have the same problem. Years ago, I thought I would try to live without tea, to see if I could restrain myself or not. For approximately six months I totally left tea drinking—and I had no headache. I think that means that although I'm habituated to tea, I don't have any sort of addiction.

THE ART OF TEA MAKING

One hundred and fifty years ago, the English ruled in many parts of the world. They searched for tea-tree seeds and found some in China and planted them here in the Himalayas. At that time there were no roads, no cultivation, just jungle. The English must have tested the weather conditions and soil and found that something unique could be produced here.

In time, the unique tea that we call Darjeeling was exported to the United Kingdom. The reasons it is unique are simple: The Himalayan range is a hilly area; the soil conditions are suitable for tea; the climatic conditions are favorable; and finally, the bushes here are excellent.

Growing tea is an art because you can easily destroy what we call the quality that remains in the leaf. At any stage the quality can be destroyed. The quality remains in the field, not in the factory. The raw material is the quality. Factory tea doesn't have the same quality. So tea growing is more of an art than a science.

I should say that each and every tea tree has life, like a human, and the same care is required of the trees as of humans. What a seed produces depends on climatic conditions. During certain periods, the bush may not be able to give more leaves but may give you more seeds. One seed makes one bush. One seedling is one bush. A tea bush may be around for two hundred years.

When people reach the highest perfection, it is nothing special; it is the normal condition.

—HINDU SAYING

But the main qualities of Darjeeling tea are: *aroma, aroma, and aroma.* When you can get aroma in a cup of Darjeeling tea, it is bound to be a wonderful aroma.

The following passage from the Gita means that when you do anything "you must be a devotee and you have to love it," whether it is God or your work. This passage contains every meaning when you say it with *pranayam,* or *concentration.* *"Whatsoever you love you should be devoted to it."* That is the main meaning of life. But you have to choose. If you remain a devotee, you'll succeed. This is the main meaning of life.

This passage is very much connected to tea, because when you are drinking tea you have to love it in a similar way. Tea is the equivalent of this depth of love. The way we think about tea is the same way we think about the other people in our life. Tea plants are connected to everything in life. There is no separation between nature and human beings. The tea plant has as good a life as a human being.

For instance, when we speak with others we know we are communicating; but when tea plants "communicate" with each other and with nature we don't know whether they are speaking or not. We know they have a life and we know they are giving something to us. But we should know they are also asking something back, just as our own body is asking for something back when we work to maintain our life. That is why we eat to sustain our body.

In a similar way, a tea bush is also working when it grows a leaf. It is asking to eat as we are eating. If we give back—feed it—the tea bush gives us tea leaves. This is the duty of the tea plant. Our duty is to eat well, so we maintain good health. But we are also doing our job when we maintain the health of the tea plant. Our job as humans and their job as tea plants are similar: to give life.

So in my opinion, there is no difference between the life of a human being and the life of a tea bush.

BASANTI & PHULMAYA RAI

BASANTI RAI: The meaning of tea is *now*. Everything is here and now from the tea leaves. Everything is good for us because of the tea garden. Tea leaves give us a place to live and give us work. We can hold our head high because of this. I've been here ever since childhood and grew up among these bushes. We are a part of the tea gardens. I am seventy-six years old now; now it's time for me to die here only in the garden. The meaning of tea in my life is that I drink it well. I drink tea well.

PHULMAYA RAI: I like tea; it makes me feel good. I can't start the day's work without tea. I feel fresh after drinking a hot cup of tea. My grandchildren also have tea in the morning. I still continue to pluck leaves in the garden. I still get my earnings from the garden. My rations come out of these earnings. Even now, I keep plucking leaves in the garden. The first flush tea is tastier. I drink from a porcelain Chinese mug. I am not young anymore. We've all become old. There is no time for humor. In old age one falls ill. My granddaughter was ill. My grandson can't walk or talk. Grandpa is also ill. He is about eighty years old. My father is also ill now with gastric problems. That is life. My life has been full of sadness.

It is true: There is no difference between people and tea bushes. A human being is similar to a tea bush. A tea bush grows, becomes old, and is thrown off. Our lives are similar. We also grow and become old and then have to die. Isn't that similar?

Until now, I've enjoyed plucking leaves every day. All my life I've been plucking leaves and I enjoy doing that. I've taught the children about the problems of work on the estate. When you work in the sun, you get sunburned, or you get wet in the rain. We teach the children all that. The boys and the girls are now married. They are living separately from us now.

Nobody has asked me these questions before. What I would like to tell people in America is that it is good to have tea.

SHIV SARIA

The Pokharia Bong village is eight kilometers away from here and is the place where I was born. I was the first in the family who was born here and so for me it is an emotional bonding. After I graduated, I started looking after the tea estate. Out of all the original owners of tea in Darjeeling, I think I'm the only one left. Other owners have migrated to other areas. The Gopaldhara Tea Estate sits on the opposite hill of the Sangma Tea Estate. A hundred and twenty or thirty years ago, my grandfather migrated to this area and established that village and so he was the first resident. It was built up from that one house and the village now has close to two hundred homes.

Around five thousand people live in the village now and they support the nearby gardens. Sunday is a holiday for the workers when they go shopping for their provisions. It is mainly a market village with stores and a cinema hall and is surrounded by five tea estates. Most of the money coming into the village is from the workers of the estates.

Some entrepreneurs transport stores and supplies, so the economy of the village is totally dependent on the estates. There is no other commercial activity in that area.

Tea is a very meaningful part of the existence of our village and of the entire district of Darjeeling. The tea here is renowned worldwide for its flavoring characteristics. No other tea can replace Darjeeling tea. About 60 percent of all money coming into Darjeeling is revenue generated by the tea industry, which is close to sixty million dollars annually.

Most of the workers in the tea industry are Nepalese. They are a very proud lot and have much self-pride. They are proud of what they do and enjoy their life. They are not very materialistic; whatever little they earn they are quite happy with. They love flowers, watching movies, and wearing very good clothes. They are 100 percent part of the success story that is my Gopaldhara garden. With their cooperation and our initiative and finances, we have been able to plant more than a hundred acres of tea at this elevation of six thousand feet. Now our garden is yielding very high quality tea and is appreciated worldwide.

China is not very far from our estate. If you drive through Sikkim for maybe three hours, over a hundred kilometres, to Gangtok, and then another three hours drive to the border, you are in China. On the Gopaldhara Tea Estate, the choicest clonal tea is planted at about a seven-thousand-foot elevation. No other garden in Darjeeling or in the world grows tea at this elevation. Generally, Darjeeling tea has been planted up to a five-thousand-foot elevation. This used to be barren land that was lying idle. When we started rooting the plantations, our senior planters advised us against planting here. They were against it because of the low temperatures, fewer daylight hours, and frost, and hailstone damage.

In spite of their advice we went ahead with the planting program that started in 1982, and the land now yields about sixteen thousand bushels of very good quality. Twenty-five percent of those tea areas earn close to 60 percent of our revenue. The apprehension of the senior planters that this area would not give economic yield has been proved incorrect.

OUR PHILOSOPHY OF TEA

Darjeeling is known for its flavor and aroma. Any type of stress that can be induced on the tea plant and its leaf will enhance the flavor level. Instead of a leaf being green, here it is yellow. We get less sunlight, so there is less chlorophyll. We also have ladybugs. At this high elevation, the temperatures are low, so we hardly get very much pest attack. Ladybugs indicate we don't use chemicals, which harm the ladybug as well as the human beings who are ultimately going to consume the tea.

We don't want to use chemicals, so all our weeding operations are done manually. Over the last four years, we have done away with the use of herbicides. Instead, we make compost and half of our nitrogen requirements are met this way, and the other half by fertilizers.

What divine drink would you have, my God, from this over-flowing cup of my life.

—RABINDRANATH TAGORE, TRANSLATED BY WILLIAM BUTLER YEATS

BALANCING NATURE AND HUMANITY

God has found His own way of balancing nature. We have tea bushes here at Gopaldhara that are more than a hundred years old. At this high elevation, the weather conditions are harsh, so yields will be much less than what would have been in the lower elevations area. But that is compensated by exceptional flavor. It's possible that we might be harvesting leaves from the same bush over a hundred years from now. But production goes down with passage of time. Some plants should be replaced with new clonal material, which can give very good quality. Clonal material refers to plants selected from similar trees. They are not identical, so each bush is different from the other.

DARJEELING'S MYRIAD TEAS

There are basically three different types of teas. First is green tea. The leaf is steamed and the enzymes are killed so that the fermentation process, which is an exothermic reaction, is arrested once the enzymes are killed. Those teas are rich in polyphenols. That is one type of manufacture of green tea. Green tea is mainly produced in China, but India has a production base of about ten million kilograms.

Behold! My heart dances in the delight of a hundred arts, and the Creator is well pleased.

—KABIR, INDIAN POET, TRANSLATED BY RABINDRANATH TAGORE

During an exothermic reaction, heat is released as well as moisture while fermentation or chemical reactions take place with the aid of oxygen. The oxygen is absorbed; carbon dioxide, heat and moisture are released.

The second basic variety is black tea. There, we have two or three basic types of production. One is the (CTC) variety, where only around 30 percent of moisture is removed during the withering process. After that, the tea is macerated and small-size teas are formed in pellet form, which is very useful in the Masala chai that is gaining popularity all over the world. The next black tea that we have is the Assam orthodox variety, which is also being produced in the low-elevation gardens of West Bengal. In the withering process, about half of the moisture is removed. After being sent through rolling machines, the teas are laid out on the floor or in racks to ferment.

During fermentation, oxygen is required. Carbon dioxide and a little moisture are released, then the teas are fired for the more orthodox variety. But for the Darjeeling variety, much more moisture is removed. A small amount of moisture is left in the leaf to aid the fermentation process and to give the leaf its roll.

In the process of rolling, some leaf damage takes place. But because of less moisture, the movement is restricted and total fermentation, which takes place in Darjeeling tea, is less and so you get a lighter cup. It develops aroma, character and briskness. In the orthodox variety, total fermentation takes place more than in Darjeeling leaf. That type of tea is consumed more with milk and sugar and is commonly known as breakfast tea. Darjeeeling tea is consumed mainly as a stand-alone, without milk; sometimes you may add a little sugar.

The third type of tea is Oolong, where the amount of moisture removal can be anywhere between twenty kilograms right up to one hundred kilograms of leaf. In the Oolong style of manufacture, the supply of oxygen to the leaf is constricted to prevent excessive fermentation from taking place and to prevent a dense color. So the fruity note is very prevalent in an Oolong tea. And it is because of the free movement of enzymes that the polyphenols get converted into flavinoids. This Oolong is a more complete tea. We have combined the benefits of both. Instead of removing 67 percent moisture like other Darjeeling producers, we remove 55 percent of the moisture and constrict the supply of oxygen during the rolling process. We are now in a position to have the best of both worlds, having retained the characteristics of a Darjeeling tea and yet having developed the fruity flavors that are present in Oolongs.

I've been making tea now for close to twenty-five years at Gopaldhara. Now I am a satisfied and happy man. Maybe someday I'll retire here.

CHAPTER FOUR
THE ART OF TEA TASTING

WITH
MRIDUL TIWARI, HARKMAN, NIMISH PARIKH,
& J.P. GURUNG

Mridul Tiwari

*The beauty of tea is that it gives you an opportunity
to notice yourself, to tend to yourself, and to
really be here clearly in all your senses.*

—Susan Borg, Weed Farm, Vermont

Mridul Tiwari was born on the premises of the Tea Planters-Club, to which she attributes the reason why tea seems to run in her veins. In 1860, during the period when India was still under British rule, her great-grandfather settled in Darjeeling district and is credited with the honor of planting the first bush of tea there, in 1902, and having the vision to plant his own estate, a three-hundred-acre garden he called "Soureni." After growing up in Darjeeling, Tiwari joined the Contemporary Targett Ltd. auctioning company as a management trainee. She studied under one of the finest Darjeeling tasters, Amarjeet Singh, and went on to become one of the few women tea tasters, and the only female tea auctioneer in India, and eventually, she became an auctioneer in all six tea centers of India. Today, she runs her own specialty tea business for the burgeoning "premium hospitality" tea industry.

MRIDUL TIWARI: I was born in the tea fields, and that's why I think it's in my blood. Tea "liquor" runs in my veins. We used to go out for evening walks on these paths with many families. All the gents used to go hand-in-hand and take a walk on a different path from the ladies, who used to walk together in another direction. All the children used to go jumping, shouting, screaming, playing on the paths, along a different way. We would all go out around four o'clock and come back home at six for dinner. I have innumerable memories here, every moment is a memory for me, including memories of our staff, Harkman and Maila, who have known me from childhood. They actually brought me up. I have sweet memories of every single moment that I spent here. I just love this place. I want to die on this land.

I thought I was being detached from my own home, my family. I have a very strong emotional bonding with this place—and why not? This is, I think, the most beautiful place in the world. If anybody gave me a choice to go to Switzerland or Soureni, I will come to Soureni to stay here with my family.

If I could replay my life, I would have my family standing right here next to me— my cousins and my friends—to just look at this beautiful view forever. Today, I have a feeling of detached loss here, a feeling that this land doesn't belong to us anymore. My family is not here anymore. The people are different now, because they are loyal to somebody else, because, of course, the tea estate has been taken over. So the emotional bonding I have with these gardens is gone.

> *He whose law is within himself walks in hiddenness.*
> *His acts are not influenced by approval or disapproval.*
> —CHUANG TZU

If I could speak with my great-grandfather again, I would thank him for coming all the way from Rajasthan and choosing this land and exposing the generations after him to this beautiful place. If it were not for him, I don't think we would have come here and found this beautiful spot, where he established this garden in 1902. Without him, I would have missed a very beautiful part of my life. I never got to interact with him because he died when I was very young. I have no memories of him, but I believe that he must have loved this place.

Looking over these fields I feel extremely nostalgic. But along with this nostalgia comes a kind of pain. I don't want to come back to live; I have to go. That's the way destiny is.

TEA ETIQUETTE

Tastes are made, not born.

— MARK TWAIN
(1835–1910)

There is a lot of difference between having tea all by yourself and having tea socially with friends. When a friend comes for tea, there is hospitality attached. Over tea you get to talk. You may be working out relations with someone over tea; you may be fixing your daughter's marriage over tea; you may be discussing business over tea. And then there are guests who come to your house who will naturally ask, "How did you prepare this tea?" So you tell them, "This tea is from our estate and this is how we prepare it." There is a significant difference between interacting with someone over tea and interacting with someone without tea.

HARKMAN

Along with the family, I drink tea when a guest comes, and make sure that we look after all vistors in the right way. We drink tea whenever we get a chance, and when we drink tea we are happy. But for those of us who live on a tea estate, frankly, we aren't so deeply interested in tea. It is in our lives, our livelihood, isn't it? As long as we get to drink tea once a day, that's enough. Of course, this tea has provided us with a home, food, and livelihood. This tea has helped us improve our children's future. The children are small, nine or ten years old, and it's this same tea that has helped raise and educate them. After learning the ropes about the tea fields, I was sent straight away to work at the bungalow. I remember a lot about living with Mridul's family. I don't remember anything else. Now it is time for us to go away. The children should grow up and do well in the gardens. What is their fate, I cannot say. I have to leave and go. My age is around seventy. There's not much age left for me. In another sense, tea has a lot of meaning and an important place in the life we live here in these fields. This is our home, for generations and generations before us and after us.

NIMISH PARIKH

Basically, you're just rolling tea on your tongue and spitting it out. That's how you know how to get the taste of tea, whether it is a *gatia* cup, whether it is brisk, bright. That's what you're judging once you roll it on your tongue. You're looking at a combination of infusion, liqueur, as well as leaf appearance, and to a certain extent, aroma. Normally, in CTC tea, there is no question of looking for aroma. What you're looking at is the cup quality, how thick the cups are, how bright they are, the briskness they have, and a combination of good leaf appearance and leaf color. I've been a tea taster for the past twenty years, and I'm extremely dedicated to this job. In fact, I love my job.

> *Everyone eats and drinks, but few appreciate taste.*
> —CONFUCIUS

What we do throughout the week is tea tasting and auctioning the tea. In fact, we speak and meet with buyers and go to the tea plantations where we give technical advice. The buyer wants feedback on the quality of tea or the manufacturing process that it's gone through. The pricing is based on the quality of the tea. The number-one issue is the quality of the tea, then the second is the pattern of demand and supply and the market prevailing price at that point in time.

Through the years, I have been tasting an average of two thousand cups of tea a week to determine if people will enjoy the tea. You see, a tea taster doesn't go through any formal training, as such. It's basically on-the-job-training. One problem is that if you are tasting tea on a regular basis it definitely stains the teeth. Normally, I see the dentist thrice a year. My gums are healthy, but the color of my teeth isn't good enough due to all this tea tasting.

The first few things the experienced tea tasters tell you to do are to check out the sizing of the grades, look at how the cut of the leaf is, and whether the tea is clean. Thereafter, you come to the infusions and look to see how bright they are or how dull they are. Then you go to the cups and, basically, look at the brightness and the strength of the tea in the cup. I won't say tea is a serious subject, but it is definitely an interesting subject.

A TEA TASTER FROM SINGELL ESTATE

We know tea by taste. After tasting, we will get to know the tea. When you taste tea, you look to see whether something is wrong, if we're doing something different. If the tea is harsh, we have to fix the tea. If the tea tastes harsher, it needs more fermentation. After more fermentation, the harshness goes out. Now the tea is OK. So the tea needs nothing more. With other teas, they might need more fermentation or more withering. Now, in the second flush tea we are looking for the color. The color should be bright. We have to rate color as per the demand of the market, as per the demand of the buyers, and as per the demand of the seasons. We have to manufacture the tea per these demands.

All of life is a dispute over taste and tasting.

—FRIEDRICH NIETZSCHE
(1844–1900)

J. P. GURUNG

*I sing the songs of olden times with adoration: may my own
songs follow the path of the sun.*

—FROM THE SVETASVATARA UPANISHADS,
TRANSLATED BY JUAN MASCARÓ

G urung is a self-described "tea designer" or "man for all
seasons," in the sense that he appreciates tea plucked
from all four picking seasons. In this extraordinary interview he reveals what he looks for in a great tea. He emphasizes
that his goal is to produce "exquisite" teas, which requires nothing less than "the human factor," as opposed to the mechanization that threatens to overtake the tea business.

J. P. GURUNG: If I want my tea to be exquisite, then I must take extra pains in making it. Otherwise, the product is ordinary. My effort is something that is passionate—and that is the right word for it. The result makes me feel good. *Good.* One word should be enough.

Recently, I was in the Singell Tea Garden and I was not very satisfied with the type of tea we were making. I asked the workers to change the various processes and parameters. Later, when we tasted the tea, I was very happy because I had achieved what I wanted to achieve with my tea making. I would even say this caliber of work makes me feel like a kind of tea designer.

Once I sit down to have a cup of our tea I feel a sense of satisfaction. I feel calmed down. I feel at ease, I feel happy, I think I feel everything good. It changes my entire mood, it changes my attitude, it changes my feelings.

Tea drinking is a part of life. You get up in the morning, and the first thing you look for is your cup of tea. One starts the day with a cup of tea, and at many times and at many places you end the day with a cup of tea also. To drink tea is as natural as breathing air. If you go down from the hills to the plains, you find that as soon as you go to somebody's house they will bring you a glass of water. Automatically it comes. Up here in the hills, they automatically bring you a cup of tea.

Basically, I am a Darjeeling man. I have been involved in this process of tea making and tea drinking very passionately, but only from the Darjeeling perspective. So I drink other types of tea like CTC, but I prefer to drink Darjeeling tea. When I go elsewhere and have a cup of tea, I feel afterward as if I must go home to properly quench my thirst with a cup of Darjeeling.

This preference goes beyond taste. In Darjeeling, tea making is an art. No amount of mechanization can replace the human factor. You know the taste, the feel, the many parameters that govern tea making. Any difference can lead to a totally different product all together. As a layman, one may not notice the difference, but for us professionals it is important.

MANUFACTURING PROCESS

As soon as you pluck the leaves, the process of fermentation begins. The chemical changes start in the leaves themselves. That is why we are insistent on taking the leaves as fast as possible to the factory, because we do not want them damaged.

By and large, we drink all grades because I need to evaluate them all. Normally, I prefer the leaf. Of late, we have had this tendency in Darjeeling for making specialty teas. It's a very small segment of the Darjeeling industry, but nevertheless, it is there and this segment is increasing. These days you do have teas coming out like Darjeeling Oolongs, white teas, or pearls that are supposed to be exotic in nature. But then these are not common teas. The original characteristic of a Darjeeling tea is a subtle flavor, along with a "roundness" in the cup.

WHAT I AM LOOKING FOR

I think Oolong didn't start in Darjeeling. We are only trying to imitate what other people are trying to do. I think we have to be very clear about the differences in Darjeeling tea, which come with the various seasons. When I drink a first-flush tea, I look for a specific quality. When I drink a second-flush tea, I look for another specific quality. And when I drink an autumnal tea I look for a third quality. These three qualities are totally different and cannot be compared. Actually, people look at each of these qualities from their own global perspective.

For instance, the Germans like the first-flush teas because they are lighter and are more brisk. They give you a little bit of a kick and also have a good flavor. But if you give that same cup of tea to the Japanese, they would not take it, because they tend to like a second-flush tea or an autumn tea, which is more round and sweeter in the cup. The second flush has more body and a subtle flavor that comes through. Whereas, if you went to England, you would want a tea that someone can pour some milk and sugar into.

Personally, I prefer an autumn tea. I'll be very happy drinking an autumn cup of tea in my house. I am a man for all seasons. I feel that the level of flavor in autumnal is very high. I associate that with the climatic change. You know it's colder here. It's a colder period of time. We here think that anything that comes from a colder climate is sweeter in taste; vegetables and cold-water fish, are tastier.

Quality in any tea moves in a very geographical manner, because there are various climatic conditions that govern quality, and these are subject to change. It is important for the tea maker to catch that quality when it is at its peak so you can then say, "Yes! I have got my cup of tea!"

In an autumnal tea I am looking for something that is very similar to the second flush in the sense that the cup would be much rounder. It would contain much more body; it would be slightly thicker in terms of the prominent flavor.

What I am looking for each season is based on what the consumer is looking for. To elaborate, during the first flush, I am looking for a tea that has very light liquoring, one that is greenish with bright infusions. I am looking for a tea whose flavor gives a punch. I am not looking for a tea that is harsh the minute I put it into my mouth. Whereas, when I go to a second flush, I am looking for a sweet cup rather than a kick.

If I were a female, I would possibly get married to tea! One cannot be successful in one's profession if one doesn't get totally involved. If the leaves could talk, they would tell me the buyer is not paying the right price.

When I go out to the tea field and see the leaves that are about to burst out, and all the buds are shining, I feel like sitting there and looking at it for hours. I can see the quality of the leaves when they are still in the field. There is no end to the joy. This is a feeling that can only come if you are totally immersed in the profession of tea.

THE GATEWAY TO THE PLANT WORLD

To get our customer their cup of tea, these days there are many problems to producing it correctly. It is one hundred percent true that tea drinking is a gateway to the plant kingdom. But then, you know one has to look at it from a different point of view. Any plant will respond to a human being, not just a tea plant, according to the way you are treating it. I think my wife has a green thumb; she's very good at plants and flowers. In our house, the plants are actually responding to her.

On Tea Tasting

Tea testing is important, because through it we come to know whether we have to increase the withering percentage, increase the temperature, or increase the fermentation. When something is wrong in the tea, you come to know it by tasting. I just tasted this tea and know it needs two degrees of withering. What I need to do is increase the withering and see it again in the drier. If it is still wrong, we have to rectify it. Sometimes teas need some improvement. We may have to increase some withering, then increase the drying temperatures, then increase the fermentation. This is what we learn in the tasting process.

—J. P. GURUNG

At the end of the day, we have to agree that this is a commercial product. In this making of a cup of tea, time and energy are just two problems. It's difficult for a layman to understand this problem. But at the same time, you must still do it correctly.

Tea has a special meaning to me, because I can't start a day without drinking it. I am up at five o'clock in the morning, and between five-thirty and six o'clock, I must have my cup of tea. Tea plays a very big role in my life. In my life everything revolves around tea. It's my profession; it's my passion; it's my obsession.

The time when you drink your tea is very important. If I drank my tea after coming home dead tired, I would prefer absolute silence. I may be sleepy and have the feeling I just want to hit the bed. But if I've got work to do, I may want to just sit and sip and enjoy tea to help me stay awake. After that cup, I am totally refreshed and don't feel so tired. This is because tea is such an invigorating drink.

Whereas, if I drink tea with my family or my friends, then I would like to hear some light music as I enjoy my tea. Both are equally enriching experiences. But their importance depends on the timing of when you drink the tea.

A Buddhist monk chanting prayers in a prayer hall is doing quite monotonous work. He needs to be fresh. Therefore, he keeps on sipping tea. But in Tibetan tea there are a lot of additives like butter and salt to help ensure that the monk doesn't fall asleep.

THE HIDDEN QUALITY

Tea is a part of everyday life for us. Tea is also definitely mood altering. But I don't think anything special is hidden in tea. It is simply that by drinking tea, whatever is hidden in your mind or heart comes out. At the same time, tea enables you to generate thought and enables you to bring out your most creative expressions that don't come out in the normal course of the day. Tea is something that enters into your system and brings out the best in you. And it can even generate more wisdom in you. That's why you find that people who are working long and hard are often sipping a cup of tea.

When tea itself is a culture and a way of life, one needs to enjoy it to the very fullest, to actually feel what it is all about. Tea is a healthy habit. I think in the States there is a tremendous amount of emphasis on tea as a health drink, and I think this is one of the very reasons why the habit of tea drinking is increasing and catching up with coffee. So using teabags is not "my cup of tea." They are for the man who is in a hurry.

Today, a basic problem is coping with the stress of modern life. Tea is an antidote to this stress. Not only tea itself, but the lifestyle behind it. It's more relaxed; you are not trying too hard; you are not running. Tell someone you know that tea is good for their health. When you offer someone a cup of tea, you are actually bringing them a world of goodness. That's why tea is catching on all over the world. That's why tea has become a part of me.

with
Ronen Dutta

Ronen Dutta

*Tea, n.s. [a word, I suppose, Chinese; thé, Fr.] A Chinese plant, of which
the infusion has lately been much drunk in Europe.*

—Dr. Johnson's Dictionary, 1755

Ronen Dutta started his career in tea as a planter in Assam.
Later, he switched from being a planter to joining an
association where his role was largely advisory to its
member gardens. After he came to Darjeeling, he became involved
in the marketing aspect of the tea business. He retired from his
association work in 2002 and continued to be consultant advisor
to various tea companies functioning in the Darjeeling hills, an
administrative district in West Bengal. "I am smoking a pipe now
because I am playing the last innings of my life. Why the devil
shouldn't I enjoy it?"

THE MEANING OF TEA

RONEN DUTTA: Now I want to just ask *you* one question. What do you mean by *different* meanings of tea? Do you mean the connotation of the term or the actual meaning—because there is no actual meaning of tea. It must be the connotation we are talking about. It's just that tea, *thé, chai*—whatever you call it—doesn't actually have any meaning. It's just a name, but I'd love to be educated about this soothing brew.

> 🖎
>
> *Tea, n. camelia senensis. An infusion of leaves in hot water.*
>
> —OXFORD AMERICAN
> DICTIONARY

When you use the word *meaning* it can be taken in two different ways: one is what it means to you; one is what it means to me, which really is the connotation of the word. Now, if you open the dictionary to look up the word *tea*, so far as I know (not that I am a well educated man) the word itself does not have a meaning.

Now, does tea have any special meaning for me? Very difficult question to answer. No. It is just a part of social life, so far as I am concerned. At practically any time of the day, if you go to meet someone in India, whether you're in his or her house or office, and vice versa, if somebody comes to visit me, it is customary to have tea. It's been a part of my social life ever since I can remember. Any kind of social intercourse is accompanied by, preceded, or followed by, a cup of tea. After the social conversation is over, we might also invite a person or persons to have a cup of tea. Whether it actually facilitates social intercourse, I don't know. But I do know if you go to see somebody or if somebody comes to see you and there is no tea offered, then it leaves a bit of a void. Something is missing. And if we cannot offer tea we normally apologize by saying, "Sorry, I've got no tea" or "Sorry, I can't afford tea because the gas has run out."

Tea drinking is a part of Indian culture and has been for close to three hundred years, but it has nothing to do with our early Indian civilization. An indigenous variety of tea was discovered in Assam, but this was subsequent to tea being introduced at our tables and also in the field by the British. Prior to that it was always the Chinese variety. It is possible that our indigenous people chewed tea leaves, but I am not very sure there is any historical evidence of that.

As for me, I have always had tea. Since I was a child, the drinking of tea has always been a part of my life. I like the brew. I feel better after my morning cup of tea, a little more awake. When I pick up my book, a newspaper, or a magazine I can better understand what I am reading. Tea helps it penetrate into my brain. After I've had a morning cup of tea, I feel more ready to face the world, face the day. I am refreshed enough to do whatever reading I choose or listen to music along with my cup of tea.

I am a very ordinary person and my meditation is not really connected with tea. I am afraid I don't actually live on that level of "probing the depths of my soul" by reading poems. When I am by myself, usually I have a cup of tea. But I do not know if a cup of tea brings about any meditative tendencies. When I am sitting quietly with a cup of tea to accompany me, it is pleasant. Contemplation is a state of mind and I cannot really truthfully say that I begin to contemplate because a cup of tea is next to me or because there is a pipe I am smoking. But it seems to work the other way; when I am in a contemplative mood then I'd like to smoke my pipe or have a cup of tea but the causative thing I am not very sure about.

When I do drink my Darjeeling tea, I drink it without milk, without sugar or light. I usually drink other teas with milk and sugar. I will add hot water if I don't use milk and sugar when I find a tea very strong.

The wisest thing is time because it discovers everything.

—Thales, Greek philosopher (624–546 bce)

Human beings have this tendency to follow a routine—a traditional timing—whether it is for a cup of tea or a meal. So I think a human being is a creature, possibly the only creature, created by God who eats because he looks at the clock, not necessarily when he feels hungry. But in India, when we feel like having tea we have tea. Although the traditional time of having tea is in the afternoon or early morning, and most go along with that. We abide by those habits. But then if you are connected with tea, you drink anytime. It could be ten o'clock in the morning or two o'clock in the afternoon; it could be before a meal or when you sit down with your meal or after your meal.

Anytime is teatime.

THE TEA INDUSTRY

In a very broad sense, India is the biggest producer and the biggest consumer of tea in the world. We produce on average nearly eight-hundred-million kilos per year. Of this total we normally export over two hundred million kilos. The balance is consumed within the country. Darjeeling produces about nine million kilos. It is the most expensive tea, a little more than one percent of the total Indian production. I presume it's because of quality that it's become the flagship of Indian tea.

The Darjeeling tea industry employs about fifty thousand workers, 60 percent of whom are women. During the harvesting period, which stretches from the end of February to the end of November, we engage another twenty thousand workers just for the plucking, the harvesting of tea leaves. There are many more connected with the industry who are not necessarily working in the plantations, such as the suppliers of the input materials, the transporters, the repairing workshops, and the office support system where needed.

Trees are the earth's endless effort to speak to the listening heaven.

—RABINDRANATH TAGORE, "FIREFLIES"

The Darjeeling tea gardens house approximately 50 percent of the total population of these hills. For every worker, we have four or five nonworkers who reside on the tea gardens. I would hazard a guess that out of a billion people in India, about three million people are in one way or another involved in the production of tea.

THE TEA LIFE

When we talk of tea, whether as a consumer or from the perspective of an industry, I would say, yes, it is a major beverage. Certainly it is in this country, and in many parts of the world. But I don't think that really describes what goes behind producing tea in a cup. Tea is a way of life.

If you're planting tea, then your tea-garden life is entirely different from any other kind of livelihood. If you're selling tea, you will find that the business is a very closed shop. It's quite difficult for an outsider to get into the tea trade. It's a way of life that is not available in many parts of the world—practically in no other part of the world—because tea plantations are becoming more mechanized. But tea in India has not really been modernized.

Darjeeling tea industry is about a hundred and thirty years old, and the process of production from the fields to the delivery end of the factory remains virtually the same as it was when it began. It's been very good for the Darjeeling district for another reason that is apart from the fact that it is really the major economic activity in these hills: Tea has also been a boon for the environment.

The Himalayas, particularly the eastern end, are supposed to be the youngest mountains in the world. So the soil is still relatively pliable, which is why we are prone to having massive landslides. In fact, we've lost a lot of our topsoil. Now with the growth in population, more and more of the hills are getting built up. The only saving factor is the presence of the tea gardens, because there is no building on that land where tea is grown. This means that tea is actually quite essential for protecting the environment in those hills.

INSTANT TEA, INSTANT LIFE

People who use teabags are missing a lot. Teabags are a manifestation of the instant life. There is more to tea than just the taste that is contained in the brew. It is a part of culture. I may be straying into other areas, I am not very sure. But I believe in sitting down, allowing the tea to brew, and pouring it out of a teapot into a nice porcelain cup. There's more to tea than just sort of dipping a bag and taking it out. When you're eating a lovely beef steak there is some pleasure in actually using the right kind of knife so that you can slice through the meat easily. Or, if you're drinking an excellent scotch whisky, you would rather have it in a crystal glass than out of a teacup. Or if you're drinking wine, the wine glass should be appropriate so that the wine should look right when you hold it against the light. The whisky or the wine is not something just to provide you with an alcoholic effect. In all kinds of consumption I feel that there is more to the act than just putting something tasty into your mouth and chewing it or gulping it down.

This is, of course, an absolutely subjective observation.

CHAPTER SIX
THE GIFT OF TEA

WITH
HARKAY & JITENDRA AGARWAL

HARKAY AND JITENDRA AGARWAL

The long, dying silence of the rain over the hills opens one's touch,
a feeling for the soul's substance, as for the opal neck spiralling the
inside of a shell.

—JAYANTA MAHAPATRA, INDIAN ENGLISH POET

JITENDRA: We prefer living in Darjeeling due to the weather. It's very cool here, compared to other places. Right now in the plains, like Delhi, it will be so very hot we are not able to live there. We love Darjeeling's weather first and foremost, and it's a calm and peaceful life. Since we are surrounded with the mountains, we get lots of fresh air and our health remains very good. It's a wonderful place we live in. We have been gifted by gods with our Pashmina shop.

HARKAY: The people are very cooperative here. It's like living together with a family. So if we need any type of help we get it from all directions. Life is very busy, very calm. The biggest business here is tea.

JITENDRA: Tea. Just tea. Tea is the biggest business. Actually we have three "t's"—*tea, tourism, and timber.* Those are the three biggest businesses in Darjeeling. Tea is the biggest, because Darjeeling is famous for serving the best tea in the world.

HARKAY: Once you say, *Darjeeling*, people will just say *tea*. Darjeeling is rather more famous for tea than for itself.

JITENDRA: Actually, it's become part of our life. As soon as we are getting up in the morning, the first thing we do is drink tea. *Without tea we can't get out of our beds.* That is the first and foremost thing that we do in the morning. We have our tea. We can avoid drinking water, but we cannot avoid drinking tea.

HARKAY: If anybody comes to our shop and asks us for a cup of water, we prefer giving them tea. Once you drink Darjeeling tea you feel fresh and it is also very good for blood pressure and diabetes.

JITENDRA: It's like an addiction. Just opposite to our shop is a famous restaurant called Planery's. Sometimes when we are sitting idle we smell the aroma and the flavor of the tea and we can't resist it. The aroma and flavor makes our bodies tingle so that we have to have a cup of tea even though we might not be thirsty. So we have to order some tea for

ourselves. It's unavoidable, you can say. Tea is one of the most precious things in our life.

HARKAY: Once we feel lethargic, we have to have tea. That is the only solution. Once we have the tea, we feel more fresh. If we have a headache, we don't go for medicine, we just go for a cup of tea. That solves our problem. Once we have two or three sips, the exhaustion is over. Altogether, we might have six to ten cups of tea a day.

THE TEA PACE

HARKAY: Actually, our life is not that fast, not like the ones they have in the big cities. Here, we have time for everything. We have time for business; we have time for our families; we have time for our friends. But it all depends, because you can make life very fast for yourself anywhere.

JITENDRA: Still, it's not like the very fast life you have in foreign countries. We have time for our children and time for our guests. We have time for everything. It's a routine life, but it's a very free life, a very calm and quiet life. We open our shop at nine o'clock in the morning and by six or six-thirty, we close the shop and go home and have a cup of tea and watch our TV. In the Hindu religion when there is a wedding or a marriage in the house, tea is served in all the places.

HARKAY: When a baby is born and you go to the family home you will definitely see tea. If somebody dies, you go to the funeral and they serve tea. In marriages or in any important occasion, tea is always there, especially in Darjeeling. You won't get water, but you'll definitely get tea. You can say it's become like wine for us.

JITENDRA: Yes, you can say it is like Indian wine, but to be frank with you, *it is* Indian wine. When we have customers from abroad and we always offer them tea and say, "Sir, would you like to have a cup of tea?" If they say, " No," then we say, " This is an Indian wine." When they hear that our masala tea is an Indian wine they say, "OK, now we want to have it!" Then they like it a lot! There are also various ways of drinking tea. Some people drink it only black, without milk or sugar.

But we Indians at home put the water at boiling and we put in tea leaves and different kind of spices. India tea prices vary according to the quality. If you go to a railway station in India, you get tea for two rupees, sometimes three rupees or four rupees. The people who are in the higher classes use the green leaf tea, which is very expensive, above a thousand, three thousand rupees per kilo. All this green leaf tea is exported abroad. In India, people go for the CTC leaves, the blended tea, which is manufactured.

HARKAY: That is what we have in Doars, the Assam area. There are two types of tea in India. We have the pot tea and the other where they just put in water and milk and tea and sugar. A lot of people drink that tea in India, which is a very nominal rate, around hundred rupees a kilogram. Only fifteen to twenty percent people have the leaf tea, which is from Darjeeling.

JITENDRA: Everybody has tea.

HARKAY: People can stay alive without food, but they have to have tea.

JITENDRA: If you happen to go to Calcutta, tea is served in a small earthen pot, which is very hygienic. There is a small market and a tea

seller along with his kettle and earthen pots. He doesn't keep an account of how much tea you are drinking. He charges a fixed rate per month, and he has to collect this much money. Every few minutes he is there with the kettle and the earthen pots. The quantity is so little, around fifty milligrams, and people take earthen pots and have a cup of tea, just a sip only, and they throw them away. There in Calcutta, if a multimillionaire happens to come to a shop and is served tea, he doesn't deny the custom; he takes the tea the customary way.

DESERT ISLAND WISH LIST

JITENDRA: If I was on a desert island, I could survive without everything, but not without tea. If a camel is in a desert that is very hot and drinks water, it can survive. If I am really in the state of dying in a desert and somebody pours two drops of tea, also I can survive for five or six hours more. That much I can tell you.

HARKAY: Tea—it is more important than water.

JITENDRA: Yes, it is more important than water.

HARKAY: If we are in the desert and it is very hot and we are far from water, I think we can survive without food for four or five days—if we get tea, just a cup of tea, everyday.

JITENDRA: First and foremost in importance would be tea, second water, and third food.

HARKAY: If our shop is empty for a while, we tell our staff to go and get us a cup of tea. With our tea, we can go ahead and work for three or four more hours, even without food.

JITENDRA: During October and November, when the tourist season starts, we just have our breakfast, no lunch. We can survive with tea throughout the day. This is a fact, sir. Not with us only, but if you go throughout Darjeeling, people will tell you the same thing.

One instant is eternity;
eternity is in the now.
When you see through
this one instant,
you see through the
one who sees.

—WU-MEN
JAPANESE ZEN MASTER,
(1183–1260)

HARKAY: This is a fact. We come from Siliguri. The first thing my wife will give us when we go home is tea. She doesn't give water or anything because she also feels that after having a cup of tea we'll be more relaxed.

JITENDRA: When I go home and tell my wife I'm feeling lazy, she tells me to have a cup of tea. If I have a headache, she tells me to have a cup of tea. She says that will do. Serving tea is a routine. We drink a minimum ten cups a day, although we may go to up to twenty cups. Let's suppose you are coming from Siliguri to Darjeeling in a shared taxi. When the driver is halfway, he stops the car and says, "OK, do you want to have a cup of tea?"

RITUAL REFRESHMENT

HARKAY: Tea means *freshness*. That is what I feel because once you have a cup of tea you'll feel more fresh.

JITENDRA: Tea, to be very honest, is the main part of our life. We are unable to resist it. If we don't take a cup of tea a day we feel that we haven't done anything and we feel quite lazy. Once we have that cup of tea life is really charming; tea gives freshness to our life. Some people say that if you have tension or have a headache you should have cup of tea because it removes all this tension. It's fresh as morning dew. Instead of going for a morning walk we have a cup of tea. Then we feel as if we have done something good for ourselves.

HARKAY: If we don't have a cup of tea during the day, we get a headache and next day we are liable to fall sick. When we are traveling from Darjeeling to other places, to visit our relatives or some important person, we definitely carry a packet of tea. When our tea is presented this way, the person we are visiting knows that we have remembered him. The present of tea makes him think he is very dear to me. By this custom you can see how tea has affected us.

THE MEANING OF
TEA

THE SECOND CUP
MOROCCO

The second [cup] banished my loneliness . . .

—LU TONG

If the first cup of tea satisfies the most elemental of physical desires—thirst—the second cup attends to the most basic of emotional desires, that of companionship. One way to appreciate this aspect of tea is to consider the role of ritual, whose traditional function has always been to give structure, form and meaning to life's moments of transition and transformation, which is to say that ritual reconnects us to the community. In this sense, ritual provides a prescribed order for religious ceremonies, fraternal organizations, and even everyday acts, like enjoying a cup of tea.

"In Lu Yu's time," writes Derek Maitland, the 8th century author of the *Cha Ching (The Tea Classic)*, "the act of drinking tea itself was a masterpiece of life, a moment that summed up all moments of tea drinking, as if the moment had not existed before and might not exist again." Lu Yu, the Sage of Tea, believed that tea symbolized the very harmony of the universe. His book provides us with the earliest historical evidence for the ritualizing of tea drinking. In his "tea bible," which may have been a commission by local tea merchants, he lists precisely nine steps for the manufacturing of tea, seven for its brewing, and exactly 24 implements to be utilized in a ceremony. As if that wasn't enough ritual, he lays out guidelines for conversation over tea and for the most sophisticated means of judging the tea itself. Maitland writes that this high degree of formalization enjoyed a "brief vogue" during the Tang and Sung Dynasties, but eventually fell away in favor of a less formal approach.

In Part 2, we travel to North Africa to explore a fascinating branch of the tree of tea rituals: the Moroccan tea ceremony. To illuminate this little known history, we turn, in chapter 7, to Professor Abdelahad Sebti who reveals its surprising origins in the exchange of cultural diplomacy with European diplomats in the late nineteenth century. Eventually, he says, tea displaced wine as the ceremonial beverage in his society. The implements, preparation and serving all ritualize—give form to—social life by promoting familiarity, trust, and a respect for the skill of the tea host. For Mamine Mohamed, tea, prayer, and ceremony are inextricably interconnected. The traditional Moroccan tea game, he explains, occurs after evening prayers. On average, three cups of tea are drunk every time it is served, the number itself signifying the union of mind, body, and spirit. Mamine also describes the selflessness at the heart of Moroccan tea ceremony. While it is a pleasure to imbibe tea, he reveals that it is actually an honor to serve it to family and friends.

In the following chapter, we learn from Moroccan café owner, Rhabaoui Abdellatif, that "When tea is a part of you, it becomes a true love story." The marvelous metaphor of a love affair helps describe the stirring depths of emotion he feels for the complexity and even the "sensuality" of tea. Abdellatif is motivated by a desire to restore the nearly forgotten tea traditions of Morocco, and to revive respect for tea for the younger generation who grew up thinking it was more of a nuisance than a "deep part of your soul." For those who appreciate these depths, he remarks that tea is a fraternity of kindred spirits, which lends modern insight to Lu Tong's ancient description of tea's powers to "banish loneliness."

In the second half of his wide-ranging interview, in chapter 9, Professor Sebti describes the relatively recent accent on ritual tea ceremony in Morocco as a modernization of the old ritual of imbibing wine. In his vivid words, tea represents a return to the ancient tradition of "a drink of togetherness." Likewise, the public tea house, he reminds us, is a return to the Arab invention of the café as a "public space" and a boon to community life.

Writing about the power and beauty of tea ceremony, China scholar and Qigong master Kenneth Cohen has followed the way of tea for over thirty years. For Cohen, tea ceremony reenacts an ancient situation, and more, it is a divine medicine. In "Tea in My Life," an essay published in the late 1970s, Cohen states that the meaning of the actions in a ceremony is evident in every action, and cannot be explained in ordinary language. "It puts us in touch with an archetype," he writes, "a vestigial energy which comes not so much from a remote past as from the timeless dimension of our own present being.

This is a quality not only of tea but of most religious and secular rituals from most ancient times onward. It is the ritual nature of tea, which shows most clearly the part it plays in my life."

Cohen goes on to say that the importance of the ritual partly derives from the fact that tea speaks a language beyond words and communicates directly and immediately without intellectualization, like music or dance. "Ritual has meaning far beyond any set definition, and this meaning reveals itself differently according to the depth and readiness of the participant." The influence of the ritual was most poignantly described to him, he has recently written, by Soshitsu Sen XV, descendant of the founder of Japanese Tea Ceremony, who told him, "A cup of tea is a cup of peace.".

If the function of ritual is to lend form to the chaos of human life, then the rich range of tea rites and ceremonies around the world gives us ample opportunity to experience our lives in far more depth and with far more clarity, more immediately and more sensuously, than we would otherwise.

—P. C.

Chapter Seven
The National Beverage of Morocco

WITH
ABDELAHAD SEBTI & MAMINE MOHAMED

ABDELAHAD SEBTI

The man stepped inside the stall and sat down, and his friend poured
him a glass of tea. They sat for an hour or so, talking and smoking
and sipping the tea.

—MOHAMMED MRABET, *The Sea in the Street*

Professor Sebti is a historian teaching at the University of Rabat. He wrote *The Book of Tea: Customs and History* with his friend Abdel Hamr Sassi, which was published by the Rabat University Press in 1999. It deals with the cultural history of tea in Morocco, documenting how it progressively became a national beverage in that country. The book also shows how a tradition comes into being, and what processes led to its development in the daily life of Moroccans. Two primary interests converge in its pages: the history of daily life and elements that exemplify daily life and everyday culture. By focussing on the study of tea, the book captures different aspects of society, cultural change, and the evolution of cultural change.

ABDELAHAD SEBTI: My friend Ibrahim el Sassi is a specialist in poetry, especially of Berber song. We realized how interesting those poetic works are from the beginning of the nineteenth century, which establish the different levels of tea's history, tea practice, the aesthetics of tea, the European incursion, and the development of colonialism. Our common interest in tea is closely tied to our interest in the relationships between popular culture, high culture, and ancient history.

TEA COMES TO MOROCCO

As for the introduction of tea in Morocco, what is striking and para-doxical is that Moroccans believe and feel that tea has always been a native beverage. But historically, tea is actually a recent phenomenon in Morocco. It would appear that it came to this country at the end of the seventeenth century or beginning of the eighteenth. But it wasn't widely distributed. In fact, tea was basically a gift that European diplomats would offer to the King of Morocco. Tea only became distributed in quantity and commercially available during the nineteenth century when introduced by the British, who got it from China. At the same time, sugar, which is an important part of tea consumption, was coming in from France. So, tea arrived progressively, infiltrating the Moroccan population, society, and topography. But you can't say that tea was a general phenomenon permeating all levels of society and all regions until early in the twentieth century.

As far as cultural history is concerned, the origin of ceremonial tea practices seems to be complex and is not yet entirely clear. The first question is that there are many imported elements and foreign components, notably tea itself, which come from China. Moroccans chose green tea and not what we call black tea. And some of the tea instruments are not Moroccan, either.

For example, here in Fez, luxury china is what we call in Arabic "reyad." In fact, reyad is a deformation of the English manufacturer Wright. The company produced luxury china according to the specifications of Fez merchants living in Manchester, and it became very well-known here. Although still available here, it is rare.

What did Moroccans drink before? Was there an earlier tea ceremony? What did Moroccans drink before tea? The answer is that several elements show that the tea ritual originates in a displacement of the wine ceremony. That is to say, in the manner of drinking, there are many components showing that the ritual is a transfer of the way wine was drunk. It is also important to mention that some groups, especially religious ones, were opposed to tea.

Moroccan poets wrote verse celebrating tea drinking that was modeled after the manner of classical Arabic poetry praising wine. On the other hand, Moroccans did construct their own tea ceremony. It is based on a combination of things, such as the company in which you drink it, the accessories, the china, the gestures, the actual preparation, the way you serve it, even how you are supposed to drink your tea. All these things make up the Moroccan tea ceremony. Contrary to assumptions about Moroccan tea, the ceremony differs from region to region and between social classes; there's a great difference in the way you serve tea in Fez, in the Sahara, or up in the mountains.

Within your own house dwells the treasure of joy; so why do you go begging from door to door?

—SUFI SAYING

THE RELIGIOUS CONTEXT

The notion that there was once an objection to tea is something a Moroccan of today can barely imagine. As far as how the opposition was quelled, we must go back and look at the context of the nineteenth century. At that time, there were two forces. First, there was the economic context, a systematic and deliberate penetration of the Moroccan market by English tea and sugar from France. Then you have to consider the conservatism of religious groups. These combined groups saw tea as an invasion of Moroccan markets.

When you think about it, this rejection of tea resembles what happened in Europe with another beverage. We have proof that certain social groups were hostile to coffee because it came from Turkey. So there's this resistance to otherness, to another culture. Then, there were "nationalists" groups that opposed tea and boycotted it for political reasons at the beginning of the twentieth century. They said the Moroccan economy was being bled dry by the importation of foreign tea and sugar. Eventually, tea won out and became the daily beverage of all social strata in Morocco. Along the way, it was integrated into social gatherings of all sorts.

However, the beverage that did have a place in Islam, especially in the Middle Ages, is coffee. In Yemen, it functioned primarily in religious ceremonies from the very beginning. It was a drink that aided the Sufi mystics. In contrast, you can't really say that tea found a place in religious ceremony. Tea just became an everyday drink, and the opposition to it faded because, basically, the economic, cultural, and political forces that promoted it in the first place prevailed. Royal support also played an important role in the development of tea drinking. Tea was first consumed in the context of the royal court, with the first tea ceremony taking place at the royal palace. Imitation of royalty followed as Moroccan society turns to tea, resembling Britain's history in its imitation of the court.

God is with those who persevere.
—THE KORAN

MOROCCAN TEA CEREMONY

For the preparation of the tea ceremony, there is a *place*. In some social milieus, for example in the Zarwia, the great Sufi institution, there is a tearoom. The Moroccan ceremony surrounding tea sometimes has its own room, a little like it is in China. Then there's the tea set, which always has platters, one reserved for the teapot and glasses, one for the tea box and sugar, the other for the mint and spoons. There is a brazier or a tripod for boiling the water, and a kettle. There is also the proxy host who prepares the tea. That's most important. Not just anyone can make the tea. You need to know how, because making tea requires skill; it's a sign of authority and of popularity.

The master of the place, whoever that might be, designates who will prepare the tea. Yet there's a progression from one step to the next. First, you heat the water in the kettle, then you rinse the teapot, put the tea in, add mint and sugar, and let it steep. There's some variation here. In some regions you just let it infuse. In others, you take the teapot once it's mixed, and put it back on the flame. Then the proxy host tastes it, pours it out, and tea is served. There's also the well-known practice of pouring the tea from up high, which creates slight foam on top of the tea.

There's another element as well, which is the number of pots. Traditionally, Moroccans favor "the three pots." Tea is prepared three times in a row. It's a ritual of longstanding practice. No one knows why. Simply, it's to take tea three times—*and you must accept the offer of all three pots of tea*. It takes no more explanation.

One thing worth remarking on in the ceremony is that you see the tea actually being made. That's very important. It's not a beverage that is *brought* to you. It is a drink you watch being prepared, which is an essential and unique component of the Moroccan tea ritual.

MOROCCAN MINT

How did mint become part of the tea? We really don't have any concrete evidence that would allow us to answer that precisely. What we can say is that mint preceded tea. Mint was here before tea. Moroccans must have drunk it as an infusion, as a hot beverage in combination with other herbs, and also for cooking some dishes. They used it as a pharmaceutical product to treat certain medical conditions. I remember when I was young, my parents would place mint on me when I had a fever.

The conjunction of mint and tea is, in fact, typically Moroccan, so it's annoying the immigrant population from the Maghreb to France say "mint tea" as though it were a North African phenomenon, whereas it is specifically Moroccan. That is to say, Algerians and Tunisians don't generally take tea with mint. While it has become a Maghreb phenomenon, it is actually a Moroccan innovation.

To be more thorough, I should also mention that among the variations worth noting with respect to mint, the first is practiced by the Jewish population of Moroccan cities. Moroccan Jews use a lot of mint and very little tea. So little in fact, that they often say, "I'll have a glass of mint," meaning a glass of tea. The other variation comes from the

Saharan areas in the South, where people take their tea without mint. So it is a very strong tea. There are places where there just isn't any mint and so other herbs take its place.

A French friend told me that when he was in Lebanon, he asked for mint tea but the waiter was astonished because, of course, they don't drink mint tea there! When my friend insisted, they brought him regular tea, and then brought a leaf or two of mint, just as a joke. They just don't drink it. So mint tea, which is really Moroccan, has wound up, for Europeans and sometimes Americans, representing an Arab, or a North African, or a Muslim, phenomenon.

To cite another example, take absinthe, which we call *shiba*. I remember when I was a child, in the winter, we used absinthe, in addition to mint, because it warms you up.

> *It is the destiny of mint to be crushed.*
> —WAVERLY LEWIS ROOT
> (1903–1982)

There are other herbs, like sage and marjoram and in some cities, like here in Fez, we also use orange flowers. But herbs are seasonal. Something that's typical of Marrakech but found nowhere else is a market specializing in herbs for tea, right behind the *Jama' al-Fna*, the place in the heart of the city. There's a market where they sell *"trallats,"* meaning *blend*, and it's a mixture of herbs. In Marrakech the blend is very sophisticated because there is such a wide variety of herbs. They're used because they contribute to the scent, for the aroma, or for their warming qualities.

What's striking is that right from the beginning Moroccans chose green tea from China. In this we are distinct from most Arab countries, and notably from Lebanon and North Africa, where people developed a taste for infusions of black tea. Why, it's difficult to say. It may be a function of its conservatism. Moroccans got used to green tea, in the form the British accustomed them to, which preserves better and is better suited for the Moroccan tea ceremony. It's difficult to imagine the brewing of black tea being compatible with the tea ceremony in Morocco.

As far as tea glasses are concerned, there has been an evolution over time, bringing change and variation. To some extent, it's a geographic variation, but it's much more of a social one. I say *evolution*,

The Pouring Ritual

There are two explanations. There's one aesthetic reason; the image of the waterfall, and another practical explanation; that it cools the tea. When you pour from on high the tea foams. This too is part of the ceremony, and we call it the Rzah, meaning the traditional turban. But I think this is something that's exaggerated in folklore, which you see mainly in hotels for tourists.

because originally tea was served in cups the way coffee is served. As for variety, it depends very much on social class.

A very popular model of tea glasses can still be found today in rural areas. It is called a *haiati*, which literally means "my life." I think the word actually refers to the transparency of the glass. A *haiati* is a small, transparent glass and has colored motifs painted on it. That's the simplest version. There are also middle-class versions, tea glasses with very simple motifs that resemble grapes and others with floral vine motifs. Then there are luxury models, very high-end glasses that cost about four thousand dirams (about four hundred dollars). They are colored glasses, generally a kind that is close to crystal, and found only in elite circles.

THE TEA GAME

ZAYYAD JARMOUN: Moroccan tradition says that you take one glass and pass the next one. The one who drinks tea doesn't set the glass down; he throws it away, toward the one who prepared the tea. He just throws it down on the floor. If the glass falls in a standing up position—then I have the right to ask the one who made the tea for anything. It's an old tradition and at the same time, it's a game to break up the monotony of the day. Today, I threw the glass three times, and it landed down each time. So it is was my friend's right to tell me what to do. For example, I might have to organize the next dinner for him. But it's actually pretty rare for the glass to land standing up.

> *The beater and the beaten. Mere players of a game ephemeral as a dream.*
>
> —MUSON, ZEN MONK

MAMINE MOHAMED: Yes, if the glass falls right-side-up, then the one who threw it imposes a command on the one who poured the tea. If the glass isn't right-side-up, the one who prepared the tea imposes his will on the one who threw the glass. It always takes time—an hour or two—and occurs either after the evening prayer or around ten or eleven o'clock at night.

MAMINE MOHAMED

Making tea happens through tradition. When you are a child, you see your elders preparing tea, and soon you begin to prepare it. At the moment of preparation, there is the "time of tea," as the English say. We say the same thing in Arabic: *teayu* is the same word, meaning tea time.

On average, we drink nine cups a day. Every time the tea is made, we drink three glasses. It's an Islamic tradition—you know, in Islam, Salat? It's the Tuesday Prayer. Normally, when you travel, there are the graces or the prayers, and you are allowed to say only two. But when you are in North Africa, you have to do all three. That's the way it is. It has to do with the time it takes to pray. When you're traveling, your prayers are fewer. When you are present for the tea ceremony, you must drink all three glasses. But if you are traveling, you cannot reduce your prayers on Tuesday. You can't shorten them; you can't do two, even if you're traveling. When you are engaged in a ceremony, you have to drink three glasses of tea. Of the five prayers, there are four besides the Maghreb prayer. But the one you can't shorten is the fourth one, the prayer of the Maghreb. As with the fourth prayer, you can't shorten your tea time, you drink your three glasses and not two. Also, you always do things in threes, in uneven numbers. If you are eating dates, you can eat only three or five or seven.

We pour tea from glass to glass to make it foam. This gives a beautiful aesthetic to the glass. If you're making tea outside, you have to protect the glass, to make sure the sand doesn't get in. When there is foam in the glass and the sand comes up it stays on top and it doesn't go down into the glass. That tradition is five hundred years old.

IT'S AN HONOR TO SERVE

As soon as a man becomes an adult, reaches majority age, he starts preparing the tea for his family, for his friends, and for groups. It is an honor in the eyes of your guests for whoever gets to prepare the tea.

It was the time I loved best in the tea-house . . . the attendant stood
with his back to the sun, balancing a brass tray on his arm. Motionless
in the sea of pale light that broke around his body, he seemed for a
moment transfigured, some fallen spirit suddenly redeemed . . . [His]
unshaven head, vacant-eyed, became the haloed face of ineffable wis-
dom, the tea-tray flashing on his arm the insignia of heaven, God's gift
to mankind. Reverently, I handed him my glass: "More tea, please."

— MICHAEL CARROLL
FROM A *Persian Teahouse: Travels in Old Iran*

Whenever you give someone tea to prepare, that person is perceived in a good light. So if I pour tea, I feel honored by the group for whom I am preparing it. I am happy because I feel that when I put the tea in the teapot I am expressing my real feelings.

Of course, it is usually the youngest of the group who makes the tea. If you're making three pots, once the youngest has prepared the tea, then it's someone else's turn. When we drink it in the morning we do it the quick way. But in the afternoon, it takes between one hour and two, and in the evening also, an hour or two to make our tea. That is because tea doesn't taste the same if it is prepared too fast. In the morning we have it a little weaker and in the evening it's made a little stronger.

CHAPTER EIGHT
THE SPIRITUAL ENERGY OF TEA

WITH
RHARBAOUI ABDELLATIF

RHARBAOUI ABDELLATIF

"Let's have some tea," said the Rifi. "We can sit over there
under the cypresses." He made tea in the garden, and they took
their glasses and sat on a mat in the shade. And they smoked
their pipes and talked.

— MOHAMMED MRABET, *The Kif Patch*

Rharbaoui Abdellatif comes from a family of sailors in Menasooara, but his life-long goal has always been to own and run a restaurant, which he now does, in Marrakech, Morocco. His dream come true is a place where he tries to create an atmosphere unique in his beloved homeland. To do this he has combined a 1970s touch, featuring clean lines and beautiful appointments, which has created what he calls "a simple little restaurant that relies on the best food, herbs, and tea from the local markets. Beyond the décor he hopes his customers will feel they are part of the "fraternity" of tea.

RHARBAOUI ABDELLATIF: Tea is a form of energy and spirituality in a glass. I think that tea is something that has been with humans forever. In the tradition I learned, tea is beyond being just a hot drink; it's also something that purifies your body.

In my restaurant, the idea is to get away from the monotony of Moroccan mint. My restaurant reflects what I love and am proud of about my country. Morocco is a beautiful land. It's my love for my country that I'm expressing in every way in my restaurant. In the end, it's very simple. I try to offer options that reflect my taste in tea, a place where basil tea or ginger tea or marjoram tea are imaginable. I try to make sure that people can savor a tea they can't find elsewhere. I'm happy about that. Anyone can do it at home. They can pick some herbs from their garden and make a hot beverage with green tea.

The inspiration for me is that Moroccans have unfortunately forgotten some of their tradition. Teas with different flavors have existed in Morocco since the nineteenth century. I think it's an Oriental inspiration. But with time and modernization, people fell back on mint tea, rather than saffron or ginger tea. Perhaps a century ago you could drink these teas in any house in Morocco.

There are many rich traditions in Morocco, but much of that is lost to us today. I think that tea is much more varied and interesting than only the mint tea that you see everywhere in Morocco. Mint isn't even something that's ours; we inherited it— and we inherited it badly. I try and seek out and offer different teas to my patrons.

> 𝒦
>
> *Your task is to discover your work and then with all your heart give yourself to it.*
>
> —BUDDHA

When I was a little boy and I had a serious fever, my mother used to make me tea with thyme. I think it's a shame that with all the wonderful teas, herbs, and strong tastes you can find here, so many people always stick with the same tea.

Everything is better appreciated when you are more mature. I'm from the younger generation that grew up with Coca-Cola and Fanta, so tea was a kind of nuisance. But we didn't have a choice, because it was there with our bread in the morning; it was there at lunch in our afternoon snack. When you're a child you don't have the same kind of appreciation of flavors the way someone does who is forty, sitting in his little shop waiting for tea time and making tea with love.

For my mother, tea is more like cigarettes or some other habit. If she doesn't have her tea, she gets upset. It's true that over time tea becomes something even more important than a habit. Over time, if you make it with love, and you savor it, tea will bring you peace, a lot of peace.

When you've been drinking tea all your life you begin to see it as something that's a deep part of your soul. It's like a love affair, like a wife for a man and a husband for a woman. When tea is part of you, it becomes a true love story.

THE PLEASURE OF MAKING TEA

If you like tea, making it starts with going out to choose your mint, smelling it, making the journey back from the market, and feeling eager. There's something deeply romantic about it. Whereas, when you're little, you drink your tea and that's that. You drink it to warm yourself or because you're thirsty. You have your way of making it and you want it to always be good.

As for the Moroccan ritual, I think it's pretty conventional. It's something classic. I have preferences for certain aromas. It's a little like love in that you are gentle with the leaves of mint. You heat the water tenderly, slowly. And then when you've drunk your tea, you feel like you've accomplished a mission. You have a sweetness running through you with

tea. I find tea to be very sensual. Even if you don't realize it, you feel it. It's very simple—just tea, mint and hot water. Once you really love it, it's something that gives you so much energy, so much pleasure. There's the mint that you have to clean this way—not that way, all these delicate operations—just to make a cup of tea. It's in you and it's a pleasure.

I prefer to drink one or two cups during the day, but good ones. It's something that should touch you, a moment in your day, so if you drink too much it's no longer that delicate aromatic event that you think of as you wake up. I prefer to drink tea for the spiritual energy it gives me, rather than a banal drink with no savor. If I had to have a plain cup all the time, it would be just a drink.

> *Men's natures are alike; it is their habits that separate them.*
> —CONFUCIUS
> (552–479 BCE)

In a way, I'm keeping or reinforcing the tradition—and then breaking or changing that tradition. I'm changing it in the sense of wanting to astonish and awaken the savors, the extraordinary aromas you can taste in teas. I think that change, whether it's an evolution or a return, is always a positive thing. If you have the opportunity to drink a cup of ginger tea or saffron tea at home, that's another flavor added to life. When life is good and you are happy, you appreciate everything. It's not really a resurrection or a change. You are able to appreciate the beauty in everyday life.

Over time you can become dependent on tea and you start drinking more and more. Human beings are like that. They either decide to stop or not. With tea, there's no real problem because it's something that's not unhealthy. I know my mother drinks six or seven pots a day. You can get to be an addict in daily life if you wind up drinking five or six pots. Well, maybe not addicted. Can you say, a "tea fiend"?

For myself, I use the standard green tea and I like basil tea because of that very fresh feeling in your mouth. When it's cold, I sometimes prefer an absinthe tea. I feel like a basil tea is more refreshing, more aromatic, so it's good for an afternoon or a morning, for an ordinary moment in the day. Absinthe, it's true, is stronger, and it's something you find in the autumn, when it's cold. It reflects the season, so an absinthe tea is good; it's best at night when you're all warm.

THE FRATERNITY OF TEA

𝒦˜

Dear friend: Your heart is a polished mirror. You must wipe it clean of the veil of dust that has gathered upon it, because it is destined to reflect the light of divine secrets.

—ABU HAMID
AL-GHAZZALI
(1058-1111)

Saffron tea is very sensitive, so it's something I prefer to drink before going to bed at night. It heats up your body. I like having that warm feeling that all the qualities of the tea are being transferred to me. Ginger and Royal Tea, with camellia and rose petals are very delicate and I have to be careful, so I like to have them at night. You can't drink a tea like that and go out into the cold. You want to stay home in the warmth. Your body reacts to it directly. Tea is like that. Our ancestors must have reacted like that. Teas must have been medicinal treatments for them. If something hurt, they would have made a tea for it.

I remember that when I got back from Italy, about the first thing I did when I got home was to have my first tea with my friends. I was eager for that, because tea has something that binds people together.

So tea is a fraternity. The ceremonies don't change because it's more than a drink to have by yourself—something that unites people in peace.

CHAPTER NINE
THE EVOLUTION OF TEA

WITH
ABDELAHAD SEBTI

ABDELAHAD SEBTI

*" . . . and we drank Arab tea with roasted almonds, two tastes that
didn't know each other, and became one in our mouth."*

—Amichai Yehudi Amicha, from *The Language of Love and Tea
with Roasted Almonds*

Tea took a long time to infiltrate Morocco. What's striking about the
phenomenon of tea is that foreigners, Europeans, travelers who came
to Morocco in the nineteenth century, all said that tea is something
very Moroccan. They observed that Moroccans were tea people. There
is an external vision that established tea in the mythic Morocco of
European imagination. However, when you look more closely on the
Moroccan side of history, you find that the practice of tea was slow in
developing.

So what is the underpinning of tea? I think there are several levels.
On the first level, tea is tied to the slowness of its progression, the dif-
fusion in Moroccan life. Originally, tea was not a common beverage.
Tea was an elite drink, so it carries the connotation of luxury, the court,
the upper classes, the city dwellers.

The second level and another surprising aspect is that in Morocco,
tea is a man's drink. Only men drink tea. We have evidence that even

in the first decades of the twentieth century, in some social groups, like those up in the Moroccan mountains, as well as with women and children, they were not permitted to drink tea. Or if they were allowed, they had the last pour, that is to say, what was left over from the tea preparation. When tea is not drunk among men, such as when a man drinks it in the company of his loved one or his wife, it is associated with sexual desire. Over the years, I have collected stories from men who explained that even in urban settings when they take their tea in the evening, and they were in the familial space, it is always associated with intimacy.

The aspect of tea being a man's drink has to do with the local culture and social relationships. How else do you explain that in rural areas, like in the mountains, men drink tea, but women or children do not? This is tied partly to the fact that men do not eat with women and children. They eat alone. The male tea tradition is an adaptation of tea in keeping up with social practice. The exclusion of women is absolutely certain.

Of course, these are stages in the development of tea culture that are now completely forgotten. But traces linger. The other thing that contributes to the significance of tea is how it has been described with beautiful metaphors when it was still the center of a very elaborate ritual. Nowadays, the real ritual intensity of the tea ceremony exists only down in the region of the Sahara, and perhaps a bit in the mountains. But the ceremony is especially strong in the south.

The greatest productions of art, whether painting, music, sculpture or poetry, have invariably this quality—something approaching the work of God.

—D. T. Suzuki

So, tea has been the subject of metaphor. When tea was still closely associated with the elite, there was a whole aesthetic of tea. This aesthetic of tea recalls the aesthetics of tea in Japan, that is, as a very weighty aesthetic. Some of this metaphoric use was recorded in classical poetry, for example, in the dialectal Berber poetry of Al-Mazir.

There's a Berber poet from the south of Morocco who wrote a very beautiful poem of almost two hundred lines, at the end of the nineteenth century, in Berber. Among the things he develops is the following image or metaphor. The poet says that the tripod for boiling water represents the minaret, the kettle is the *muezzin* that calls you to prayer. The round tray is the oratory, where you pray, the *mossalah* and the teapot is the imam, the man who directs prayer in the mosque. The glasses represent the faithful placed all around: the community.

No man fears what he has seen grow.

—AFRICAN PROVERB

Tea acquired these elaborate images over time. The last of the images was constructed very late, this association of tea with the community. Until then, the image of tea represented a much more, shall we say, hierarchical society.

For the Berbers, there are many varieties of mint, though in some Berber regions you don't find mint. Some types are given other names, like *timige,* which is a kind of herb. As for the question of practice, I don't think there's any specific Berber one to my knowledge, except perhaps that tea is drunk to keep warm, in addition to its usual usage.

The better-known tea ceremony and the more established one is from the Sahara. Currently, it is the region where the ritual is most elaborate and most rigid. People from the Sahara, even if they live in cities up north, go somewhere quiet and they take time with their tea. Since it is conducted in Sahara time, it is a long ceremony. They take their tea without mint and very strong; you drink it from little glasses that are only half-filled.

Has modern life had an impact on tea drinking? What is worth mentioning is that the introduction of tea itself was part of a process of economic modernization, the creation or opening of the Moroccan market and international commerce during the nineteenth century.

Historically, Morocco has this phenomenon of having culturally appropriating something that came from outside. What happened then is paradoxical. Moroccans invented a ritual, something peculiar to themselves, with a product, tea, coming from the outside.

First of all, it's a question of time—time people no longer have. They don't have time to prepare tea the way they used to. But it is also a question of space. People live more and more often in apartments. Now they have to make tea in the kitchen and bring it out, except, of course, for ceremonies like weddings or family gatherings. Even at weddings the tea is no longer prepared the same way. It's prepared away, practically in the kitchen, and served like it would be in a Western reception, by servers with trays. There again, the evolution of tea is tied to the evolution of the family. It's no longer an extended family, but more the nuclear family. You have the evolution of the family that no longer permits, or is not compatible with, the practices of tea. You also have competition from coffee and from black tea like Lipton, and from carbonated drinks, especially in urban blue-collar areas. When tea was offered to guests in the past, it was to honor them. More and more, when guests are offered a beverage, the habit is to offer them carbonated ones.

In religious festivals like Ramadan, the feast and celebration for the birth of the prophet, people go and visit as an extended family. Of course, the tradition is for tea to be offered. But today, the relationship to time has changed. While Moroccans continue to enact this ritual, they go through it much faster. They have to go to many more houses in a short period of time. So if people who are receiving no longer have time to prepare the tea, what do they serve? They serve juices. The question of ritual is tied to daily life and culture. What we're losing is at the level of unity, the level of human relationships that are associated with a phenomenon like tea.

TEA VERSUS COFFEE

In Morocco, coffee arrived from the Mash-el-eb, from the Arab east, and it permeated all areas under Ottoman rule. It is a geographical coincidence that coffee took hold in Tunisia and Algeria, but not in Morocco, other than in the North of Morocco at a very late date. So, coffee has existed in Algeria since the sixteenth century, but it doesn't exist in the same way in Morocco.

This harks back to an important sociological point. Tea is a beverage that is usually drunk inside. Whereas coffee, when it appeared in Algeria and elsewhere in the Arab world, arrived alongside the institution of the café as a "public space," like communal space. That's interesting, especially since Europeans and Westerners often don't know that the café is an invention of Arab spatiality. It appeared in the Ottoman world before it was adopted in Europe. In Morocco, there's a kind of avoidance, or distance with respect to public space. Until recently, society looked down on the idea of eating out, to say you had a bite outside. So, consuming food outside has a pejorative quality.

I remember another aspect of the question of coffee versus tea from my own youth. We rarely had coffee. Mostly, it was a beverage we had during funerals. In the social rituals associated with burial you have coffee. The difference is that tea retained its associations with pleasure, so you would decline to drink tea in situations like that of a funeral. Later, I learned that this was true not only in Fez, where I grew up, but in other Moroccan cities as well.

In general, Moroccans drink more tea than coffee. But they also drink a lot more coffee than they did before. That is an effect that's partly tied to advertising for Nescafé coffee. It's also tied to lifestyle. For example, in some ads, drinking coffee is associated with the active and fast life of cities. Other coffee ads emphasize the difference between the city and rural areas. So more and more people drink a lot more coffee in urban areas than in the country. We see more meetings at cafés—because there's no time to visit at home—which is a major contribution to the advantage of coffee.

Contrary to Europeans, Moroccans never associated tea with Asia. In the Western imagination, tea represents Asian exoticism, but for Moroccans, tea is a practice they've completely appropriated. For Moroccans, tea and tea sets came indirectly from Britain. The classic Moroccan teapot shape is a copy of the common English teapot from the beginning of the eighteenth century. All these things contribute to why Moroccans have forgotten the Asian origins of tea.

Overall, Moroccans drink less and less tea at breakfast and drink it regularly, especially in the context of the family, after lunch and after dinner. In in the country and in the mountains, people also have tea before lunch is served, if they have guests. Then there's the tea of what we call the "*gouter*," a taste, in the middle of the afternoon, the tea that accompanies meals, the tea associated with pauses and rests, and the tea that is a form of hospitality for a guest or someone who doesn't live with you.

In some social contexts, tea is also the time for negotiation and business. During the French Protectorat, from 1912 to 1956, the first resident General Lioté, the one who was responsible for French policy toward Morocco, invented the expression the "glass of tea policy." This means a policy that relies on close ties to the Moroccan elite, confirming what I said earlier, that it is intimately tied to negotiation.

But finally, why do we stop and take time for tea? I think tea is essentially a drink of togetherness. Tea is a conversation beverage; tea is for being together and talking. Remember, in the southern regions, notably in the Oussous, and also the Atlas Mountains, tea is the equivalent of a literary salon. Many poems and literary works give accounts that describe the tea ceremony as a kind of salon for conversation and literature. Obviously, in this setting, time stops.

THE MEANING OF
TEA

THE THIRD CUP

AMERICA

The third expelled the dourness from my mind . . .

—LU TONG

Throughout human history there has moved a strong current of belief that when people lose their connection with nature they become cut off from their deepest selves. The practices of philosophy, art, and religion have served as a means for people to "get back in touch" with what cultural historians such as Aldous Huxley have called the "ground of our own being."

Broadly speaking, there are three main movements for those who are determined to regain their accord with nature. First is the practice of the *inward way*, that of mystics and saints, such as Meister Eckhardt and Sri Auribindo, those who realign their spiritual and physical beings through meditation, contemplation, and other rigorous aesthetic practices. Second is the *outward way* of the scientist and artist, from Leonardo to Mary Oliver, the path for those who try to ground themselves through inventions, research, painting, sculpture, music, or words. Third, I dare say, is *the way of tea*, what the Chinese call *chatao*, and which has been for centuries a path that includes many of the attributes listed above, as well as the intriguing one mentioned by Lu Tong in this section's epigraph. By regrounding us in nature with every sip we take, tea has the capacity to alleviate the "dourness" from our minds by lifting our spirits.

As we learn from the tea aficionados in Part 3: "America," the uncanny brew can "expel the dourness," the gloominess or sullenness that can make our hearts heavy. Tea affects our moods, of course, by dint of its sheer chemistry; but also by simplifying our lives, allowing room for everyday pleasure, and by "inducing inspiration," in the words of James Norwood Pratt.

For Pratt, a highly respected tea scholar, the question of how his spirit can be affected by the "spirit" in a tea plant is one of its "noble qualities," and lies at the core of tea's "charm and its mystery." He believes that tea is one of the great "civilizing forces" in human history, and that it has transformed us in innumerable ways, not the least of which is by giving us the opportunity to experience the dimension of the numinous, the "windless calm" in our fleeting lives. For him, tea deals with the "dourness" of life (from the Latin *durus* or "hardness") by being "our solace in solitude," and by inviting us to participate in "the oldest fraternity on the planet," the circle of tea friends.

In chapter 11, Pratt's close friend and colleague, Roy Fong, speaks about how Taoist philosophy permeates his work in the tea world. For Fong, the importance of "the way of tea" is less in the manufacturing than in the opportunity to communicate directly with nature. Communication to him is intimate; it refers to the moment of bringing tea leaves back to life. This is most effectively done, he believes, in a gonfu tea ceremony, where people open up their hearts to each other in a way they would not otherwise do. As with so many other commentators in this book, Fong shows how the ritual act of making and sharing tea helps anchor people who find themselves adrift in a world racing at "warp speed." For Fong, the closer you look at tea, the more you will understand "the true meaning of life," which is why, he says, "the way of tea is infinite."

Since the early 1990s the idea of the teahouse as a sanctuary for contemporary America has gained great popularity. To Nicky Perry and Michelle Brown, two teahouse owners in New York City and Washington, D.C., respectively, the role of tea is almost too obvious to even talk about. Michelle Brown, speaking at her Teaism café, says that tea teaches patience in a culture riven by impatience. "We do have our Type-A personalities," she says, customers who can't even wait for "the three minutes it takes the tea leaves to release their flavor." For her, tea is an antidote that can alleviate the particularly worrisome form of modern anxiety that some social commentators are calling "time-sickness." For Nicky Perry, the teahouse was an opportunity to offer Americans an alternative to the "terrible tea" that has been our only option for decades. When she moved to New York from England, she says, "So I decided right there and then that that's what I wanted to do—I wanted to open a tea house where Americans could find out what tea is and what tea should taste like." After growing up in England she confesses to wanting to share her belief that tea leads to "a moment of pause," an invitation to stop, morning, noon, and night, and appreciate life a little more.

Chapter 13 features two devoted tea companions, Roy Fong and James Norwood Pratt, who reflect on what Fong calls "the wisdom of tea." This sagacious quality, he says, occurs when there is the right balance of the five elements, which provide a profound sense of inner peace. Tea is an "antidote to modern excesses," he remarks, due to the beauty of its ceremonies and variety of tastes. Meanwhile, Pratt expatiates on the influence of tea by reminding us that its true pleasure derives from the steady repetition of each stage of its preparation and its consumption. For him, tea ceremony is a form of physical and social renewal, since it replenishes not only one's energy, but also one's friendships.

The folks of Tea, South Dakota reveal, in chapter 14, a unique perspective. Ironically, they speak of the pride they feel for living in a town named after a beverage they respect, but they admit they don't consume quite as much tea as the town's founders. Nor as much as curious visitors assume. John Lawlor, the mayor of Tea, recalls how tea once gave his town respite from "our rush, rush, rush world." Luella DeJong, of the Historical Society, muses about the loss of tea in daily life because of the loss of time and the absence of family meals. Her comments strike a note of wistfulness as she remembers when tea was synonymous with neighborliness, and it was inconceivable not to ask a visitor if he or she wished to sip a cup of tea. Her comments reflect an ardent belief in the social aspects of tea and its attendant cultivation of conversation, relaxation, and reminiscing.

Vermont herbalist Susan Borg, in chapter 15, admits she is a tea drinker who is mainly interested in its "medicinal qualities." She catalogues a number of herbal teas, from dandelion to milk thistle, calendula and spilanthes, raspberry and bergamot. She lists their benefits, including aiding digestion, easing stress, and providing the opportunity to "slow down and relax," despite, she adds, the cultural bias that any form of contemplation is an excuse for being "lazy or frivolous."

In the final chapter of Part 3 we turn once more to the voice of James Norwood Pratt, who delivers with a poetic flourish a defense of what he calls "Our greatest civilizing force . . . one of the treasures of the world." For it is tea that holds out the possibility of "a portal to a wordless realm." Pratt believes that tea has the capacity to unlock the secrets of the heart, and to allow human beings to be touched by the "divine spirit of nature." In his translation of the Lu Tong poem that has provided a crossbeam of inspiration for this book, he suggests that a tea drinker needs all seven cups to achieve the longed-for sense of transport, the refining of the spirit, and the humble sense of awe and wonder for this "miracle of vegetation."

The peace of mind and soul that can come with the magical influence of sipping tea is fleeting and capable of renewal. By teaching us what we need to unlearn, it makes a space for something new to enter—the spirit that revives and enlivens us. Perhaps this is why we crave the drama of tea, the beauty of its theater and of its renewal. Or as his friend and mentor Roy Fong concludes, "The tea takes center stage and we all play around it."

—P. C.

WITH
JAMES NORWOOD PRATT

JAMES NORWOOD PRATT

To the thirsty, a single cup of water is like sweet dew.

—Chinese proverb

O ne of the world's foremost authorities on tea and tea lore, Pratt is a native of Winston-Salem, North Carolina and was educated at Chapel Hill. As a wine aficionado, he first published the widely-admired *Wine Bibbers Guide*. Lured by the similarities between great wines and great teas, he went on to write *The Tea Lover's Treasury* in 1971—considered to be one of the definitive books on tea. He has been given the distinction of being made the Honorary Director of The Imperial Tea Court, in San Francisco, the first traditional Chinese teahouse in America. While he lives in San Francisco with his partner, Valerie Turner, the two travel extensively promoting tea in all forms. He is also a scholar of the classics, particularly Latin. He pursues the art of fine living on a daily basis, which for him always includes several cups of the best teas with the company of good friends.

JAMES NORWOOD PRATT: Tea is the essence of the middle way. It is the stream down which the middle way itself finds its way. Not too formal, not too involved. Not too exhilarating, but not too bland. These are all the noble qualities of tea. It is never so exotic that it isn't rather humble, and never too pretentious that it's inaccessible. All of this is part of the teaching of the plant or perhaps we should even say of the spirit that inhabits the plant. Surely, I am a manifestation of some kind of spirit that's alive in this body. Surely, this body isn't all there is; likewise the tea plant. Surely, tea is a manifestation of the spirit that is expressing itself by assuming that physical form. We know it through the leaf, which is like the human skin, as an organ. You know how quickly the skin dehydrates in just a few hours of dry heat. That is how sensitive the leaf of the plant is to the ambient conditions. So it is sensitive to heat, cold, even the wind. The weather is what makes the leaf have the different flavors that it has.

I do know that tea speaks to me, and I do know that it is alive, and I do know that life is somehow divine. There is a spirit that is living in that tea leaf and it will speak to anybody who becomes one with it, who drinks or ingests it. Moreover, it is perfectly intelligible. It enters our own spirit and it *exhilarates* us. That I think is the best word for the tea effect, because it does calm you at the same time it's energizing you. But what it mainly does is turn up the corners of your mouth! It makes you smile in a way that you wouldn't if you were without tea! The total effect is one of making you feel better and making the world a more amusing place. Tea does enliven us because there is *life* in it.

All these musings would be something you would keep to yourself in most company. It takes a very simpático friend to discuss this with. As the poet said, "I have no will to try proof-bringing." Someone who has never tasted fine tea, has never had the effect of tea inside him, would put up an argument, perhaps. As tea drinkers, we would just have to change the subject.

TEA THIRSTY

Tea has arrived to save us. In this society, which demands more and more and delivers less and less, we are thirsty for tea, as Rabandranath Tagore says in his poem: "Come ye, tea thirsty ones." Those are the

Americans of the twenty-first century. We don't have the opportunities to talk to one another about what's on our mind, about what's in our hearts, and to get beyond the state of monkey-mind. We are simply repeating the headlines, the fashion news or something else that the media have been paid to put into our brains.

How often do we get to step back into that moment of windless calm that tea can make a space for? How often can we, in the bluster of daily events and busy lives, take time for tea?

Tea is our solace in solitude.

We all know that different drinks have different effects and different uses. We know what it is to need a drink to relax us in a social situation where we feel strange. We all know also how coffee can perk you up when you have quite run out of energy. Well, tea is an all-purpose drink; it does both of these things in its own way, and unlike alcohol and unlike coffee, it's something that doesn't stop being your friend. Alcohol can turn against you and coffee can treat you poorly as you get older. No way is somebody in his fifties drinking as much coffee as in his thirties. But tea is a steady companion through life. And when I say tea, I always mean the leaf of the tea plant *Camellia sinensis*. If it's not the leaf of the tea plant, the *Camellia sinensis*, botanically it's not really tea. Now we can't legislate language, so of course we speak of herbal tea when we should simply say *herbal*—that's what it is—it's an herbal and it might be very pleasant. But none of them I drink very often. I love French vervaine. I like hibiscus and certain other leaves from other herbs. But I like *Camellia sinensis* so intensely that I can't think of anything more interesting than to have yet another tea. And by tea, I mean real tea.

TEA AS TRANSPORT

The most famous of all poems about tea is one I have reworked from an old friend's translation from the Chinese. So this is John Blofeld, plus James Norwood Pratt. It is by Master Jade Spring (Lu Tong), who wrote it around the year 1000 during the Tang dynasty days in China. He was retired and was living in the countryside when he wrote this poem about receiving a gift of freshly picked tea from his highly placed, very important friend, the Imperial Censor Man.

The Story Behind the "Song of Tea"

I was lying asleep as the morning sun climbed high when a thunderous knocking
at the door shattered my dreams.
An officer of the law delivering a letter from the Imperial Censor; its three great
seals slanting across the white silk cover; Opening it, the words I read bring
him vividly to mind. He says,
Enclosed are three hundred caries of moon-shaped cakes of tea for me. Well, the
first drink sleekly moistened my lips and throat. [These are the thimble cups,
you see.]
The second banished my loneliness.
The third, expelled the dourness from my mind, inducing inspirations borne
from all the books I had read.
The fourth broke me out in a light perspiration, dispersing a lifetime's trouble
through my pores.
The fifth drink bathed every atom of my being.
The sixth lifted me higher to kinship with the immortals.
The seventh is the utmost I can drink. ·
A light breeze jets out from under my arms. [His huge sleeves, you see.]
And Master Jade Spring it is, who rides upon this breeze
To some place where immortals come down to earth
Guarded by their divinity of course, from rain and wind.
But how can I bare the fate of those countless beings,
Born to bitter toil, amid the towering peaks? [These are the people who make
the tea, who grow it.]
How can I bear the fate of those countless beings?
Born to bitter toil, amid towering peaks.
I must ask the Imperial Censor Man if he can tell whether such human beings,
as they are,
are ever allowed any rest.

—TRANSLATED BY JOHN BLOFELD,
AS RECALLED AND RECITED BY JAMES NORWOOD PRATT

How many things in this life can we—the most privileged people
on the planet—touch with our very own fingers something that has
been handled by the humblest workers on the planet? The tea leaf is
one of the very few things we can name that has been touched by their
fingers and touched by our own.

This poem expresses communion between the poet, a friend of the Prime Minister, so to speak, and those people, whose toil made this tea that was worthy of the Emperor himself. He had given it to the Censor, who disbursed it because this was tribute tea, a gift to his friend. This is a great poem. Wouldn't it be wonderful to hear this in Chinese?

Tea is second only to womankind as a civilizing force in China, and probably everywhere else that it has ever gone. It is impossible to make tea for long without developing a fetish for the wares that are used to make it. So we wind up having an affair with a teacup. We wind up cherishing a cracked teapot. The equipment means something to us and we want it to be beautiful and not just to look at, but beautiful to handle, to hold as well as to behold. In its aesthetics, as well in its affects, what the drink does inside us, tea has been a very civilizing force.

TEA AS REALITY CHECK

Clearly, for so many of us tea is our only contact with reality. As a city dweller, I have to go out of my way to actually stand on dirt, stand on the earth for a few minutes in the course of a day. I have to be deliberate in doing this. I think it's a good thing to do. I do it every day in the same way that I drink tea. Everyday it connects me with not only that person who plucked that leaf, which actually had a life, which grew on a plant. It was rooted in the soil and benefited from the weather, the rain, and the wind, and the sunshine. All of this is so elementary, maybe that is why it is so important to me. How can it be unimportant to other city dwellers? If you make certain kinds of tea in certain kinds of ways, you can see in the bottom of your cup a floating forest that you can enter. Perhaps it is there only in fantasy, but there it is, a forest for you.

THE OLDEST FRATERNITY

In five thousand years, tea has grown from a regional tonic in the south of China to mankind's favorite drink. It wasn't the result of some great advertising campaign; it was because tea speaks for itself. Now I am simply the spokesman for the spirit in this plant here in San Francisco, California. But I take my place in a long ancient brotherhood and sisterhood of tea lovers. We may be the oldest brotherhood, fraternity, and sorority on the planet. People like myself who love tea get together to drink it with other people who love it and talk about what's on our mind. We exchange stories about things we have discovered, and our favorite this and that. Also, because of its effect on us, we will exchange more than that. By the time we have talked several times, we will have in a way, opened our hearts, one to another. Soft drinks don't encourage this kind of tendency.

What makes me want to be a praise singer is that tea makes us lift up our hearts. Tea tells us, "Lift up your hearts!" You don't have to be a Christian to have to say we lift them up unto the Lord, like the Anglicans do, for instance. You could be a Jew and say, "L'achaim!"— "To life!" When you lift up the heart, that is life. That is joy. That is what tea wants you to feel. It's an example of how tea has a conversation with me. It's what I hear tea saying in my own interior silence. Tea will help us discover what is not true about that understanding. Perhaps it will be through a direct relationship with a plant product.

THE WORLD OF THE SPIRIT

It's a very good question, what is this natural world and how does it relate to the world of the spirit?

Tea is the subtlest of things, perhaps, that we can ingest. We can know every microscopic variation in the leaf of that plant will have a corresponding effect inside our own sensibility. This is simply amazing. Here is the nexus of body and mind or what the Buddha called the mystery of body, speech, and mind. So how is it that my spirit, which is nowhere at home in this world, is so connected, so affected by this leaf, which is the material product of the molecules of the time, the space, this place right here that we inhabit? And, of course, no one can answer that. That is tea's charm and its mystery. That is why tea is the portal indeed to our existence. Whatever tea allows us to enter into is not some kind of motionless realm. As long as we have the body, we are about motion. The heart beats, the lungs expire, the body moves. That's the nature of existence as we know it as human beings.

As the poet Rilke asks, "When shall we, like these plants, be open?"

Perhaps tea can help us glimpse a way of that, but what it can do for us most definitely here and now is give us an adjustment. There may not be anything wrong with you before a cup of tea, but that tea will give you an adjustment of body and spirit so that there is something more right with you after you have that cup of tea.

EVERYTHING YOU NEED TO KNOW

It makes sense to me to say that you can learn everything you need to know from tea. It makes sense to me from my experience as well as my understanding of how far it has developed the truth that all traditions are teaching us. The experience I have of tea has been my principle study for years. I have learned that you could follow this single thread through history and you could learn much of the essentials about the human enterprise. Through times of war and times of peace, times of healing ourselves, times for fun and entertainment, tea goes on and on. It relates to all of those aspects of human life at all times. It is a high road to understanding human history and culture.

PROFOUND PLEASURES

There is a simple way to live your life. Every day you should hear a little good music, look at a few fine paintings or drawings, try to have some good conversation, get in some good reading, and take some tea.

The pleasures of tea are a whole. People who are simply served tea instead of preparing it themselves are missing half of the pleasures. Once you are involved in many kinds of tea, you know that preparation is critical: the temperature of the water; the amount of time you need to steep this leaf versus that leaf. These variables come down to a question of timing and interludes. This is again part of what tea teaches. If you are simply waiting for the cup to appear before you, with the tea being prepared, you've missed a great deal.

I think that it's also true to say that the pleasure of tea is not over once you have finished the cup before you. If you are expecting someone else to whisk it away and wash that cup, then you're again missing something important. The handling of fine porcelain or earthenware or silver is a pleasure of its own. A tea ceremony, which begins with warming the water, only concludes when you have finished cleaning all of the utensils and vessels that you have used, and you've put them away ready to be used next time—that is the complete tea ceremony.

HOW TEA ASPIRES TO ART

To make the observation that tea is an agricultural product, like wine, which at its best aspires to art, is to place tea in the company where it belongs. Of the great triad of tea, wine, and tobacco, tea is the most refined of them all.

What tea tastes like is a result of actual microscopic changes in the leaf and the ability to control that leaf and make it sing the song that you want it to sing. Of course, there are limits to what you can do. A great

Never say just a symbol!

—Carl Gustav Jung
(1875–1961)

tea maker works within those limits. That's what a real tea man is trying to do every time he makes tea. Even though a certain cup of tea may not be great, we should still lift it and give a thought or a nod to those tea makers whose efforts and skills and traditions made it a tea worthy of drinking,

Now the art of tea is such that you can actually go beyond any boundaries. So here's to our Chinese forebears! They taught us something important about the significance of the foundations of the ancestral ways.

I think you can indeed actually taste the work of the tea maker in the tea that you're drinking, if you are attentive to it. Some might not know what they are tasting, *but how to be attentive to tea is the whole question.* Tea is so quiet, it requires a quiet palette to appreciate what's going on and what it has to say. What's going on not only on our tongue but down our throat and through our bodies as the tea warms the belly and quickens the nerves and generally perks us up. So it's not the taste only, you see; it's the entire fact. At that point, are you distinguishing between art and craft? After a while, not only do you respect any tea that you know is honest, however humble you are glad to get it, but also you begin to erase those distinctions. It's something that's great on its own. If a great painting or a great wine or a great tea knocks your socks off, you don't need to be told it is great. It is its own demonstration.

I have long believed that everything is emblematic. What we call reality is representative of a realm that lies beyond what we can perceive. For instance, the human race has a craving for gods and forms. But why the crucifix and why the cross-legged Buddha? Why again and again do we create an image of a god and why an image that is supposed to point beyond itself, an image that is not of this realm where we live?

If we hunger after some forms that can be symbolic, pointing to a realm beyond their own reality, why shouldn't we also respond to certain natural forms? The curling of tea leaves comes to mind. They are not abstractions; they are the simple truth about the way it is, the way it works. Flower fades to fruit, fruit fades to make earth. *This is the natural process, a circular process.*

TIME AND THE ART OF LIVING

It's a brilliant formulation, the difference between taking time and making time. Tea is firmly on the side of making time for one's friends. This is in fact making time for our life. The rest of the time we are immersed in business, aren't we? What I call "monkey-mind" goes nowhere. There is just so much energy. So making time, whether for friends or for tea, is making time for life.

This concept of time would make sense to the very orthodox Anglican Samuel Johnson. He was the first to define tea time in a dictionary. Dr. Johnson's definition was, "Anytime tea is served." In those years, tea wasn't only a matter of serving at four o'clock in the afternoon; it was anytime tea was served. That's tea time. I think it's very beneficial to live as much as possible on tea time and in tea time versus whatever clock time prevails in your corporation or in your city. Tea time is the caffeine version of nap time. It's time for recreation. For tea can stop time so you can receive a passport to a timeless place, and there you can be at peace.

The first advertisement in the English language for tea was: "By all Chinese physicians approved! Drink!" Then, tea was a nectar, an ambrosial passport to paradise. Later, in 1657, a broadside for a coffee house in London describes the virtues of tea. It's amazing how well it was understood. The writer makes exactly the claims that clinical science later substantiated in the twentieth century.

Historically, you do have to ask yourself what was driving those European explorers to sail around the world, because our Asian cousins had no such compulsion. They sailed with much greater ease, much greater distances, and they decided they didn't need to do that. I am referring to the Ming Dynasty, when the Chinese Treasure Fleets journeyed all the way to the Cape of Good Hope, thirty or forty years before Vasco de Gama did it. But the Chinese found nothing of interest to them. The Europeans knew what interested them, and spices were at the top of the list, followed by the luxuries they were without—jewels and fabrics, the textiles of India and China, things that they couldn't imagine in Europe. They had no way of making a dish that would stand up to boiling water, because they couldn't find a kiln that would fire clay at high enough temperature for it to be china.

So all of the luxuries of life originated from the Orient, and tea was one of the last to be discovered. The European explorers knew about China and all of the spices, not to mention the jewels, the fabrics, furs, and luxuries, lacquer and printing, gun powder and paper.

So when the first Europeans arrived in Canton, in 1513, they were dealing with an altogether higher civilization. They were amazed to find a city that had running water, street lights at night, and people who smelled good and who bathed regularly.

THE MOST CREATIVE DRINK

So what is it about tea that transforms us? You can't isolate the taste and the form from the ceremony, the preparation of tea, and the washing-up after tea. It's inseparable from the enjoyment of tea. I think it's the whole package. It's tea that centers me; it's tea that allows me to focus, and it's tea that gives me a moment of peace. These are all true statements, different ways of saying the same thing.

Wine and tea are dissimilar in this respect. The lover of wine doesn't have to participate in its preparation, except perhaps to have it at the right temperature, let it breathe a little, and take time savoring it in little sips. Wine appreciation requires no skill greater than pulling a cork, whereas tea appreciation requires you to know what you are doing when you are making it, or at least be willing to learn. When we get a new tea, none of us knows what we are doing,

By definition, tea is more creative than wine or other illustrious beverages because at its root *to create* is to make something. So tea is more creative in the sense of having to make the drink, starting with the leaf and the water. It is the processing of that leaf that determines whether you have black tea, green tea, white tea, yellow tea, Oolong tea, or scented tea with jasmine or other herbs. So it's the processing of the leaf, and this has developed very slowly over human history.

Pleasure is far too serious to take lightly. Taking tea is a moment of windless calm, amid the bluster of daily events and has always been one of humanity's favorite pleasures. But beyond pleasure, tea can always provide glimpses of the ultimate reality, usually when we least expect any.

I believe it was Owl, in one of the Winnie the Pooh books, who said so wisely, "Come inside. We'll see if tea and buns can make the world a better place."

CHAPTER ELEVEN
THE SOUL OF TEA

WITH
ROY FONG

ROY FONG OF THE IMPERIAL TEA COURT

Man follows the way of the earth, the earth follows the way of heaven,
heaven follows the way of Tao, and Tao follows its own way.

—CHINESE SAYING

A native of Hong Kong, Roy Fong is the founder and proprietor of San Francisco's Imperial Tea Court, and an ordained Daoist priest. He was introduced to tea at an early age, and has spent many years developing close relationships with tea growers and producers in mainland China and Taiwan, as well as historic pottery workshops in Yixing, in Jiangsu province. In 1997, an international jury awarded his "Imperial Green" tea first place at the Tea Masters annual conference. Currently, he devotes himself to reestablishing the ancient rite of tea dating back to the time of China's greatest tea master, Lu Yu, whose classic book, *Cha Ching* ("Tea Scripture"), first appeared around the year 780.

ROY FONG: I am the owner of the Imperial Tea Court, near Chinatown, in San Francisco. I have been in the tea business for twenty-five years. I decided to have this kind of teahouse, which is a northern style, rather than a southern style Chinese teahouse, because I feel like I am more of a northerner than a southerner, even though I was born in Hong Kong.

We Chinese people don't just make tea; we communicate with nature. We vitalize the leaves. So the tea itself is like a cycle of life. It starts from the soil with water and grows into a plant, and from a plant it gets harvested and processed into tea, and then dried and stored. Then you revitalize it by adding water and it comes alive again and gives out its aroma. While people make tea differently, they all learn to communicate in subtle ways, by smelling the fragrance, by looking at how the leaves unfurl, by observing the color of the tea, and the reaction that tea gives you.

That's my way of talking to the tea. I don't look at it mystically. Instead of making tea by measurement or by time, I make tea by reacting and communicating with the leaves.

The *soul* of tea can be explained this way. You communicate with tea when you try to bring it back to life, when you share the experience together. I am involved from the soil management to the growing of the tea, the shipping of tea here, to our refinishing and making it. So I feel I have an intimate knowledge or relationship with certain teas. When you make tea and you feel some of these experiences, then the spirit of the tea is revealed.

When the heart is at ease, the body is healthy.

—CHINESE PROVERB

I am a simple man, but to me the Taoist way says it all. This is everything in life. To the simple farmer, it says it all. Most Chinese know in an intimate way about the earth, the heavens, and man. In order for the universe to be in harmony, each of these three elements has to play its role correctly. But it's man who plays the pivotal role, because we are in the middle. By understanding and listening to the messages from heaven or from earth, you can do the right thing. There is no difference between growing tea, running a small business, or trying to make a film. Listen to the messages. If you follow the heavens and the earth, the Tao will open the way, and you'll probably be OK.

RECEPTIVITY, RESPONSIBILITY, AND REGRET

There is really nothing that's singled out in life and stands completely on its own. Everything is interrelated. Tea plants are extremely receptive to seasonal change and in a practical way to temperature change. Generally, when the temperature hits about ten degrees centigrade during the spring, tea starts to bloom. The plants are receiving signals from the air, from the roots, and from the soil, about whether it's moist enough or not, whether it's nutrient enough or not. When all those signals are complete the plant starts to blossom and bud. Man's job is to take what heaven and earth, in combination, give us and to make it work and present it correctly. Then the whole cycle starts over again.

But this natural knowledge is being lost in China because of the breathtaking acceleration of things there. Obviously, I feel a sense of regret. Things are moving so fast that people are starting to forget their past. I understand things in simple terms. Tradition requires that the responsible tea merchant does the responsible thing. That means taking care of your farmers, taking care of your soil, explaining to the farmers the reasons to do things correctly, and then explaining to other people, who are maybe not so in touch with nature, what's right and what's wrong. In my small way I am trying to do the right thing. I am hoping to be able to pass some of the little bit of knowledge about tea that I have accumulated to those who are ready to receive it.

I do this because I am a tea merchant. I can't think of anything better than remembering and honoring the past through the making and selling of tea. If you read Lu Yu's *Cha Ching*, which was written in the Tang dynasty, everything he said is still relevant today. As far as tea is concerned, it is made the same way now as it was made five hundred years ago.

If you have ever been to a tea farm and looked at some old guy making tea, you cannot help but be humbled, because these people have this tea making idea in their blood. This is not something you can learn. It is passed down from generation to generation, through bloodlines.

Let's put it simply. Even if I live next to a tea plant for the rest of my life, by the time I die I *still* won't know everything about how to make tea from that plant. Just think about it. The discovery that this plant was capable of doing all these things was just wonderful. To me, there is nothing else better than to remember the past and to honor it with tea.

THE ROOTS OF LIFE

Tea can definitely help you anchor yourself better in life. First of all, something that is in fashion for thousands of years has got to have a lot going for it. The hard fact is that we are going at warp speed with computers and cell phones, which can, ironically, help you understand that you need tea a lot more than you need all this new technology. I always say to people who ask me about the pace of life: *You can drink more coffee to help you speed up, but you should drink tea to help you slow down so you can do more.*

Tea gives you a more clear presence of mind and it gives you more energy. Tea revitalizes you so you are actually better prepared for the everyday challenges that you have to face. So I don't think tea is going to be out of fashion anytime soon.

A piece of time is like a piece of gold, but this piece of gold is not enough to buy this piece of time.
—CHINESE PROVERB

If you are looking at tea to see if it can give you everything in life or even a philosophical point of view, I think it depends on what you mean by the word *look*. If you just look at it, the tea will show you fragrance and color and maybe taste. But if you gaze a little bit deeper into tea, you will be able to think about the people who toiled for hours and hours and weeks and weeks and months and months to make it all happen. *Then you will understand a little bit more about the true meaning of life.*

If you look still further, at those thousands of years and the millions and millions of people who put their heart and soul into the art of making tea, you are still just looking at a drop of water in the ocean of knowledge about tea. There is no end of the unfolding artistic display of tea. However deep and however you want to look at it, there is a level of tea for you.

The Chinese people originally discovered writing as painting or pictures. If you look at the word *cha*, tea, in Chinese, it's not in letters; the word is in pictures. So if you look at the first two strokes on top, there are the leaves, and on the side are branches, and the word in the bottom means wood or a tree. If you look at the whole picture it's actually a plant.

So it is *chatao*—and Chinese people don't use the term *tao* very loosely. You have to be talking about something immense, and that is almost impossible to ever finish learning about. It is those things that have always been associated with the word *tao*. The word itself is immense and infinite.

Chado, the way of tea, is infinite. So *chatao*, the way of tea, is also infinite. The word comes with a character that represents a boat, like you are a person riding on a boat. This character means the head. Chinese people at that time looked at the ocean as infinite so you ride the boat into infinity. At least that is my understanding. It's up to each person to interpret.

THE TEA WAY OF LIFE

When I take people to my tea farm to harvest tea and to pick tea, the number-one importance that I try to convey is that you have to look at the local people. You have to learn the local dialect, you have to look at the local land, look at how the foliage looks, look at the poetry, look at the culinary aspect of how people eat. All these things in combination make the tea the way it is. Each region has tea that is unique to that region, but is connected to the complete cycle of life. If you are a Chinese person, tea is *so important* to you that you don't even know it is important.

When my wife and I got married, we did the most important thing you can do, which is thanking your parents by serving them tea. Even now, when people get married they give each other gifts of tea, because tea is from the earth where you are from. It's a deep part of you that you are giving. Some Chinese people like to give a Pu-Er tea from the Yunan region as a wedding gift. This tea gets better with age, so the hope is your relationship gets better with age. You don't think about it but it's so important. It's like the air you breathe. Nobody thinks about how many breaths they took today. Tea is like that. So tea is in every-thing in life.

Chapter Twelve
The Reeducation of the Public

with
Nicky Perry & Michelle Brown

Nicky Perry

Anytime is tea time.

—Dr. Samuel Johnson

N icky Perry got started in the tea business when she first came to America at the age of twenty-one. "Within about a year, I realized that the tea here was absolutely foul." No matter where she went, she found it to be the same. "In fact, it still is, even though I've been here for sixteen years," she adds. So Perry decided right there and then what she wanted to do. Her aim was to open a teahouse where Americans could find out how fine tea should taste. "Really," she concludes, "the tea in this country tasted like it was fished out of the Boston harbor and put into the microwave."

NICKY PERRY: For English people, drinking tea has been par for the course, the norm, the everyday, all day, every day, for many, many years. It's second nature. We don't think about why we drink tea. We just do.

But for Americans there has been such a lot of press about how good tea is for you. Many people have heard by now how tea is full of antioxidants, how green tea can stave off this illness, or white tea can stave off that illness. That is why I think Americans are so obsessed with the whole health thing. It's become much more in vogue in the American consciousness, and they are drinking way more tea than when I first came here twenty-five years ago, partly because you can now buy decent tea.

When I first came here in 1981, there wasn't anywhere to get a good cup of tea. You had to have it flown in or shipped in or your mom would send you a box of tea, or every time you went home you'd have to bring a suitcase back full of tea.

My husband, when he first came to America, went to a coffee shop. When he ordered tea they brought it to him, as they do in coffee shops here, in a big thick ceramic cup with lemon on the side. He thought, *Oh, how civilized are these Americans. They've given me a finger bowl.* So he squeezed the lemon into the lukewarm water and then rinsed his finger because he thought it was a finger bowl. The restaurateur was horrified.

HOW TO BREW A GOOD CUPPA TEA

All I know is that good tea is good tea. In this day and age I think a lot of people believe loose-leaf tea is better than a teabag. In my restaurant at Tea & Sympathy we serve it loose in a teapot with a tea strainer and with china cups and saucers, because that's the traditional and pretty way to do it. But there is nothing wrong with using teabags if you start out with a really good-quality tea. The more spice you have for the tea to infuse, the better the tea will be. It is also very important to use fresh boiling water. It is no good letting it sit for twenty minutes and reboiling it, because if you lose oxygen from the water, you lose some of the flavor from the tea.

For most loose-leaf tea you need three to five minutes to sit in the pot and brew before you drink it. If you leave it in the pot for too long, it does get stewed and it does taste a little dry and a little strong. You can add a little more hot water to that. Actually, restaurants in England serve your pot of tea with a pot of hot water so you can weaken it, if you wish.

I drink about three cups of tea a day, mostly in the evening, and I drink, believe it or not, decaffeinated tea because regular tea gives me a terrible stomachache. I discovered that when I went home to England to visit, I wasn't drinking as much tea as in the past. When you go home and you visit people, they just lash tea on you every twenty minutes. I discovered it would give me a terrible stomachache if I drank too much.

Nowadays, Americans seem to enjoy a much broader selection of tea. They'll be much more adventurous with their tea, and if they don't like to drink caffeine then they'll drink what's known as tisane or what's known in this country as an herbal tea—and in the restaurant we do serve quite a lot of that: apple, peach, and pear. There's nothing wrong with drinking herbal tea. A lot of people drink mint tea or caramel tea to soothe their stomach or their nerves, but an herbal tea is not real tea. Real tea comes from the tea plant and herbal tea has absolutely nothing whatsoever to do with the tea plant. I think the reason that people call mint tea or caramel tea *tea* is because it's made in exactly the same way as real tea. They're both infusions with boiling water.

Making a Pot of Tea

For a proper pot of tea you need to start with (a) really good quality tea and (b) freshly boiled water. The classic way of doing it is this. As soon as the water is boiled, pour a little in your teapot, swirl the tea pot to warm the teapot, and then dump the water. Then you spoon your loose-leaf tea or your teabags into your teapot and you fill the teapot with boiling water. You leave it to set with the lid on for two, three, four minutes, depending on how strong you like it. Most people, before they serve it, will lift the lid to give it a quick stir to make sure the liquid is all even and it's not dark at the bottom and light at the top, and then you pour. If it's loose tea then obviously you pour it through a tea strainer into your cup. It's actually very simple.

—Nicky Perry

CLASS

Tea does not have a class distinction anymore. When tea first went to England, only the rich drank it. In fact, what would happen in rich houses is that the ladies would have their friends around for tea and then they would brew the leaves and save them. They would pass the tea leaves down to the top layer of servants, either the butler or the cook. They would make their tea from those tea leaves and would drink their tea. They would give those leaves to the scullery maids, and the scullery maids would have their tea from leaves that have already been used twice—"Upstairs, Downstairs" style. We don't have this routine anymore, because we wouldn't think of giving our old tea leaves to someone else for any reason.

Love and scandal are the best sweeteners of tea.

—HENRY FIELDING, "LOVE IN SEVERAL MASQUES"

Of course, in England, if you got to visit somebody, whether a friend, an aunt, or uncle, the first thing that happens when that front door closes is that the kettle goes on and tea is served. That happens in every household across the country—whatever class you are in. It's not like I have studied this or know a great deal about it. I just know what tea should taste like and I know automatically how to make it.

During soccer matches in England, as soon as it's halftime, there have been times when the national grid has gone down. If it's a big foot-

"O," said Bilbo, and just at that moment he felt more tired than he ever remembered feeling before. He was thinking once again of his comfortable chair before the fire in his favorite sitting-room in his hobbit-hole, and of the kettle singing.

—J. R. R. TOLKIEN
The Hobbit

ball match and everybody is home watching their TVs, as soon as the first half is over, everybody rushes to the kitchen to put their kettle on, because in this day and age in England it's all electric. So there is a massive electricity surge during the big matches when the grid has gone down, because the whole country is having a cup of tea at the same time! That is the truth, because that's just what we do. We all drink tea at once.

I have been in America for a long time. Now, I don't think it odd if I am not offered tea at an American's house. But I would think it was odd if I came to your house and you didn't offer me anything, because Americans are very hospitable. If I came to your house and you were a Chinese-American, who had just brought back a wonderful Oolong from China, I'd say, "Oh, yes!" and I'd drink it.

TIME TO PAUSE

Having a cup of tea is a time to pause. As soon as I get in at night, the kettle goes on immediately. After the first few sips of the tea, it's "Oooh, tea!" To have your cup brings a moment of pause. My husband can't live without a cup of tea at nighttime; most English people can't live without their cup of tea. Let's face it: Americans could take it or leave it because it's not in their culture. It's not like every time somebody comes to the house the mom says, "Let's put the kettle on we are going to all have tea." But there are nursery rhymes about tea in England.

In fact, the name of this business is Polly-Polly Ltd., as in "Polly, put the kettle on!" When we put the key in the door at nighttime what's the first thing we do? We put the kettle on.

Tea is significant in my life because it's always been in my life. It's part of my life. It's not something that I was introduced to—and all of a sudden realized how much I loved it. I've always just had it. It's very rare that you meet an English person who doesn't like tea. If I had English people in a restaurant and offered them a pot of tea and they said they didn't like tea, I'd be taken aback. It's unusual to meet English people who don't drink tea. So tea doesn't really have any special meaning—but if I was without it, *then* it would be a big deal!

MICHELLE BROWN

Ten years ago, when we opened Teaism in Washington, DC, there really weren't many teahouses around the United States. We have expanded slowly while tea has grown throughout the country in a very special fashion, by way of small, independent tea shops.

When we first opened Teaism, we used to have tea events. At our first one we were very nervous about how the guests might react. We suggested to the gentleman who was teaching the class that we should serve some wine or sake to loosen up the conversation. He assured us that twenty minutes into the tea drinking, he would not be able to keep the place quiet, that they would all be involved, excited, and in the process with him. He was right. We have learned that the first cup of tea of the day or a cup of tea over conversation is like a lubricant that just opens people up. Tea just makes language flow more freely.

As I arrive at Teaism, I go directly to the tea station and make my first cup. I love tea. I drink it all day. I start the day with either a black tea, a Yunan Gold, a Darjeeling first flush, or a lovely Ceylon tea. I try to make something strong and caffeinated, a drink that will linger on my palette. Through the lunch hour I enjoy some iced tea, especially in the hot summer months. At Teaism, we have a lovely iced tea on the menu called Moroccan Mint, which is a green tea with spearmints added to it. I enjoy that often through the lunch hour. We do our own blending here, using actually a Vietnamese tea, which carries a lot of astringency but also a lot more complexity than a Gun Powder tea.

During the course of the day I have four or five cups of tea. After the lunch hour here, I make sure that all of my guests are fed, and then I sit down and usually enjoy a cup of hot tea with my own lunch. This tends to be a green tea, maybe a Japanese Genmaicha or a lovely Oolong. We don't utilize the gung fu service in the restaurant because of the need for all the ritual and time and space.

Ecstasy is a glass full of tea and a piece of sugar in the mouth.
—ALEXANDER PUSHKIN
(1799–1837)

Tea drinking for me means finding a moment of calm and peace and quiet. We use huge lidded mugs that really allow you to smell the aroma of the tea and feel the steam coming off from the brew. Sometimes this confuses our guests who might say, "Where is my teapot? I need a little teacup to go with this!" But we insist on serving tea this way, because we don't want tea drinking to be a delicate operation. Instead, we want to include it as a manly thing to do as well. The large mug is about making tea more accessible to men.

EDUCATING THE PUBLIC

We spend a lot of time trying to educate the public about tea. We try to do it in a gracious way, offering information, but not too much to overwhelm them. We say just enough to help them discern what they might enjoy as their first step into tea. To do this, we simply open the tea chest and show them all the different kinds of leaves and allow them to smell and touch and feel and see the diversity of the leaves. Of course, this tends to excite people, but the real idea is to get them to open up to the possibility of drinking loose-leaf tea.

When we look at tea we think of it on a spectrum; one end is black tea and the other end is green tea. White tea is the bud of the plant, the first picking of the season and it's simply dried. As we move up in the spectrum, we find green teas. Oolongs span the spectrum between black teas and green teas. They carry some of the characteristics of the black tea because they are partially oxidized, some more partially than others, so they reach into the qualities of black tea. Some are oxidized less and have characteristics of green teas. Green teas are simply dried and Oolongs are partially oxidized, then roasted and dried, while black teas are allowed to fully oxidize before they are dried.

There is a lot of confusion about this spectrum. My colleague Kim Barnes and I are always in the process of educating our customers and trying to keep tea as simple as possible. Our goal is to bring people into tea through the lushness and the elegance of the product. Then they can find their way through the notion of how tea is processed and maybe reach out for more information.

I think people are increasingly turning to tea for its health benefits, and also to find a moment of calm in their lives. Tea can help them to get on better with the stresses of daily business. One of my favorite sayings is that "Tea teaches us patience." I say that because we do have our type-A personalities who come to our tea shop and obviously don't want to wait the three minutes that it takes for the tea leaves to release all their flavor. To be honest, we kind of force those people to wait; we don't allow them to demand that they want their tea now—before it is fully steeped. Carefully, we explain to them that tea teaches us patience, and ask them to give the leaf a few minutes so it may release its flavor.

Tea drinking occurs all day long. We are open seven days a week for breakfast, lunch, and dinner, so we have a lot of people who come in for their first cup of tea with us, to have a little dose of caffeine. During lunch hour, people tend to enjoy an iced tea, something refreshing.

Tea drinkers are very wedded to their rituals. Every afternoon, a lovely couple on bicycles comes in for their scones and a bit of Earl Grey. It's quite lovely to see them ride their bikes across town to come to Teaism.

On the weekends, we see a lot of afternoon tea drinkers; four o'clock on a Saturday afternoon is a crazy time for us. People are in and out of the house doing errands or sightseeing, and to them a moment of calm is very important. We are on a mission to get them to understand the elegance and beauty of whole-leaf tea.

When we opened Teaism, there were some hard decisions to make about our line of tea. We knew that some people might be caffeine sensitive, so we designed a minimal line of herbal blends for those who chose to drink tea throughout the day.

Our mission has always been to teach people about the diversity and elegance of whole-leaf tea drinking. What we do feel is that there are health benefits of tea drinking coupled with the ritual aspects of tea drinking, the calm that we find in our lives through tea drinking.

Our tea offering is designed around pure teas, because we wish to develop knowledgeable tea drinkers who will drink with us on a regular

basis. For those who have a discerning palette, they can find teas here from all over the world, a broad range of teas from scented to adulterated and blended. We also try to sell pure leaf tea, a pure Ceylon, a pure Darjeeling, to give the customer the purest experience of the tea leaf.

American tea drinking has evolved over the last many decades. Tea sales grew from a quarter-billion dollars to over a billion dollars between 1990 and 2007. While Americans began with Lipton, I think a lot of people moved to Twinings tea or maybe loose-leaf tea. Twining teas would represent lovely Darjeeling, a lovely Lapsong Souchong. Twining tea was the first inroad into educating the American public to the broader spectrum of teas available. The tea that is found in a teabag is often described as "dust and fannings," the bottom of the tea chest. It's also described as CTC, which is cut-and-torn tea leaf. The quality and the grade that goes into a teabag tends to be so far down the spectrum that it's hard to even imagine that there are any health benefits left over. So our mission is to expose the public here to quality loose-leaf tea drinking, and it doesn't take long to persuade people.

Our customers are fiercely loyal, because there is a ritual to tea drinking. Some people are in three times a day, some people are in three times a week. I think the healthy aspects of our food menu support their lifestyle in such a way that they find Teasim to be a very important part of their lives.

So tea is both a solitary and a social activity. To offer someone a cup of tea is in a sense a preamble to conversation. Everybody gets involved in the preparation, and then the talk starts and rolls on as we drink tea together. It's a shared pleasure. There is something very friendly about asking, "Would you like a cup of tea?" Even deciding what kind of tea to match the person's emotional state is friendly. Do they need something comforting or stimulating or calming? At that point, we will make something together that's fun.

The cultivation of tea plays a special role as a metaphor for civilization.

—JOEL, DAVID & KARL SCHAPIRA, *The Book of Coffee and Tea*

Tea is about making everyone comfortable. This might entail two friends having a serious conversation, a business discussion, the appreciation of something beautiful, or listening to music. The tea sets the atmosphere and the time. It makes everything warm; it makes life tasteful, literally.

For me personally, the meaning of tea is *calm*. I find calm in tea, a moment to still the waters and breathe and relax. If I have my tea, I can do that anywhere, even if there are three hundred people coming through the door for lunch hour. If I have my tea, I have my calm.

Chapter Thirteen
THE WISDOM OF TEA

WITH
JAMES NORWOOD PRATT & ROY FONG

JAMES NORWOOD PRATT AND ROY FONG

ROY FONG: Chinese people prize tea. But to us, tea is not just about how it tastes; tea is about how it feels. A perfect cup of tea leads to perfect timing. A perfect cup is a fusion of self and tea. Once you reach that point, you reach a perfect cup of tea.

JAMES NORWOOD PRATT: Yes, tea is timing and the interludes that are required. It is the result of someone who makes tea well, Roy. You can make that tea so it would have more or less aroma. It is your *gongfu* tea ritual style that brings out the depth, the quality of your Tie Guan Yin tea.

ROY: The art of gongfu style tea means working further, or practicing more. It is a simple term that people use for martial arts, but in this case, the work is always different. You never finish your gongfu training; there is always further work to do. You get to know the tea better as you get to know yourself better, and you continue to progress. Your practice gets to a point where you don't think about how to make the tea. You just make this personal connection with the tea, and then everything just happens. I never really think about measuring tea or deciding what to do next. I just make tea.

NORWOOD: Yes, after thirty years constantly making tea in this fashion, you can do it perfectly just about every time.

ROY: Well, you know perfection is an illusion and an elusive term. What is perfect today I am sure is not going to be perfect tomorrow. I don't really think of it that way. I don't think about making perfect tea, I just make tea and it happens. I suppose I could make it better, and obviously time does help. I've been doing this for thirty years because tea attracted me and it continues to allow me to grow. Somebody who has been doing it all their life may have it in their blood, but sometimes somebody from out of nowhere can see the flaws or other ideas or other avenues that just do not come to those who are actually doing this everyday. Somebody like me comes in with fresh ideas, and sometimes it does help. I don't know why I know these things, but to me it makes sense that I just approach the experts and speak to them.

Is it not wonderful to put one's learning into practice? Is it not wonderful to welcome friends from afar? Is it not a gentleman who will not be offended if others fail to notice his great qualities?

—CONFUCIUS

THE IMPERIAL TEA COURT

ROY: Traditionally, you call your best tea the "monkey-picked," because it is supposed to flag your own personality, your outlook on life, your personality in tea, and your philosophy. Somebody who drinks monkey-picked tea is supposed to be able to tell, "Ah! this is monkey-picked!"

NORWOOD: There is a signature to tea. It is someone's calligraphy and allows you to recognize a person's particular tea.

ROY: Absolutely. That's what it is supposed to be, so you don't lightly call tea the "monkey-pick" because it is your name card. If you don't do it well, people will remember you for bad "monkey-picked" tea.

THE WISDOM OF TEA

ROY: If you want to think about *the wisdom of tea* or the *perfection* of tea, you can think of it this way. The Chinese believe that the universe is comprised of five elements: metal, wood, water, fire, and earth. Making perfect tea is an attempt to combine the five elements. If you combine them *eloquently and completely,* you create harmony, and, you may come very close to perfection. Metal is the mineral content in the soil that allows the plant to be molded and allows the plant to grow properly. The earth grows the plant and the earth makes the teapot, which makes the tea possible. Fire is the sun that makes everything grow; you heat the water with the fire on the pot. So the questions are: how much tea leaf? How much heat? How much water? How do you make the pot and what *kind* of pot? In this case, we are asking the water to revive the tea in the pot and bring it back to life. All of these things create an attempt to reach a kind of perfection each time that I make tea. Philosophically, I try to think this way so I can attempt to try to balance the five elements. Sometimes it all works out and you didn't even think about it. To me, it achieves such inner peace that I can't even describe it except to say that it is like a long bout of meditating.

NORWOOD: It creates harmony.

ROY: Yes. I remember when I first started to make gongfu style tea. It seemed like an hour flashed by in just a few moments. Thirty years later, I still have these moments of harmony. I am not a scholar or a philosopher. It doesn't happen often, but when it does, I think I've come close to a kind of harmony.

NORWOOD: Perhaps if we prepare ourselves as carefully as we prepare our tea, it would happen more often.

ROY: Perhaps—but the whole idea is to prepare tea without having to prepare tea. You don't measure your tea by measuring your tea; you don't measure your water by measuring your water. You do it all in such harmony that everything happens properly.

NORWOOD: You quoted your Chinese forefathers. Allow me to quote mine—Dr. Samuel Johnson, my Anglo-Saxon forefather—on this question. In his great English dictionary he defines tea time in a very Chinese way. "Tea time," he says, "is anytime tea is served." The English had not yet settled on a set hour, and for Johnson, in the 1700s, it was anytime that tea was served. Dr. Johnson was prepared to drink tea in quantities, and he had such a clear conscience and such a keen mind that I am convinced that it's the tea that helped bring us that dictionary.

ROY: There is a level of tea for everyone. If you want to be artistic, there is tea for you; if you want to be philosophical, there is tea for you— even for small children.

TEA AND THE SCHOLARS

NORWOOD: There was a young artist from Hong Zhu who visited me soon after you had made a tea gift to me. After he walked into the room, I was preparing it and he's smelled the *Longjing* (Dragon Well), and said, "Ah, for me that is an aroma that is always mingled with the smell of ink." That was because as his father and all of those scholars in Hong Zhu were practicing their calligraphy, they were also drinking their Dragon Well tea.

ROY: Hong Zhu is a magical place; it's always been the basket of civilization for China. Hong Zhu was the center for a lot of scholars, calligraphers, and painters; even a lot of the most famous court officials are from there. Fortunately, with tea it's easier. You can definitely take the approach, but you don't really have to go back there. In my experience with tea and Taoism, fortunately, it's rather easy. You have to directly experience it; you have to touch it, you have to feel it to experience it. But you also need to quietly allow it to happen and not be so conscious of form. When people have asked me about learning about tea, I must tell them that I feel like I am more the messenger than the teacher. The messenger shows you the door and you have to decide to open it or not. Nobody else can do that for you. Tea is that messenger. You don't have to say much. When you have opened the door enough times, you have experienced the Tao.

THE POWER OF METAPHOR

NORWOOD: The experience of tea itself is in a realm that no word has even entered. Therefore, you can only imply metaphor to speak of tea, as in poetry. To describe tea requires a poet of the appetites. First and alone, a poet can talk about the tea in the cup, but it's still talk—and talk is cheap. Tea is an experience and an experience is dear.

ROY: *It's as if the tea actually communicates with you.* The better you learn how to deal with tea, the better it rewards you. It tastes better. I am not aware of any teabag that has this kind of quality. With a well-made tea that really connects with you, you can almost feel the hard work and the care that went into the making. The more you drink and understand it, the more you appreciate it. This is a depth of value that cannot be purchased.

NORWOOD: What you are weighing is not just one pound of pedigree tea, which has been carefully nourished in Ang Shi county in Fujian, and very carefully manufactured to your specifications, but the care of that particular leaf. When it is handled respectfully, you have exactly that sense of harmony.

ROY: If you are a painter, you don't want to paint something that nobody wants. You want to paint something that is sought-after, because you are good at it. You want people to feel good looking at your work. To me, tea is like that. I can't draw a straight line. So tea is as close as I can get to the feeling of the painter. There are paintings that have been looked at for centuries, and you can try to figure out what the original intent of the artist was. Perhaps tea is easier because you can touch it and you can feel it. So you can sense the way tea talks to you. Whatever you do to tea, it will react in a particular way. For the Chinese, it is more important how tea feels in your emotions.

NORWOOD: Tea does enter you. In that sense, we do become one with the tea and the tea becomes a part of us.

ROY: That's because you are able to do something about it. You could either make it stronger by brewing it differently or by altering the temperature to make it more suitable for the moment, your state of mind.

I don't think any sort of art can react in this way. You certainly cannot change how a painting is talking to you, but you can certainly change the way that tea talks to you.

ALERTNESS

Roy: As far as having an alert mind for preparing tea, I think that's precisely what you *don't* want to have. If you are totally worried about it and you are completely focused, you are too nervous, and good tea is not going to happen. It's only when you are now communicating directly with tea that you can be making adjustments without thinking about it. If everything you do with tea is from the heart, it is moving deep into your being and you don't have to worry about measuring it. When somebody is very good at making tea, he or she *wills* the tea to be this way or that way. In some way you do it without thinking.

Regarding the process of having to be completely alert and focused, *you really just need to pay attention.* You need to give the tea this moment out of the cycle of life, this one moment, and the rest of it will happen itself. The more you worry about it, the more you want to do something, the more you take away from the moment. I never really bother about it. Sometimes your best doesn't turn out to be the best. That's life. I don't allow it to bother me. I preach to everybody who will listen to me to just relax, just listen to yourself, just listen to what the tea wants. Sometimes, when I make tea for other people, I ask them to smell the aroma. I explain that the aroma tells you everything about the tea. In that regard, when you smell the tea, or taste the aromatics, it can transport you to that eighteen-hundred-meter altitude where the mist and the clouds congregate and the tea just blossoms. You know the lushness itself. It definitely tells you all this. When I drink the tea, I try to imagine the whole cycle of this tea's life—it shows you that. It's difficult to explain. Sometimes words just don't do it. But it is like the clouds and mists in Chinese paintings that made them wonder, "How could any place be like this?"

I drink my tea and say Hm hm.

—Jack Kerouac
(1922–1969)

NORWOOD: My teacup is one of my principle teachers on how to be happy. If my teacup could talk it would say the same thing from one day to the next: "Happy, happy, happy. Have you forgotten you are here to be happy?" When I do forget how to be happy, it is time for another cup of tea. I was taught by my tea master how to say thank you for tea. It is by tapping the table. This was the way some wise soul said thank you to the emperor centuries ago, and the Chinese are people who have long memories.

THE TEA JOURNEY

ROY: Tea can be a messenger. Tea can take you on a journey. Tea is an intricate part of life itself. When people say they want to learn about tea, I tell them that they can't just learn about tea by drinking it. That's not enough. Eventually, you are going to find what you are going to want to learn about the poetry from that area where the tea come from, and you'll want to visit there and step on that soil where the tea comes from and get your shoes dirty. You'll want to sit in the marketplace and watch the people go by, and you'll want to eat in a local diner and get really infused with the local energy. Only after these experiences will you understand how intricate tea is. You can't just take the tea out and say to them, "This is Dragon Well tea." But you can say that it's Dragon Well tea and tell them where it came from and what that means.

> *The true purpose of the journey is not for the self-aggrandizement of the hero, but for the purpose of bringing a boon back to the community.*
>
> —JOSEPH CAMPBELL
> (1904–1987)

NORWOOD: The Western world has had a romance with tea ever since we had our first sip. Your ancestors had tea four thousand years before my ancestors ever had their first sip, which was only four hundred years ago. Even then, they didn't just take to the tea itself. They also adopted the tea wares, the architecture, poetry, and furniture. All over Europe there was a fascination with Chinese fashion, for using beautiful things to make the tea in. That's the nature of tea. When you think of any culture that has adopted tea you are also thinking of the art-works that tea inspired there.

TEA CULTURE TODAY

ROY: There is a revival of tea culture in a positive and a negative way, especially in China, but really worldwide. Everybody thinks they know about tea, but they don't *really* know about tea. There is a new urge to learn about tea, and in China, there is a revival of tea. Everybody was drinking tea because this is the thing you do and it's a cheap beverage. Now people drink tea because they can. So people are fighting, clamoring for more expensive tea just because they can. The challenge people like me or people who really care about tea have is, Where do you maintain this balance to produce good tea? Chemicals have been a blessing, but also have brought a hell of a lot of difficulty because once farmers discover chemicals, they tend to use it and overuse them. I feel that the teas of yesteryears are probably gone; they might not ever happen again. Teas that you and I drank when we first met may never be as available again.

NORWOOD: That's right. Now you can get Tie Guan Yin only every third year.

ROY: That is because you have to do ten times the amount of work that you did fifteen years ago to get maybe twenty percent of the tea you used to get. I know a lot more about tea than I did fifteen or twenty years ago, but I feel like it's almost a losing battle. This new urge to acquire the best tea makes it less of an incentive to make better tea, because you can sell it for whatever. The tea doesn't have to be that good, because there is a new group of people who are willing to pay *anything* for it. With pollution and smog at the lower altitudes, around six hundred meters, you can't see the sky. If smog is blocking out the sun, how is the plant going to produce food? How will tea taste any good?

If one does not work the fields, another goes hungry.

—EMPEROR WE CONG,
TANG DYNASTY

NORWOOD: Those air problems are a factor at the agricultural level of the countryside in today's world. It has its parallel with the cultural attitude of the people who are living in cities. I feel very strongly that urban stress has everything to do with the importance of tea in today's world. Roy, you have often said that you and I are apostles of this tea plant and that we are just its messengers. You've said the reason that anybody has shared our pleasure in tea is because in a society that is demanding more and more of people and delivering less and less, tea becomes one of those rare links to nature. That's what tea is a product of and that's what it leads us back to, and that's why we desperately need it. It doesn't make any changes in the tea drinker, perhaps, but it gives him an adjustment. He can see more clearly for a little while.

ROY: We have been saying that for about a decade, because we have been steadily getting worse, quality-wise. But the number of people who are willing to accept less for more is steadily increasing, so it's a sad stage if you have never had tea like *this* before, the way it should be.

NORWOOD: We have never equaled the Longjing.

ROY: This year's Longjing is probably the best in four or five years, and it's a shadow of what it used to be. The greatness that was achieved effortlessly not so long ago I don't think can even be achieved anymore. When the weather does not cooperate, there is very little you can do. The seasons are out of order—when it's supposed to be warm it isn't; when its supposed to rain it doesn't. Scientists can measure all they want, but the farmers know what's happening here. This is where they live and this is what they do; all good farmers are feng shui masters. They just cannot help but know where the plant is, where the sun is at the correct position, where the best air is moving through, where the best energies are. This comes from many, many generations working the land and being in tune with nature. Feng Shui teaches how to position yourself correctly, and farmers are feng shui masters. Farmers know more than anybody else when the sky is not right, heavens are not right. So people can deny all they want. They can sit in their comfortable air conditioned office and say there is no global warming; they can claim that the proof is not in yet. Everybody who is involved with tea will tell you that in the last ten years, the harvest has been worse every year. Perhaps tea is paying the price. I think farming and tea transcend national and cultural boundaries.

NORWOOD: You don't have to believe in the existence of Shen Nung, the Divine Cultivator or Immortal Farmer, who is reputed to have discovered tea. Of course, he was one of the first four emperors of China, supposedly legendary. Nobody can say for sure.

ROY: Back then, there were no written records. But you know that this is how farmers are. People who live closer to the earth just know. Now we are talking about tea as an antidote to modern excesses and how tea is not what is used to be. I think tea is not even a shadow of what it used to be.

NORWOOD: We may remember a certain Tie Guan Yin that we believe would rank higher than the one we are drinking now. But that does not detract from our enjoyment from the Tie Guan Yin that is in the cup before us.

ROY: It's not just how it tastes; it's like wine. Tea is a matter of who you are with and how the day is going. But overall, the quality of tea by any standard is certainly not what is used to be not so long ago.

NORWOOD: But it's still the closest thing we have to an antidote to an antidote to civilization and its discontents.

THE SWING OF RECOGNITION

ROY: I don't think that I am a teacher. I have certain information that may be helpful, and again, we are only the messengers.

NORWOOD: The audience wasn't there twelve years ago, it just didn't exist. In 1996, the entire tea market in the United States was less than one billion dollars. By now, in 2006, it is well over seven billion dollars. We have seen an explosion, a renaissance of tea.

ROY: And these numbers do not include sales in restaurants, because you can't really track sales in Chinese restaurants, since they don't serve coffee. They only serve tea. I challenge you to find a Chinese restaurant—no matter how bad it is—that doesn't sell some kind of tea. This is precisely what tea is—it is so much into your daily life and such a part of you that you don't even think about it. It's like your skin. You don't think about a patch of your skin, because it's a part of you. Tea is like that.

NORWOOD: Even Eskimos drink tea. It would be indispensable to any group in any country that I could think of. I was reading about Pygmies of the Congo not so long ago, and they were pictured drinking tea. This was an exotic novelty for them. It had come from who knows where? They would have been amazed as to where it came from! The article said they had a myth as to where it came from, but they had already learned to prepare and enjoy it, and I'll bet you would have trouble with Pygmies if you cut off their tea supply!

ROY: Yes, there has been a big swing of recognition of tea. People are no longer willing to settle for just any sort of tea. When I was a child a teabag was fine. I thought the best thing to do to tea was to add sugar and water. But until you have a chance to compare a high-quality Oolong to teabag tea with milk and sugar, you'll never know the difference. Teabags are made entirely for convenience. There is no artistry. It's a nice beverage, but you would never think about it as an art form. The complexity of the fine tea is one story, and the preparation is another story, and the multilevels of flavor and feelings is another story. No, I don't think you can get a good story from your everyday teabag.

NORWOOD: You just put your finger on it. Half of the pleasure of tea is in the preparation, and so you are denied that part of the pleasure if you resort to the convenience of a teabag. The pleasure of the tea doesn't end when you sip it; there is still the aftertaste. There is the sensation throughout your body. But the pleasure of the tea doesn't really end there. As a matter of fact, I believe that it's only when you have finished washing your tea equipment and put it all back in place, ready to be used again, that you have completed your tea ceremony.

ROY: Let me put it to you this way. Drinking out of a teabag is something like someone saying to a painter that from now on, you can only paint on a two-by-two-inch canvas, and you can only do ninety strokes, never more, never less. What kind of art would that be? While it could be precise and it could even be enjoyable to some people, it would certainly be no art form. The whole thing about creating art is that you are allowed to go beyond any boundary that you could ever imagine. Similarly, if you try to tell a tea maker that he must exactly measure his tea, and he must exactly measure its temperature, and he must exactly measure the steeping time, all this instruction would not allow him to feed and grow his ability to serve tea, because everything had been prearranged. There would be no meaning. In contrast, when you make tea, you should allow it to decide how it wants to go along with you.

NORWOOD: Spoken like a true Taoist.

THE MOST ENJOYABLE ASPECT OF TEA

ROY: My friendship with you has not been something that you could have looked for or found. It just had to happen. Actually, I don't think we could have stopped it from happening, despite ourselves. We've been friends in the way that tea takes its own course.

NORWOOD: That's right. When the student is ready, the teacher appears. This is a clear example of how we are taught. You needed a student, and I showed up on the spot.

ROY: Tea can be enjoyed with music and poetry and flowers, fine paintings and other works of art, but most of all, tea can be enjoyed with friends.

NORWOOD: Music is supposed to be the universal language, so it must be accompanied by tea.

ROY: In the end, the most enjoyable part of having tea is when you share it with friends, especially when we make gongfu style tea. It's a perfect time to share time together without infringing on each other. We communicate without having to speak too much or trying to entertain each other, or trying to lengthen a meeting together. The tea takes its course and you follow. To me, it's perhaps more important than tasty treats or other elements like music. Tea is music without having anything played.

NORWOOD: However, when your friend shares a certain taste for luxury, it does make the tea taste better. I will never forget drinking Dragon Well tea with you on the dragon boats in Ghiangzhou to the accompaniment of classical Chinese music, with the scenery of West Lake all around us. I thought your company and that tea were unusually enjoyable. Of course, the earth is the mother of all things. The earth brings forth all things, which includes tea. So tea is one of her chthonic messages. What the earth's truths are and what the earth teaches through you is renewal. This is our earthbound way of learning. Tea not only expresses these truths, but refines them. Imagine this leaf and its tenderness just at the beginning of its youth, with all of its promise still inside plucked from that leaf and preserved. To preserve the nectar of the leaf in its natural state and to be renewed and reawakened thousands of miles away in a strange country where someone brings it together again with life giving water and nectar—this is to free something that you and I can imbibe. That is the renewal at a remove in time, and at a remove in space, which is even further symbolized here in our beloved tea plant, isn't it? That is what the leaf is teaching us. *Tea is renewal.*

ROY: For me, the future of tea is very clear. I know exactly where I want to go and I know exactly what I need to do. I feel like the last thirteen . or fourteen years have flown by. But I am not doing what I think I am good at. I never had a chance really to spend one hundred percent of my energy devoted to the one thing that I really enjoy, which is to learn the way of tea. I want to learn many more different aspects of tea, how to make tea better, or maybe read some tea poetry, or how to grow tea better. During the Tang dynasty, tea was powdered and whipped in the bowl like they do in the Japanese tea ceremony now, and you drank the whole thing. The tea at that time was referred to as *tea congi,* because it was white-colored. I want to make that tea. In those days, you would take freshly harvested tips of the tea, soak them in water until they soften, and then strip the outer skin off until white inside. You would steam them, press and grind them. This is one of my ambitions. The future to me means going back to learn more about tea. Before I am gone from this earth, I need to buy or lease land close to a tea field. I want to feel the seasonal changes with the tea so that I can make the adjustments based on how the tea should be feeling. I am a very basic person, so I don't have any grand plans, but I do have a clear set of goals. In the Chinese thinking, you feel that the clouds and the mist are in high places, which is where the immortals live. How can the tea be bad there if that is where the immortals dwell?

NORWOOD: My own ambition is also simple. I want to go to heaven in a teacup. I found that you fill the cup with the teas to take me to heaven. One of the highest honors I have ever received was when you made me Honorary Director of your own Imperial Tea Court, here in San Francisco. I should simply not let you out of my sight. As you continue to do these things, I want to be close by and to shout encouragement, but also to drink the products and talk about it with you. It's been a wonderful ride.

ROY: The journey is so long with so much to do. No matter how bad things are, or how good things are, there is more in tea than you can ever do. So for me, there is so much more to learn. I have spent thirty years of my life pretty seriously trying to learn about tea, and I feel I can finally answer a good question once in a while.

TOP 20 TEA DEFINITIONS
A Selection of Essential Terms from
The Tea Dictionary
by James Norwood Pratt

The nomenclature and verbiage of tea is complex, colorful, and important for any serious tea aficionado, connoisseur, or entrepreneur. While it's tempting to use casual slang or personal variation on centuries-old terms, standardization of terminology includes: cupping descriptives, leaf styles, origins, and much more. Although it's all but impossible to pick the absolute most relevant or important tea definitions for a given individual or company, there are a few that must be reserved for the prime "top spot," or Top Twenty, in this case.

The World of Tea is as rich and various as that of wine, but vastly more subtle and mysterious. As our sleepy old tea trade begins to wake up in the United States, we are realizing the need for a dictionary of the worldwide language spoken in the World of Tea. Just as any devotee of fine dining must understand "Menu French," American tea lovers increasingly need to know "Tea Chinese" as well as a host of other terms variously derived from Hindi or Japanese.

Preeminent tea sage Pratt declares, "None of us knows all there is to know about tea, but to benefit the age-old Tea Society to which we all belong, let our knowledge, like our tea, be shared and our ignorance, like our thirst, overcome."

ANTIOXIDANTS: Antioxidants are any substances that prevent or slow oxidation in the body. They neutralize the damaging effects of free radicals, which are byproducts of cell metabolism. Free radicals may be likened to rust; they travel through the cells, disrupting normal cellular functioning. Such damage, it is thought, assists the body to age and causes many other ailments. Like a rust preventive and remover, antioxidants are free radical scavengers that mop up and counteract the damaging effect of these free radicals within the cells of the body.

BERGAMOT: Literally, "Prince's pear" (Turkish), bergamot is a four-meter-high citrus tree (*Citrus bergamia*) that is the source of oil of bergamot, the key aromatic ingredient of Earl Grey scented tea. Grown in Turkey, Greece, Corfu, southern Italy, and principally, today, in Sicily, bergamot produces a bitter, orangelike fruit that is not eaten fresh, but can be made into marmalades and liqueurs, although it is principally raised for the oil its rind yields for use in perfume and scenting tea.

CAFFEINE: 1, 3, 7-trimethyl-xanthine, or caffeine ($C_8H_{10}N_4O_2$), occurs in some sixty plants, including coffee, tea, mate, guarana, chocolate, and kola nuts. It is a feeble, basic, colorless compound with a slightly bitter taste, which acts as a central nervous system stimulant and a diuretic. In tea, caffeine has an important function in performing the "cream," or precipitate, which appears on the surface when a tea infusion cools. Caffeine does not play an active part in the changes taking place during manufacture. In a tea infusion, its bitter taste might possibly make up part of the briskness of the liquor. Caffeine in tea has a different effect than caffeine in coffee.

CAMELLIA SINENSIS: Literally, "Chinese camellia"—the botanical name for tea—is an evergreen shrub that grows to tree heights in some cases. There are eighty-two different species of *Camellia sinensis*, of which tea is the most complex, with three major varieties numbering almost four hundred recognized cultivars. The varieties are *Camellia sinensis var. sinensis*, known as China bush; *Camellia sinensis var. assamica*, known as Assam bush; and the commercially unimportant *Camellia irrawadiensis*, called Cambodia tea. Most cultivars fall under China bush;

among many others, for instnace, Shuixian, Dahongpao, Rongui, and some several dozen others best known for producing Oolong.

CATECHINS: The primary polyphenol found in tea, catechins account for 30–40 percent of dry leaf weight. The four main catechins in green tea leaf are; Gallocatechin (GC), Epigallocatechin (EGC), Epicatechin (EC), and Epigallocatechine Gallate (EGCG). The EGCG type also gives green tea antimicrobial properties that defend the body against various food-poisoning microbes.

CHAI: A Western term for sweet spiced tea from India, where chai is known as *masala chai: masala* is Hindi for spice; *chai* is Hindi for tea. Chai is incredibly popular in India, and since the early 1990s, increasingly popular in the United States. There is no fixed recipe or preparation method for masala chai. All chai has four basic components: tea, sweetener, milk, and spices. As a secondary meaning, chai is the word for tea in Russian and many other languages. It no doubt derives from *cha yeh*, the Chinese words meaning tea leaf.

CTC: The crush-tear-curl method of processing black teas; with this process the leaf is made into the stronger tasting, higher-caffeine dark teas typically found in teabags. Not all CTC is necessarily low-grade tea, but it does provide a much more intensely flavored cup than the more delicate whole-leaf teas.

CULTIVAR: Literally, "cultivated variety," cultivar refers to any plant subvariety within a particular cultivated species that is distinguished by one or more characteristics. Thus, wine-grape cultivars include Chardonnay, Pinot Noir, Cabernet Sauvingnon, and others, while cultivars of tea include Ti Quan Yin, Shuixian, Yunnan Dayeh, Quimen, to name a few. By definition, every clone—the CR-6017 developed for Nilgiri Estates or the AV-2 widespread in Darjeeling—is a cultivar. More famous black-tea cultivars are China's Keemun and Da-Yeh, or "big leaf," from which Yunnan Black is made. Longjing and numerous other green teas are also made from specific cultivars, just as Fujian's white tea Yinzhen is made exclusively from the Da Bai, or "big white," cultivar. China's widely propagated "wild" tea strain called Jiu Keng is a recently discovered cultivar, though numerous Oolong cultivars have been known for centuries: Da Hong Pao, Ti Quan Yin, Shuixian, Rongui, Fenghuang, Dancong, Maoxie, Ti Lohan, White Rooster Crest, Qilan, Taoren, and many others.

GOLDEN TIP: Buds, and sometimes the first leaves that have picked up tea juices during the rolling process and show "hair" gummed into a mat, are called "golden tip." After fermentation and firing, these buds and first leaves, being practically devoid of chlorophyll, turn golden in color and are most desirable.

GUYWAN: Alternatively Gaiwan; in Cantonese, a method called *Cha zhong*, literally, "covered cup." Another Chinese invention, this simple, elegant way to prepare tea is older than the teapot. It consists of a porcelain cup that has a saucer and a lid but no handle, and the three elements are always used together. The guywan can serve as both a steeping vessel and a drinking cup. After steeping tea, it can be decanted into other cups or one can drink directly from the guywan, using the lid to restrain the leaf and keep the tea warm.

"HIGH" TEA: Decidedly not the same as "Afternoon Tea," High Tea is served at the end of the day as a workingman's meal, usually of leftovers. Unlike afternoon tea, high tea consists of heavy savories such as meat and cheese as well as various kinds of desserts. In England, it is sometimes also called Yorkshire tea.

MUSCATEL: Tasting term derived from the flavor and aroma peculiar to grapes of the Muscat family, muscatel is named for the captial city and port of Oman on the Persian Gulf, and source of historic wines mentioned in the Bible and throughout the Middle East, as in Omar Khayyam and friends. Though of many subvarieties, muscat grapes have a character all their own and usually are used for sweet dessert wines. Resembling musk, *musky* is the usual dictionary definition of this term traceable well over a thousand years back in Western languages to Old Provencal as *muscadelle*. In tea, it denotes a unique muscatlike fruitiness in aroma and flavor found exclusively in the most highly prized Darleelings—usually Second Flush—when it is found at all. So rare is this taste characteristic that many American colleagues say they've never encountered it, and a Darjeeling tea estate owner said that his father congratulated him in 2003 for producing teas with the most pronounced "muscatel" flavor the father remembered since the days of the British Raj. As rare as it is unmistakable, muscatel remains a mystery even for those who have experienced its charm. One Darjeeling estate manager suggested to me it is somehow related to infestations of green fly in the gardens. Howsoever explained, muscatel is greatly to be wished for all concerned.

ORANGE PEKOE (OP): This manufacturing term applies to a long, largely unbroken leaf grade that sometimes contains leaf buds that fall between Pekoe grade, the only larger unbroken grade, and Broken Orange Pekoe, the next smaller. The OP classification is often confused by consumers who mistakenly believe it refers to tea flavor, as opposed to leaf size. The name conjures up a vision of a flavory and exotic variety. Early Dutch traders seem to have used "orange" to imply Holland's ruling House of Orange.

ORTHODOX MANUFACTURE: Traditional method of tea manufacture that uses machines to mimic manual methods employed in old China. In this process, each batch of leaf is withered and then put into rollers, which bruise and shape it prior to oxidation. Following oxidation, that is, "fermentation," the leaf is fired to arrest further chemical change and preserve it free of moisture, and then is graded by leaf size. All of the world's great black teas are produced by Orthodox Manufacture, which preserves the integrity and full flavor of the leaf. It is expensive and time-consuming compared to CTC manufacture.

OXIDATION: This stage follows rolling in orthodox manufacture of black tea, when the leaf is left to oxidize. The time required for oxidation varies widely, depending on the nature of the leaf, the rolling method used, the temperature of the leaf, and the ambient atmosphere's warmth and humidity. Various chemical changes that take place during oxidation are responsible for the briskness, strength, and color of the resulting tea. The aroma of the leaf develops markedly as oxidation proceeds. The term *oxidation* has replaced the old misnomer *fermenta-*

tion to describe this process, in which, after all, nothing ferments—that is, produces alcohol.

PLUCKING TABLE: For uniform growth and ease of plucking, tea bushes on estates outside China and Japan are kept pruned to provide a waist-high flat "table." From this plucking table, in season, the tea "flushes," that is, sprouts young shoots consisting of two leaves and a bud, at predicatable intervals called "plucking rounds" so that this fresh growth may be harvested.

SHRIMP EYE: The Chinese term for the stage during boiling of water when the first tiny bubbles appear on the bottom of the kettle. After *shrimp eye* comes the *crab eye* and then the *fish eye* stage before *string of pearls* and finally, *raging torrent*.

TANNINS: "Tannins" is the now obsolete term for the polyphenol content of tea, principally catechins. The color of the infusion, its pungency, strength, color, and tartness of liquor depend largely on these "tannins" and their combination with other constituents. The term was adopted in the 1800s before it was understood that tea pholyphenols have nothing in common with tannins found in tannic acid.

TISANES: Herbal infusions, tisanes are often mistakenly referred to as herbal "teas," although containing no *Camellia sinensis* leaf. Tisanes use a variety of flowers, berries, seeds, peels, leaves, and roots of different plants, such as chamomile, ginseng, rose petals, hibiscus, peppermint, valerian, lavender, and jasmine, to name a few. Tisanes are typically caffeine-free.

WATER TEMPERATURE: Different teas require different temperatures of water: Black and Pu-Er tea need boiling water, but this will "burn" or "cook" green and white teas. For these, water should be considerably cooler at around 165–185°F (73–85°C), depending on the tea. Oolongs are best steeped in water just below boiling point, at 185–200°F (85-93°C), always depending on the particular tea. The darker the Oolong, the higher the temperature.

Chapter Fourteen

THESE CHANGING TIMES:
The Folks of Tea

WITH
The Folks of Tea, South Dakota

TEA, SOUTH DAKOTA

There is a great deal of poetry and fine sentiment in a chest of tea.
—RALPH WALDO EMERSON (1803–1882)
LETTERS AND SOCIAL AIMS, 1883

The story goes that the town's name at the time, Byron, was no longer a good choice—there were too many similar names in the area. So some settlers were asked to come up with ten names from which one would be chosen. They wrote a list, but got stuck on number nine. They couldn't seem to think of another name. Some say there was a crate of tea sitting in the store; some say that it was tea time for these German folks. For whatever reason, the last name on the list was *Tea*, and it was the one chosen as the official name of their town, nestled into the very heart of South Dakota.

CAL: The origin story of the name of our town goes like this. When the first settlers stopped here for a break, halfway between Lennox and Suffolk, they discussed what to name the place. They noticed a box with the word TEA written on it at the old railroad station and so they decided to put the name into a hat with a number of others. *Tea* was on the bottom of the list, but it was chosen. My grandfather came here to Tea, South Dakota, in 1883. A year later, his father and his five brothers and one sister came. One brother was the first postmaster in Tea; one brother was the first mail carrier; and one brother was a partner with John Peters, who had the first store. My grandfather's cousin donated one block of land for the original school. In the old days, the farmer's schedule was to get up in the morning, have a cup of tea and a biscuit or donut. Then you went out and did your chores for a couple of hours. Later, you would come in and have breakfast. Around ten o'clock in the morning, you had coffee. At noon, you had a big meal, and at three o'clock in the afternoon you had tea, and in the evening you had your meal again. Tea feels good. It has a good taste to it, and it warms you up in the wintertime.

HENRY: I have lived here since I was three years old. A few years ago, the water quality here was very bad. After the water quality was raised, I think a lot of people went to coffee. But tea is to me a ritual. In the old days, you'd have tea in the morning and tea again in the afternoon when you'd review the activities of the day.

ERNIE: I remember the simplicity of the town when I was a kid growing up here. The homes were all heated with wood, cobs, and coal. I earned a little spending money when I'd get out of school at four o'clock in the afternoon and go hauling their cobs, coal, and water. Usually in winter it was dark by the time I got back home. There were three streetlights in Tea, and so it was kind of scary for a little boy on the outskirts of town where it got dark and it was time to go home.

We also had tea in the morning, tea at dinnertime, and tea at suppertime. My parents boiled the tea in the pot, and when we got home from school this tea was really good. This is maybe a little gross, but we'd put the spout right into our mouth and drink whatever tea was left. I enjoyed it. Nowadays, it's a Lipton teabag. Just about every night

> *Half our life is spent trying to find something to do with the time we have rushed through life trying to save.*
>
> —WILL ROGERS

I dip it in water and have tea and put in a little cream or a little sugar and sit read a book. Tea is a very good drink. I think it's healthy. It's never hurt me. When I'd go down to visit my Uncle P. D.'s—he's an old farmer, eighty years old—I'd get boiled tea consistently, and I'd enjoy it. Uncle P. D. likes to sit and talk about the past, with three cups of tea, black or with sugar or with cream. Today, people are drinking less tea than fifty years ago. I think it's because it's a soda generation. You'll see young people going shopping, and they usually have a soda with them. Even in our church they'll have a bottle of water with them during the services, which was unheard-of when I was a young boy.

DICK: I married into this community in 1961, and where I came from, I never knew what tea was. But the first thing I learned was my wife's family were tea drinkers, green tea as far as I can remember. When they had company, my wife's mother would always ask, "Would you want tea or coffee?" Most of them drank tea, but I always had to have coffee. They'd always put it out as a kind of afterthought: "Oh, maybe you didn't want tea? So would you want some coffee?" The tea I drink would be iced tea, with lots of sugar, during summertime. It's a good refresher; it quenches your thirst.

Originally, I am from about thirty-five miles south of here—from a bunch of Norwegians and some Germans down there—and, oh boy, there are a lot of tea drinkers. I am kind of acquiring a little taste for iced tea, but not hot tea. Iced tea is my thing. Now they're touting lots of benefits in green tea. Tea might make a comeback, especially with the health thing going for it—but years ago, the water wasn't so good. It came off the roofs and went into the cistern with a filter. You did the best you can. I can't ever remember anybody getting real sick because the water wasn't full of chlorine. I think people grew up pretty healthy around here because they treated their water with tea.

HENRY: I remember going out to Milo and Rose Hoffman's and helping Milo clean his cistern. We had all the water out, but I was scooping out the dirt and there were all kinds of frogs in there. Rose said, "Oh, Milo, it's got frogs."

DICK: Sometimes, I think it tastes better when you have all that stuff in it!

CAL: I was only four or five years old when I had my first cup of tea. We had gone to visit my great-grandmother, and she had little cups that were about half as big as a regular cup. It was real strong black tea that everybody had a chance to drink, no matter how old you were. I think almost everybody drank tea.

HENRY: Yes, tea was very important to everybody in the old days. Tea was a kind of a treat, and you had it with every meal and after every meal. It was just part of life.

ERNIE: One of the things about tea that I do remember is how my mother put it in a nursing bottle when we were young. We were drinking tea from the time we were a year old. Of course, it wouldn't be real strong tea, but I remember it very well.

DICK: When us young guys were throwing bales of hay we'd want *cold, cold water.* The old boys, they'd want *hot, hot, hot tea,* and that kept them *cool, cool, cool.* They said that hot tea was better for you and quenched your thirst better. I could never understand that. The old boys even wore their long johns in the middle of summer. They said it insulated them and kept the heat out. They always drank their tea hot and their coffee hot, and we drank cold, cold water. I never got with that program, but, boy, a lot of them did.

ERNIE: One of the reasons they did not drink anything but hot tea was that there was no modern refrigeration. The only refrigeration we had was a hole that had been drilled into the ground where they lowered their butter and cream. Or they'd put anything they wanted cold down in the cistern. That was the only formal refrigeration.

CAL: I can remember back when the general store had about anything you wanted to buy, like dry goods, clothing, shoes, kerosene, and gas. Folks brought chicken and eggs to pay for their groceries. If you had more coming to you than what you needed for your groceries, then they gave you chips or tokens so that you could come back and spend them at the store when you really needed things. They were usually worth a little more than if you took cash. When you bought groceries, you also bought a box of tea. At that time, tea just came in a box, not in bags. If you wanted a drink, you just took out a little pinch of tea leaves and put it in the pot, let it steep, poured it into the cup, and used a little strainer to strain the leaves out. All I remember is the tea was black. I think it was called Old Law Tea.

QUALITY OF LIFE

HENRY: Well, I think the three stoplights in Tea are a safety factor, in order to move the traffic. We used to have sixty cars a day and now we have six thousand, so it requires more regulation. I think the main difference between New York City and Tea, South Dakota, is the choice of how you like to live. You'd find a kind of openness in Tea that you don't find in New York City. Today, you would probably find people who are a little more leisurely than in New York City. I think that people here still have some friendliness about them, and everybody here has time for everybody else.

CAL: If a local farmer gets in trouble or somebody dies, all the neighbors get together and harvest or put in his crop. They do whatever is necessary. Everyone kind of pitches in and helps; probably you wouldn't have that in New York City. But I think time itself is changing in Tea. Before, it used to be a lot slower and now it seems to be getting a bit more like bigger cities. People have more things going on. People have kids in school, so they're running to everything after school and before school. When I went to school, we went to school at nine o'clock in the morning and got out at twelve o'clock; we went back at one o'clock, got out at four o'clock. That was about the end of it. Everything is different now. I suppose that would be progress, in a way, as far as time is changing.

DICK: When you go from a population of a hundred to three thousand, there are lots of new people who have no roots here whatsoever. The history of Tea doesn't mean nothing to them. You've really got to be dedicated to want to cling to the old stuff. Sometimes you got to look back to look ahead. That's what we've been trying to do. This spring,

we had a run for mayor of the town. One of the things I was asked was, "Why did you run?" Well, I'd heard the historical society and other folks in town talking about losing some of these old ways and thought that we might want to keep up with some of our heritage and tradition in Tea. You know, once it's gone, it's gone.

Tea Community Dinner

WOMAN #1: Do I drink tea every day? I do drink tea quite often. I'm also a coffee drinker. I like black tea the most.

WOMAN #2: Do I drink tea? You know, we should. It's healthy.

WOMAN #1: Maybe once a day at least, I have a cup of tea. I usually just drink either green or black tea, whichever. Lipton, just plain old Lipton, usually. I don't know, it kinda makes you feel relaxed, I guess. It's good.

WOMAN #2: Well, it is an antioxidant. Most of the time now it's alone, 'cause I live alone, but sometimes with family, friends. My mother used to drink tea. I suppose she's what got me started drinking tea. I drink quite a bit of iced tea, which I like. My husband was from the South, and of course Southern people, they love their iced tea. I like mine sweet, my iced tea, but just black tea. This is more formal and sophisticated. Nice teacups. I usually just grab a mug. It holds a little more! But tea is healthy.

WOMAN #1: My mom used to make loose-leaf tea. She had her big old teapot and that little old strainer. Everyone's looking for an easier way now. But it would be good to have one of those old teapots again. I wish I did have one of those. It'd be nice. The food is excellent, the company is excellent, a good way to spend a Sunday afternoon. I don't know why I don't drink more tea, because I like it. Too much else going on, I guess, so we should get back in the habit.

WOMAN #2: Yes, I think it relaxes you. Maybe you can even lose a few pounds, if you don't eat all the goodies!

WOMAN #1: I think we're part of history! Remember, we're having tea in Tea—on the hundredth anniversary!

WOMAN #2: This is my hometown! My dad was a carpenter. I'm the youngest of eight kids. We were all born and raised here. I still have one brother who lives here and an older sister. So it means a lot to come back to where we were born and raised, because our home is still here, and the home that my first husband and I built, on Main Street, when you come into town. We were married here fifty-seven years ago.

John Lawlor

· "Teapot Days" started out as an annual event to try to promote the community by bringing people back into this town, where I'm the mayor. This year is our centennial so we have a few more activities going on to help us celebrate our "Teapot Days."

We have to do this nowadays because of the influence of the Internet, the video games, and the play stations. Today, all those other things are vying for the attention of the people of Tea. Cell phones! I cannot believe how often you see young kids walking down the street or riding their bike while talking on a cell phone! There are so many things that really do try to pull at their attention or distract them from just being a kid. When I was growing up, it was baseball and football. You went outside and played. Today, we have kids who spend hours chatting back and forth with their friends on the Internet. It amazes me. It's such a fast-paced society now. I look at the activities that my children are involved in, versus what I was involved in at their age. At some point, we parents have to take responsibility and say, "OK, you need to go outside and get away from all this technology. Use your mind and create your own ways to have fun!"

We don't take time to really sit back anymore and enjoy our time for what it is, for what we have right now. It's a go, go, go, rush, rush,

rush world. We can all be guilty of trying to make too many things happen in one day. We're all wondering what's the next activity we have to be doing, instead of enjoying life and then really reflecting on the things that have happened to us. Tea is a place where people can take the time—if it's a priority to you.

LUELLA DEJONG

I believe that sharing roots in Tea means someone who was born and raised here, went to school here, has lived here for quite a number of years. Ironically, people in Tea don't drink a lot of tea. We're more into coffee, coke, and beer. With their rich German background, most people drink tea in the afternoon, but we're not heavy tea drinkers. But still, we're wondering why we don't have a tea shop in Tea.

I have found that just taking the time to drink tea slows everything down.

—SUSAN BORG,
WEED FARM, VERMONT

Tea was a farming community and when you're a farmer you want your roast beef and potatoes and gravy, and lunch in the afternoon is some sandwiches and a piece of cake and a couple of cookies. Little tea sandwiches would never, never do for these farmers.

*No matter how hard you try, you cannot accelerate enlightenment.
Every religion teaches the need to slow down in order to connect
with the self, with others, and with a higher force. In Psalm 46, the
Bible says: "Be still and know that I am God."*
—CARL HONORE, *In Praise of Slowness: Challenging the Cult of Speed*

Prior to getting the water piped in, most people had a cistern. If you had a cistern you either had a pump like this, a larger one that stood up outside the cistern. Some of the cisterns had the one where you turned the handle around, and that was the system for getting water. Then Tea got their water piped in, but that was a very poor quality of water. Your water heater didn't last very long with Tea water. The business people didn't really like to sell water heaters in Tea anymore because it would rust out before your warranty was up. They didn't appreciate that.

But this kind of a pump would likely have to be primed. The water in the cisterns came off the roof. It was rainwater that was collected, and they had a charcoal box on the side of the building that the water filtered through. A couple of times a year you'd rinse out the filter box so the water was clean, and you'd also probably once a year or so clean out your cistern. But cistern water didn't always last. Back then, families had an average of six to eight kids, and rationing it out by the pails full, you know, your cistern won't last. There were people who had good well water who would sell it. You could order a truck full of water and have it delivered into your cistern. If you had a dry spell in the summer you'd have to order a tank-load of water from good soft water wells.

The water that comes off the roof is the best water for tea, and I still use it at my house. When you make tea or coffee, you get no scum on it, which a lot of the city water has in it. There's no chlorine. It makes the best tea. It makes the best drinking water. We use two large cisterns, because when we built the house there was no rural water. So we kept the cisterns for our hot water heater and for our cold water in the kitchen.

Most of the time I heat my water in a hot pot. I have a thermos jug pitcher there that I make it in so it stays hot, so I can enjoy a cup of tea a little later on, and it's still hot. It isn't like on the cook stoves where you set it toward the back and it would stay warm. What I don't drink I put in a jar in the refrigerator and then I got iced tea.

My mother used loose tea with the little metal containers. Of course, back in the turn of the twentieth century, almost everything in the grocery store was in bulk, whether it was sugar, tea, whatever, and they'd dip into the bag and dip out however much you wanted. So you would have a sack of tea at home to make your tea.

The old-fashioned way to make tea would be with a teakettle on the stove all day. Well then, when you wanted to make tea, you would pull it to the front where the stove was hotter and get it to a good rolling boil—my mother-in-law still does this—it has to almost steam up her kitchen boiling so hard. Then she pours it over her tea. And then you have to leave it set for a few minutes, of course, before you can drink it. Now, like I said, in the olden days they would set the teapot back on this part of the stove and it would stay warm for quite a while. You don't want to boil it again, but it would stay hot enough to be good to drink.

A human being is part of a whole, called by us the Universe,
a part limited by time and space. He experiences himself, his
thoughts and feelings, as something separated from the rest, a kind
of optical delusion of his consciousness. This delusion is a kind of
prison for us, restricting us to our personal desires and to affection
for a few persons nearest us. Our task must be to free ourselves from
this prison by widening our circles of compassion to embrace all
living creatures and the whole of nature in its beauty.

—ALBERT EINSTEIN (1879–1955)

In those old farming days, if you came to visit somebody's place and weren't invited into the house for a cup of tea or coffee, you felt offended. If you came to my house, I would invite you in and offer you tea or coffee, plus probably some cake or cookies. If people weren't invited in, they wondered what the problem was.

Tea that was boiling hot, because you just made it, you would pour into the saucer and drink it from there, because that way it would cool off. My father-in-law would drink it that way all the time, because it was his wife that had the good boiling water that would steam up the kitchen. So he would pour his in the saucer and drink it out of the saucer.

I think tea time has disappeared because everybody is working now. This was an agricultural community. They needed a break and their horses needed a break. They worked very hard. By mid-afternoon, they were hungry. Now, there's nobody home in the afternoon in most houses, to have tea. So they don't have lunch anymore. When we kids had to bring lunch out to the fields for my dad, it would be a jar of tea, sandwiches, a couple cookies, and it was quite a lunch. If you visited the older people for tea at their house, you got sandwiches and cake with peach sauce.

A TEA SHOP

A tea shop in Tea might get a fair amount of business, but I have not found people in Tea to be strong tea drinkers. I serve lunch, coffee, and so on over at the church quite often, and when it's my turn to serve, there's tea served. I don't have a lot of takers. This isn't true of all the German communities. When we serve tea and coffee and cake for my mother-in-law's birthday—she's ninety-seven now—we do it after the church services, and it isn't unusual to make fifty cups of tea.

My mother-in-law has tea every afternoon. And this was true of my parents too, they'd have coffee in the morning and tea in the afternoon. Now, if I understood right, I think my father-in-law also drank tea first thing in the morning. They'd fire up the cook stove—get the water boiling—not only to heat the house, but he'd have a cup of tea before he went out to do chores. And if you came there in the evening they probably would have asked you which one you want, tea or coffee. Tea has been touted now to have health benefits, and it could be one of the reasons she is ninety-seven. Tea time is also a time of relaxation, so it kind of revitalizes you after you've had a cup of tea and maybe a couple of cookies, and then you can get up and go again.

When I hear someone say "tea time moment," the first thing that comes to mind would be sitting down with some friends and a cup of tea, and enjoying a little visit with your cup of tea. Back in other times, I think people took more time to visit friends and relatives, and there was a closer relationship with your neighbors.

Chapter Fifteen
The Phenomenon of Herbal Tea

WITH
SUSAN BORG

SUSAN BORG

This evening sky may bring snow. "Come enjoy a cup with me."
—PO CHU-I, TRANSLATED BY SAM HAMILL

Susan Gallagher Borg lives and works at her home, on Weed Farm, Vermont, where she raises herbs, vegetables, and chickens, and teaches classes on educational bodywork, music, and herbalism. Borg's background includes teaching Experiential Anatomy and Kinesiology at Middlebury College and Burlington College, in Vermont, as well as acting as their director of the Resonant Kinesiology Training Program for bodyworkers. Her current passion is teaching students at her farm about the medicinal qualities of herbs.

SUSAN BORG: The main advantage of making a tea from an infusion of herbs is that it is easy to do. It is quick and something that anyone can do without any prior knowledge of either herbs or the mechanics of doing it. In general, if you just want the good taste, then any herb that you like can be used for tea. If you are looking for medicinal qualities, then you actually need to check and see that the herb actually gives those qualities to water. Some herbs won't. With those, you need to either make a tincture with alcohol, use vinegar, or put them in oil, because their medicinal qualities are dissolved in different ways.

My favorite tea for taste is the one that's called either Anne hyssop or liquorish mint, depending on who's naming it. The two teas that I drink everyday are, first, a combination of dandelion and milk thistle, and second, one that is made of nettles. The medicinal effects of dandelion and milk sisal support the liver and help it to do its job properly, which is to clean chemicals out of the body. The nettles help the liver in a similar way, and also help the adrenal keep things calm instead of antsy.

There are some other teas that alter my moods. I find that sage tea is a tea that calms me. I don't know if everyone would find that, but I find it calming and soothing. Sage tea is used also to support the female reproductive system, because it stops the hormones from flopping around.

TEAS AND HERBS

I consider *Camellia sinensis* to be an herbal tea, and I consider herbs to be any plant that we find a use for, which would certainly cover *Camellia sinensis*. The reason that I don't prefer to drink that particular tea is because of its caffeine, which doesn't agree with my body. But I know that for many people the caffeine is the reason they like tea. Caffeine is not necessarily bad for some bodies; it may be exactly what they need.

I am not sure what distinction some tea experts are making between a tea and an infusion. As far as I am concerned, tea is the name of the tea or the herb or the plant. You are going to dry it, you are going to use it in water; that makes it a tea. *Camellia sinensis* is the technical name of something that gives its medicinal properties to water. The process of getting those medicinal properties into the water is called *infusion*. So I don't really see the difference between tea and an infusion.

I think the real reason why we don't say *Camellia sinensis* "tea" is cultural. When folks began to drink tea in England, they were drinking something that had been brought to them by travelers from China. That was the only tea they thought of as tea. They were also drinking other herbs at that point, but I don't think the English referred to them as teas. Once tea became an important part of English culture, other brews started to be called teas.

As for me, I don't grow *Camellia sinensis* here on Weed Farm. We don't have the right climate here for it. The mountains in Lincoln, Vermont, are not the same as in China or Malaysia or India.

TEA RITUALS

For me, tea drinking is both a solitary activity and a social activity. I prepare my cups of tea in two different ways, depending on whether I am going to use fresh herb or dry herb. If I am going to use fresh herb, I just go outside and pick the herb, trying to find the most beautiful leaves I can. Then I cut up the leaves a little bit so that there is more surface area in contact with the water. I put them into my pot or cup or tea ball and pour hot water on them and let them steep for about five or six minutes. But if I am going to use dried herbs, then I dry them and place them in

Outside the sky is light with stars;
There's a hollow roaring from the sea.
And, alas! for the little almond flowers,
The wind is shaking the almond tree.
How little I thought, a year ago,
In the horrible cottage upon the Lee
That he and I should be sitting so
And sipping a cup of camomile tea.
—KATHERINE MANSFIELD, FROM *Camomile Tea*

a glass container. Next, I fill up the tea ball, put it in the cup, pour hot water in it, and let it wait for the same five or six minutes.

The most common thing for me to do during cool weather or cold weather when someone comes to visit is to immediately ask if they would like a cup of tea. That's a sort of preamble to our conversation. It also gets everybody involved in tea. Soon, everybody starts to talk and the evening rolls on as we drink the tea together. In this sense, tea is a shared pleasure.

Now, I don't think of tea as a ritual, but it does seem to be an act that people understand, even if just unconsciously. Rather than go into it purposefully, as in a traditional ritual; there is just something friendly about asking, "Would you like a cup of tea?" as well as the answer: "Sure, I would like a cup of tea."

Getting together over tea also means deciding what kind people would like, depending on their emotional state. Do they need something comforting? Or do they need something stimulating? Or do they want something calming? Going through the process of picking out the cups and choosing the tea, then putting the tea in it, boiling the water, and then sitting and enjoying it means we have made something together that's fun.

At my farm, when there is a group wanting tea altogether, we put out samples of the teas that we have and say, "Take your pick." Sometimes our guests choose a tea just because they like the picture on the box.

I have found that just taking the time to drink tea slows everything down. Perhaps that's one of the ways in which tea is useful. It helps people slow down so that they can focus on whatever exchange they are going to share. With all the minutia of our lives, it is important to have *the opportunity to simply be* for a while. This is so rare in our culture, almost discouraged, as if it means you are either being lazy or frivolous.

THE MYRIAD AFFECTS OF CAFFEINE

Caffeine works on different people in different ways. For some folks, caffeine is a stimulant; for others it is actually a relaxant. They find it calming. What is interesting about herbal teas is that there is not just one constituent; they have many, many qualities. Your body may respond to this particular quality one time when you drink the tea and another particular quality the next time you drink the tea, because your personal chemistry is different from day to day.

For instance, you may find nettle tea a very calming tea on one day and rather stimulating on another day. You might find mint tea stimulating on a particular day and then a calming tea on another day. Catnip, which cats find to be wonderfully stimulating, makes them want to roll around in it. But one of its main uses in humans is for calming their digestive system. We respond to it in a very different way, though some people find the smell of catnip tea wakes them up. The way that different herbs interact with your body depends on your nutrition, your chemical state, and your emotional state.

Herbs change seasonally. They also change according to their nutrients and to weather. One of the important things here is this is a certified organic farm. Our choice is organic, rather than chemical, because we believe that whatever nourishes the plant gives it its taste, its flavor, and its medicinal qualities.

If you pick mint in the springtime, or when it is flowering in the middle of summer, or in the fall when it's starting to dry, it will taste different. If you pick mint after it has been raining for two weeks, or if you pick mint when it's been hot and dry for a week, it's also going to taste different.

Most of the packaged teas that you buy are from many different places. Tea comes in bulk and then is mixed. The idea is to take all those combinations of flavors from different teas, from different places, and mix them together until there is a uniform taste among all the teabags made by a particular company.

The beauty of tea is that it gives you an opportunity to notice yourself, to attend to yourself, and to really be present clearly in all your senses. So one should consider seriously looking at tea and saying, "What kind of tea do I want to put in my body? Do I want to put tea from across the world that's been sprayed with herbicides or pesticides? Would I rather have tea that's fresh, would I rather have tea that's grown near me, so I know it hasn't traveled with exhaust fumes and all kinds of other things from long distance?"

I feel very strongly that I want only organic tea for its health benefits, for myself and for my family. I don't want to be putting chemicals into my nutrition, and I also want to make sure that the things I take into my body are as healthy as they can be. I choose organic and I choose local because things that have grown locally have not had to travel a long way, they haven't been subjected to tremendous heat, they haven't been subjected to terrible cold. They are grown right here. It is also true that you can't grow everything near where you live. On that thought, one of the teas that I grow here in Vermont is raspberry leaf, which has a flavor very similar to *Camellia sinensis*. I don't know if the *Camellia sinensis* folks would like it very much, but it's very pleasant. It doesn't have any caffeine and you can grow it in Vermont.

A SAMPLER OF HERBAL TEAS

As a tea, calendula flower is really good for the whole digestive system. If you are stressed in some way, calendula tea would be calming, especially if you are have ulcers or extra acid, because it can be so soothing. But calendula is not a tea that you pick up and drink for fun—only if you need it medicinally. We have several different kinds of herb tea plants here on Weed Farm. Bergamot is famous because it flavors Earl Grey tea. It also makes a wonderful tea all by itself. We often use this flavoring to cover other teas that are medicinally useful, but are not very tasty themselves. So it's nice to have this flavor along with it.

Spilanthes is a very funny-looking herb. It has pretty green, ruffly leaves with a little button flower and not any petals, just a bright chromium yellow and a dark-red center that looks an eyeball. As you are walking past the plant it sort of looks at you. It's called the toothache plant, because it looks so strange and has a really concentrated dose of the same kind of medicinal properties as Echinacea. If you chew on this flower it makes your gum buzz. If you have a toothache, you can go take this eyeball flower and chew on it, and the whole side of your mouth goes off to sleep.

Nettle tea is one of my favorites. I just love it. It makes my day feel good. The nettles do sting when they are fresh, but once they are dried they don't sting anymore, as long as you can snip the nettles. You can dry them and then you can use your fingers to put them in the teabag if you want.

The leaves of the plain old raspberry plant that you grow in your garden are nothing fancy, but they make a tea that tastes very similar to *Camellia sinensis*. Calendula flowers are yellow and orange; it's the flowers themselves that you make the tea with. There is a sticky resin in the petals and in their base that has the medicinal quality, the soothing quality. With catnip, you usually pick the leaves for tea before it grows into a flower. Mint tea is familiar to just about anybody, and lemon bomb has a lemony flavor, as you might imagine. Anise hyssop, or liquorish mint, is an herb whose flower you drop right in the tea. Ground ivy is something that probably people will recognize as stuff that they pull out of their yards, but ground ivy tea is wonderful because it cools your body.

GROWING TEA ON WEED FARM

Our farm is about several things. It's a family project that I decided to do when my daughter graduated from college and I was free to choose what I wanted to do with my life, as she was all grown up and on her way.

I wanted to find a place where I could grow my own food, where I could grow my own medicines, where my life could be focused, and where I could be enveloped in just the process of being.

Growing tea here on Weed Farm is a work of art that is played out in stages: choosing the seeds, planting the seeds, growing the seedlings, watering them, caring for them every day, watching them grow, seeing them become gorgeous green plants, replanting them, potting and watering them for the greenhouse, caring for them there.

A merry heart doeth good like a medicine.
—THE BIBLE

All of this is about choices I make: soil, light, and water. Choices I make are about plants so they can live, grow, and thrive. All of these things come together to make healthy plants. To do that is a work of art.

Afterward, we take the plant from the greenhouse and plant it outdoors and water it some more, make sure that it's weeded, that the soil is taken care of, and the compost is mixed in. We watch the bugs come and eat; we watch the flowers grow. Then there is the picking of the plants and either drying or using them fresh and actually ingesting them. The plant is a work of art. It's a beautiful being, and it becomes a part of me. That kind of exchange is extraordinary. That's why I want to live here; that's why I want to grow my own food. All of this is about attention and sharing. Long before I drink the tea, there is a tremendous amount of exchange between me and the plant.

THE MANY LEVELS OF TEA

Tea can offer many layers of enjoyment and medicinal help. Certainly tea also offers an opportunity to sit down and slow down and relax, either as a solitary or a social activity. That's one of the most useful things that tea can offer. It provides an opportunity to sit down. Most of us don't allow ourselves to just sit down. It would be nice if we could, but tea gives us the excuse to sit down for a little while and contemplate nothing—or something—very slowly. A tea offering is quietness, slowness, peacefulness, attentiveness. Tea gives us the chance to open up to whatever is happening in our lives.

CHAPTER SIXTEEN
THE WORDLESS REALM

WITH
JAMES NORWOOD PRATT

JAMES NORWOOD PRATT

There is a wonderful legend about the origins of the "Big Red Robe," or "Great Scarlet Cloak" tea, what the Chinese call *Da Hong Pao*. This refers to the robe of office. It was the badge of office of a very high mandarin in the Song Dynasty, who fell ill unto death and credited his recovery to drinking tea from this particular patch of bushes up in the Wuyi mountains. When the mandarin recovered, he made a pilgrimage to stand in that place on the terrace beneath the Tianxin Cliff in the Wuyi mountains, where that tea had come from. He spread his cloak over the bushes, and others would be expected to kowtow. From that time on, those plants have been called Da Hong Pao—the "Big Red Robe." Eight hundred years later, that same patch of bushes still wakes up from hibernation every spring and puts forth a few new leaves, and tea is made. The whole canyon is full of their offspring. Not all of the plants there may be eight hundred years old, but some of them date back that far.

There is a varietal unto itself. When you stand in Nine Dragon's Nest, which is the name of a famous canyon in China, you

> Opportunity must not be lost while the gods smile.
>
> —LI JING, TANG DYNASTY

understand the art of feng shui as if you have never understood it before: *feng:* wind, *shui:* water. The truth about anyplace lies in which way the wind blows, and which way the water flows; that is the lay of the land. In this canyon, the walls rise steeply. The sun can only come onto the plants directly from around eleven to one, and the wind can only blow from a certain direction and the water only has a certain flow. These are factors why Da Hong Pao tastes so peculiar. There is nothing else that can taste like Da Hong Pao. When you remove these plants and take them somewhere else, the tea from them doesn't really taste like the down-home Da Hong Pao, either.

For all of these reasons, this is one of China's legendary teas; it is very rare. The real thing can't come from anywhere else; it can't come from any other bush; and there is never going to be very much of it. This tea is always made in that dark Oolong style that is so beloved of the people of China. It is now regarded as an old-fashioned way of making Oolong, but it brings out a richness that you wouldn't believe any plant could show you. I shall say no more about the beauties of Da Hong Pao. I am omitting, I assure you, a great deal.

In the fifties when I was in high school, I learned the magical words for the first time. Of course, I learned about words like witchcraft, which were redolent with romanticism, and other ideas concerning magic. This is the same thing that makes Harry Potter a phenomena among young readers today. I carried it to ridiculous extents and wound up using the Latin that I had been taught to read of the Middle Ages. Through these portals of wisdom, I entered the spiritual path. It's not long after you discover a path such as this, that you lose interest in exercising power over other human beings.

This study of cultism, which lasted until I was about thirty years old, is over now. Of course, this is a subject of infinite interest, but I don't have room in my library anymore

Any object, intensely regarded, may be a gate of access to the incorruptible eon of the gods.

—JAMES JOYCE, *Ulysses*

for all my books. I have now taken a bold step and decided to part with some, possibly a big box, of my library of esoteric matters.

There is so much to be said about tea, because it exists in a realm beyond words, one that can only be entered by poets ready to use metaphors. A beautiful tea is really a tea to write poetry by. It would be my companion as I gazed out over the bay alone, I would choose a special time to have a tea this special. Tea itself I think of as a metaphor. After all, it's up there with acupuncture and fung shui and all of the other Taoist arts. Taoism is something embedded in nature, something that we have lifted from nature to experience it more directly through this medium of tea. If we are not really a body, then what is in tea that is affecting us in this way?

Tea is actually as much a spiritual being as we are. The actual leaf that was steeped in your teapot is just the envelope that the spirit of tea has arrived in. Tea can be a portal to that wordless realm, which was one of the definitions that Lao Tzu gave to it. He said when you are confronting this realm, there is nothing else to do but be silent and have the deep experience of knowing that *you are that realm that you are seeking*. That's what tea teaches.

THE INHERENT MEANING

Does tea have a meaning? I don't know. I don't believe life has a meaning that can be written down on a piéce of paper. It's not what you'd find on a piece of paper or in a stream of words. If tea has a meaning, it is one that we will never capture in a book or a poem. However, this is not to say that tea does not have an existence; this is not to say that tea doesn't have an effect on you. One of the effects that tea has had on every people who have used it is to inspire myths.

Where did tea come from? Who could possibly have come up with the idea of plucking this particular leaf from this particular bush and processing it in this particular way so that it yields this particular delicious beverage? What makes tea delicious, anyway? At the core of tea is its bitterness, so you see there is *something else.*

A Chinese proverb that I have always treasured says, "Tea is bitter, like good advice." That's the metaphor; that's the meaning. Where did it come from? Everybody who has loved tea has had to ask that question, and the answers are various. I have collected about seventeen origin stories so far. Some of them are creation myths, the ones from the homeland of tea in China. Others are cultural myths, such as the tale of Shen Nung, the legendary emperor, who was trying all of the herbs in China so that he could launch the herbal medicines. Of course, he had to have an antidote for those that are poisonous. He found that the leaf of the tea plant did this the best.

The story about the eyelids of Bodhidharma is another favorite creation story. He probably existed and lived in the 500s. He's the man who came to China from India and taught Buddhism. The Chinese also credit him with introducing Zen. But he is also the patron saint of tea, because Zen spread along with the teachings of Bodhidharma. There are countless myths.

Sitting by myself, tea is my solace in solitude, one of my favorite companions. Many of the teas I drink are those that I write poetry by, and these are totally different from teas that you might listen to music by, or teas that you would invite a friend over to share.

Tea does unlock the secrets of your heart when you are seated across the table from a fair tea maker, and you began to exchange personal stories and important information. I believe one of the secrets of tea throughout history is that it makes us *talky*. Look at me. Tea is the universal social solvent, you might say, because it makes us exchange matters of the heart with one another more easily.

Those of us who have come to tea as a livelihood, as a calling, believe that tea has called *us*. We didn't choose this livelihood—but we found this calling and the tea is making us its examples. We are simply the way-showers. Not everybody is going to go into the tea business, but those who do are much happier and better off. Tea makes my body sing and dance on a molecular level; that's exactly what it is doing to us.

A philosopher friend pointed out to me very recently the important difference between taking time and making time. This is tea you would make time for. In this respect, we are in some way the servants of tea. We are taking it to more people and sharing it not only with our friends, but with customers whose names we don't even know, such as the people who read my books. I seldom find out who exactly they are, but a lot of strangers have told me how tea has led them to a whole new understanding of what life can be like.

PR: Do you still wake happy but aware of your mortality?

JG: Yes, though sometimes I have to have a cup of tea first.

—PARIS REVIEW
INTERVIEW WITH POET
JACK GILBERT, 2002

So we are not the only ones to make this discovery. I think everybody who realizes this in some way wants to pass it on. This is the same as being eager to share tea that you have found with somebody who doesn't know about it. You are compelled to say, "Oh, come sit down, I have a new tea to show you."

For me, it is a deep enjoyment to have this spirit inside us. Eventually, we discover as if we feel we can't have too much of it. We come to realize that with a great tea we are in the presence of a great work of art. In fact, we are living in a time in America where tea defines a sort of sociocultural frontier between the people who are trying to go faster and faster and the people who are saying, "No!—I have gone as fast as I wish. I need to go the other way!"

THE MEANING OF
TEA

THE FOURTH CUP

JAPAN

The fourth [bowl] broke me out in a light perspiration ...

— Lu Tong

Regarding the powerful ritual of Japanese tea ceremony, the esteemed scholar of Japanese culture, Daisetz Suzuki, wrote, "Who would then deny that when I am sipping tea in my tearoom I am swallowing the whole universe with it and that this very moment of lifting the bowl to my lips is eternity itself transcending time and space?"

By the ninth century, the Japanese developed the *cha-no-yu*, or ceremony of the "way of tea." As travel writer Lafcadio Hearn wrote in the nineteenth-century, the Japanese used ritual to turn tea into "an exquisite art." In the 1950s, mythologist Joseph Campbell participated in a tea ceremony in Kyoto with a venerable tea master. Later, he wrote, "The tearoom is the realm of the sacred," adding that the ritual itself represented the very embodiment of culture, "a society in form."

In that spirit, we explore in Part 4: "Japan," the belief that one of tea's greatest virtues is its utter simplicity, and Lu T'ung's curious description of how the fourth cup compels us to break out in a sweat, as if the heat and possibly the spirit in the tea is cathartic.

We begin with Sensei Yuriko Arai, who describes the highly stylized Japanese tea ceremony that she practices as being emblematic of the very soul of her culture. The essence of cha-no-yu, she says, is the simple serving of a cup of tea; and yet, she explains, tea is also vastly complex in its ability to "train our minds and souls." To her, the rigors of her traditional practice represent a rare opportunity in our rapidly accelerating world "to let yourself take a step back" and reflect, if even for a few minutes over tea. Without such rituals, she concludes, we are apt to forget who we really are. We are far more likely to remember, she says, if we honor the simple words that summarize the "mentality of tea," which are *Ichigo Ichie*, meaning "One meeting, one time."

For Rokuhei Inoue, the Japanese bottled tea entrepreneur, the bane of modern life is the influence of coffee and soft drinks, and the Bullet Train-pace of life in his homeland. The accelerated pace of living and the lack of respect for tradition, he says, have moved people far away from what he calls the "essence of tea," which includes its medicinal qualities and its calming effects. He is driven to make innovations in the tea industry because he feels that it is necessary to restore the soul of Japan. If he can accomplish this, he says, he can spread the gospel of good tea to the general public.

Together, these reflections are reminiscent of the mnemonic practices of the sages of old, whose task it was to remind people of the wisdom of never forgetting what is worth remembering, nor ever remembering what is best forgotten. By drinking tea, we learn about the role that tea has played for much of history in enabling human beings to better enjoy the miracle of the present moment, the companionship of kindred spirits, and a deeper connection to our ancestors.

Or as Nambo Sokei wrote in an eighteenth-century Japanese book of tea, "The truth lies in a bowl of tea."

—P. C.

WITH
YURIKO ARAI, HAYASHIZAKI NORIKO,
& TWO HIPSTERS

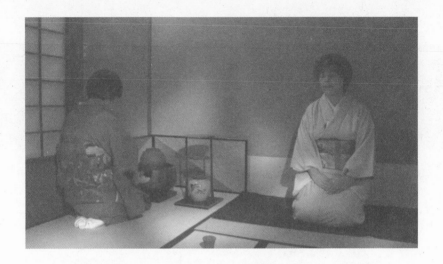

YURIKO ARAI

Enshu Kobori was the founder of the Japanese style of tea ceremony called *chado*, "the way of tea." His rules or wisdom on chado have been followed by his successors for centuries. The thirteenth-generation grand tea master of our style of chado, Sochu Kobori, wrote a scroll for my grandfather that describes the mentality behind chado. It is written that one of the most important teachings is that the way of chado is not anything special. It is simply about honoring your family, honoring your parents, and honoring each season.

For example, the tools or implements that one uses in chado are not valued by how much they cost, but by how long they have been used, and how their own characteristics have been built up over the years. Chado is not about anything special, but it is rooted in the mentality of valuing everything surrounding the tea ceremony, including the seasons, the materials, and the seasonal food you serve with tea.

Originally, I think that tea was made to train our minds and souls. The act of tasting tea is just a result of this.

—YURIKO ARAI

When we make tea in a ceremony, the entire process can take ten minutes. The

Tea began as a medicine and grew into a beverage . . . The fifteenth century saw Japan ennoble it into a religion of aestheticism—Teaism. Teaism is a cult founded on the adoration of the beautiful among the sordid facts of everyday existence.

—Kakuzo Okakura, *The Book of Tea*

actual preparation takes about six minutes. To whisk the tea powder and actually make the tea takes about two minutes; putting back the tools that were used to make the tea after it was drunk takes another two. The fact that we spend more time on preparation shows that the act of making and putting your heart into the tea for the person you are serving is the most important aspect of the ceremony. It's not just about drinking the tea, but what it took to prepare it.

THE STATE OF MIND

There is a simple phrase that summarizes the "mentality" of tea: It is *Ichigo Ichie,* which means "One meeting, one time." This saying implies that today may be the only time you and I meet in our lifetime, so I should honor this valuable moment. It means I want to use this time to serve you the best tea that I can. This is the mentality of chado.

Obviously, each of the utensils and tools are cleaned or purified before the guest arrives. But to clean each piece again in front of your guests is another way of honoring them. This act shows your generosity and your kindness to them.

If you want to be full, let yourself be empty.

—Tao Te Ching,
TRANSLATED BY
STEPHEN MITCHELL

A teahouse is very different from other buildings. Everything from the location to the height of the ceiling is meant to be appreciated. Everything inside the teahouse is meant to train one's eye for observation, including hanging scrolls, which are meant to be enjoyed by reading them. The style of the written characters is to be admired and observed. Flowers are displayed for enjoyment by evoking the observer's knowledge of seasonal blooms. In a similar way, one who serves tea thinks about the theme of the tea party they invited their guests to. If you want to use a white flower, then you choose a teacup based on this color and think about the overall decor balance. Guests at a tea ceremony are quite likely to understand what the host is trying to express through a given theme.

> 🖎
>
> *The simplicity of the tearoom and its freedom from vulgarity makes it truly a sanctuary from the vexations of the outer world.*
>
> —KAKUZO OKAKURA
> *The Book of Tea*

Typically, a guest would take the tea utensils into their hands to learn further about the way they are used. Some days I present to my guest only the tea container and the teaspoon. But if guests were to ask to see the teacup as well, it is not considered rude, and I would be happy to present it to them. As the host, I would reveal when it was made and who made it. As one studies more about the tea ceremony, the better appreciation one would have of the utensils used. That is why each one is observed carefully.

Perhaps the biggest theme in tea is the concept of *Mu*, or nothingness, in other words, zero. This is a Buddhist concept. When the host faces a guest in a tea ceremony, they are equals in the tearoom, although their social status may differ considerably. They are the bare beings of who they are with no frills. The word for this in Japanese is *Sottaku*. That is the most basic spirit of tea in Japan. Sometimes you may come across a scroll with a character of *Mu* or zero with a circle around it. This symbolizes that it takes sixty years to do a full circle, and also refers to the concept. Everything starts with nothing and ends with nothing.

For example, ceramics are bound to break. Any tool will break if you use it enough. In our practice, if someone were to break something we use, we do not punish that person, because we base our thinking on the concept of returning to nothing. That is why the basis of tea is the notion of nothingness.

THE IMPORTANCE OF WATER

In our tradition of tea, water is extremely important. Japan is a country with an abundance of water, so collecting rain for water is something we do not do. There are places where we can collect natural ground water, and we call this *meisui*. Tea brewed with meisui is exceptional. In our day-to-day training, we use ordinary water, but when we have guests to perform tea ceremony for, we fetch the meisui to use instead. Using the proper water for tea is extremely important.

Tea can be enjoyed wherever you like. For example, we bring our tea sets when we go hiking, to enjoy tea or have a tea party up in the mountains. You can do it without all the traditional tools. Often, I serve tea while wearing a kimono. This tradition only began in the Meiji period when woman started to get involved in the tea ceremony. Until that time, the ceremony existed only in men's society, and when they performed it, they wore kimonos. Naturally, women have also worn them ever since.

In this Temple Space
you become all things,
and you see
yourself no more;
and in that All-Other
you become all things,
and never cease to be
yourself.
— THE GOSPEL OF PHILIP,
TRANSLATED FROM
THE COPTIC BY
JEAN-YVES LELOUP

When you look back over almost four hundred years of tea history in Japan you notice that many important things have happened. Our country has fought many wars, but even then, men took their tea ceremony tools with them and found time to have proper tea.

So the enjoyment of tea is not about having a particular environment for it. As long as you have the tea powder and a cup and hot water, you can have tea. Throughout the long history of Japanese tea ceremony and the learning to have appreciation for all its details, a complex culture has emerged. But that is not to say you cannot have proper tea without those things.

TIME FOR REFLECTION

Today, everyone is so busy all over the world. We are surrounded by machines. I think it is extremely important to take time to reflect, wherever you are. For example, if you are on the computer all morning and right next to you is a cell phone and a camera, you are surrounded by many things. So it's important not to let those things take you away from yourself, and to let yourself take a step back. It doesn't have to be for a long time, maybe just for five or ten minutes. That's what Japanese tea ceremony offers. If we do not incorporate traditions in our modern life, I think that we will just drain ourselves, and forget who we are.

Nowadays, industrialism is making true refinement more and more difficult all over the world. Do we not need the tearoom more than ever?
—KAKUZO OKAKURA, *The Book of Tea*

HAYASHIZAKI NORIKO

Normally, my days are very busy, The tea ceremony eases my mind. When I step into a teahouse it helps me concentrate on my tea practice *chado*, or the way of tea, a very practical way of life. It's simple, but that simplicity brings calmness to one's mental state. So coming here after being out in the busyness of the city is very soothing. It's become rare to live in Japanese-style homes with tatami mats these days.

When we practice tea, we have some sweets; with a good cup of tea, it is extremely relaxing. Not only can you enjoy a good cup of tea, but you can also make others happy by making them a cup. There may be very few words said during tea ceremonies, but through tea you can communicate with your heart. When you are making tea for guests, you want them to enjoy it, just as I want to enjoy tea that was made for me. I think this way of people communicating with one another is very nice; communication through eating and drinking is calming. Also, the concept of purifying the utensils is another way tea gives me comfort. Although this is done to purify them and to show respect toward your guest, the process seems to purify my mind as well.

TWO HIPSTERS

HAIR: I like coffee better than tea.

HAT: Yeah, coffee.

HAIR: I've just been drinking it more lately.

HAT: No, I drink tea after meals. Japanese tea.

HAIR: Sometimes I drink Oolong tea to keep from getting sleepy.

HAT: Coffee goes with cigarettes. Tobacco tastes good.

HAIR: After meals, I drink coffee while I'm smoking

HAIR: Ah, I guess coffee, because of its Western image. Our style is fifties American.

HAT: Yeah, we like the fifties, so we drink coffee.

HAIR: Coffee. Well, we're basically going back in time. I like old things, I like going back in the past to America.

HAT: America in the fifties is cooler than Japanese culture.

HAIR: Yeah, it's cooler.

WITH
ROKUHEI INOUE, YURIKO ARAI, JAPANESE COUPLE,
& TEA SELLER

ROKUHEI INOUE

I've got the whole universe in this tea caddy of mine.

—BAISAO (1675-1763), FROM *Three Verses on the Tea-Selling Life*

Inoue's company, Irokuen, was founded in 1818. In Japanese historical terms, this would be the first year of the Bunsei Era. Since the very first owner until now, the company has traditionally been handed down to the eldest son of the next generation. It is the duty of this son to support the family and its business. Rokuhei Inoue is the seventh generation of Irokuen. In kanji, or Chinese characters, you would spell Rokuhei with a character symbolizing the number *six* and a character for *flat.* "When I hand down this company to my son, who will be the eighth generation, his name will become Rokuhyoei. This has been the tradition for four hundred years, since the time Kyoto faced a major historical change, during the Oonin no Ran, and the Muromachi Shogunate disappeared. Since then, our family has been only in the tea business."

A New Generation of Tea

ROKUHEI INOUE: As you know, tea was spread to Japan by a famous Buddhist monk, Eisai. For a thousand years, tea has been regarded the most basic, traditional, and fundamental beverage of Japanese culture. The tea master Rikkyu and other influences added to this rich history. However, today tea has been changing to conform to the youth of Japan. I personally think that the fundamentals of tea should not change, and cannot be fundamentally changed. But if we talk about why it is changing now, we have to say that it has most definitely to do with our modern lifestyle. Our social behavior here in Japan changed when the culture turned more Western after the war.

For instance, when Coca-Cola was introduced from America, many young people began to prefer soda over tea. To older folks, it was a bizarre drink, but it captured the hearts of our younger population. The culture of our younger generation has become a Coca-Cola culture, so to speak. Another factor is that we Japanese began to use taller tables for dining, and no longer sat on Tatami mats. Soon, a traditional tea set was no longer essential in the culinary culture of Japan.

Eventually, tea began taking on a more Western form, with such things as teabags and instant tea. Cuisine such as hamburgers began to spread, people began to drink water, juice, milk, and other beverages. We have begun to change into a culture that no longer requires tea. Even though tea has been regarded as the most fabulous beverage throughout the history of Japan, the modern reality is that our culture now has ceased to enjoy tea in the true way.

Modernization

Tea was originally brought to Japan from China as medicine. The monk Eisai came to Japan from China about a thousand years ago and brought with him some powered tea. There was a long period where we consumed tea strictly for its medicinal use. In the beginning, tea was so rare and valuable, the only people who could have it were people who belonged to the privileged circles. Soon, tea became a symbol of status for people such as feudal lords, the Imperial court, extremely rich merchants, or maybe a monk with status in a temple. The general public had almost no access to tea. Eventually, tea became more available to the general public.

Now, there are two different types of tea: the kind used in tea ceremonies and the kind that is used by the general public. Tea ceremonies, or *chado*, is our basic form of teaching manners, and a place to rest your soul. Then there is *sencha*, which is the traditional beverage that Japanese people have been consuming for centuries. This is the tea that has changed with our changes in lifestyle.

Today, the kind of tea that is consumed in businesses whose only focus is efficiency, are teas that only look and taste like traditional tea. In other words, tea was brought to Japan for its medicinal qualities and its ability to become our mental crutch. Now it's been reduced to something we drink only when we are thirsty. The true essence of tea, including its medicinal qualities and its calming effects, is no longer appreciated.

As a tea seller who works in a two-hundred-year-old tradition, I personally do not approve of the way this is going. I know that this evolution of tea is unacceptable to our future. The speedy conveniences of our times [see photo] have eradicated the true benefits of tea. So I truly want to bring the tea closer to its origins. Tea not only supported the heart of Japan, tea created it. I believe that it is my duty and my company's duty to bring back the essence of tea.

TEA SENSIBILITY

I think tea is a product of sensibility. Tea is something that is enjoyed by those with individual sensibilities. Some like their tea weak, in Japanese terms, or strong, in Western terms. Others like it light or soft. Japan also has three major tea-producing prefectures. One is Uji, in Kyoto; the others are Shizuoka and Kyushu. Each is unique to its region. Some like the tea that comes from the same place they are from. The perfect tea is one that matches your own sensibility. You would have to drink a lot of tea to see which fits best. I think it's important to find your own tea—and not to dismiss one only because you didn't like it on the first try. Maybe try another tea, or come back to it when you are in a different state of mind. I want the Japanese people to find their own tea again, with each new stage or growth in life. A middle-class tea doesn't mean it's good for everyone, no matter what.

For example, when you are getting married, or when you have your first child, or when you are old and once again have some time to yourself, those are the times when tea should be enjoyed. Gradually, you will find your own tea.

When I look back on my ancestor's endeavors, it has always been about spreading the word of tea to the Japanese public, and wanting them to enjoy a good cup of tea. I have great pride in that. It just happened to be that in my generation, a certain war ended, and after that war, society became dramatically modernized. With all this change, tea, which used to be naturally important to our culture and the mentality toward it, became less central.

If we stay on this modernized track, the only tea that will remain will be tea that comes in a plastic bottle. The traditional form of tea will disappear. The true way of tea will cease in Japan. We are facing a fork in the road, so this is a very important generation. Progress is something we all wish for, but the old ways should still be incorporated into the new ways of the world. Japanese history involves many things, such as the *Tanka, Manyoushu, The Tale of Genji, Ukiyoe.* The creators drank tea without even thinking about it. Tea was the way to calm one's soul, and that's the way it has been until now. But I cannot do it alone, so I have been promoting and encouraging people to take a look back at our culture and rediscover the tea that exists in the root of it. I don't want to exaggerate, but I think that it remains my duty or my life's work.

THE COMPANY PRINCIPLES

There are three important principles in my company: Tea is mind and spirit; tea is friendship; tea is an expression of kindness. These three points are very important, not only in my company, but to all Japanese.

I hope to bring back the true form of tea to Japan. My idea was to make this plastic bottle. Now, there are so many of these bottled tea products, each with their own charm. I thought it would be nice to have a bottled drink that contained tea that had not been brewed a long time before it was sold. I wanted to make something that was more pure.

So after a considerable amount of research, we came up with a bottle that contains the highest-grade powdered *matcha*. When you shake it, you have pure and just-made tea—*instantly*. Unlike other companies, we looked for a way to deliver the purest tea. During the pasteurization process, the color of the tea naturally changes from green to brown as it is heated. We are interested in ways to provide the tea leaves in their entirety. We've developed a product here that is a bottle of mineral water sold with a cap full of green tea powder. We've come up with a way for the tea to be dissolved into the water for the first time when the bottle is opened.

Would that some great wizard might from the stem of society shape a mighty harp whose strings would resound to the touch of genius?

—KAKUZO OKAKURA, THE BOOK OF TEA

Of course, the reason behind this is that we believe our customers will then have the natural desire to return to their tea set and brew tea the right way.

Japanese green tea is now not only enjoyed in Japan, but all over the world. Elements of green tea, like the fat-fighting *catechins*, are now known for their benefits for the human body, and are being enjoyed all over the world. I think that we in the industry need to continue to spread the word about the benefits of green tea. As green tea becomes more and more popular, we need to experiment with flavors that suit not only Japanese tastes, but also tastes of consumers in other cultures. We want to spread the taste of real Japanese tea to all parts of the world.

Traditionally, Japanese houses came with a quarter known as the *chadonoma*, or the tearoom. It came with a fire pit and an iron to boil the water, and was offered by one member of the family to another as gratitude after a long day of work. It was never just a drink.

Having learned the
ways of silence
within the noise
of urban life
I take life as it comes
to me and everywhere
I am is true.

—BAISO, FROM THE OLD TEA-SELLER (1675–1763)

In the past, I think tea was used to get to know another person, and to express kindness towards another. Tea played an important role in the samurai world during the Tokugawa reign, as well as the times of Hideyoshi, in the form of chado, where one makes and offers tea to another. Historically, tea symbolized everything in the heart of the person offering it, a form in which you expressed kindness and hospitality.

YURIKO ARAI

Let me try this. This is really funny. Is this *matcha*, too? It's not very good. It tastes a lot different from the tea I make. I think that this is a completely different sort of a beverage!

Tea ceremony is tea ceremony. I guess this is one way to get people to drink more *matcha*. It's not good. They sell iced green tea drinks like this in the summertime, and it's similar to those. I think the ratio of tea powder to water is wrong. If there was less water and the water was extremely cold, it could be good. *Matcha* is very good when you use ice-cold water. It has to be either very hot, or very cold—nothing in between.

I think they should come up with a different balance for water and powder.

Then maybe they will have a good drink. Personally, I would rather make my own tea.

Cold tea and cold rice are bearable, but not cold looks and cold words.

—JAPANESE FOLK SAYING

STREET TEA

JAPANESE WIFE: I always have bread for breakfast. My husband eats a Japanese breakfast, but we just started making coffee to match my Western breakfast. We eat Japanese sweets when we're relaxing.

JAPANESE HUSBAND: I guess we drink tea in more relaxing situations. It's like water to us, ever since we were young. We drink Japanese tea, *genmai cha* (brown rice tea) and *bancha* (late season tea), and also black tea and coffee.

JAPANESE WIFE: Before I got married, I took tea-ceremony lessons. So I've participated in things like *hatsu-gama* (first tea ceremony of the year). It was an Ikenobou, the oldest Kyoto tea-ceremony style. I stopped attending classes after I got married, but since I had the utensils, I would buy *matcha* and make it in the traditional manner on special occasions, like New Year's, or when we receive gourmet Japanese sweets. It's like you're getting your life back in order. So I twist the lid and close it again. Twist, close, and shake. Right? Oh! It's turned into tea. Is this Japanese tea? It was just plain water a moment ago! How convenient! This is the first time I've seen anything like this. The taste is pretty strong. It's greener than usual. It's good for people who like it. I like it, so it's good for me. Nowadays, it doesn't matter about how tea

comes. If you like it, you should drink it. It's important to take time to relax. *Otemae* means tea-serving manners are important. Convenient things like this are okay too.

TEA SELLER

Actually, my family is in the tea business. I'm the fourth generation in the business. I sell *bancha* and a few different types of *sencha*. There is a difference between *sencha* and *bancha*. The new leaves are made into sencha. When the tea becomes fully ripe, it is *bancha*. This *yamacha* is not tea that was grown in a field, but rather, tea that grows wild in the mountains. Using this wild tea, we process it in the same way as it was processed in the Meiji era, before automation.

Everything in Japan and the rest of the world is changing very quickly. Even conversation has changed from slow, careful communication between two people to an exchange of simple responses. The importance of listening to people carefully and communicating effectively has been diminished not only in Japan's schools, but also in Japanese society in general.

I have a personally interesting story about this that involves *yamacha*. When I volunteered for the "Social Education" branch of the Board of Education, I advised the parents that I spoke with to take time to have tea with their children after coming home from work, even if for only a short time.

> *If asked the nature of* chanoyu, *say it's the sound of windblown pines in a painting.*
>
> —SEN SOTAN
> (1576–1658)

In a world filled with computers, we have been accustomed to thinking about things in only one way, by way of our computers. When the computer provides us with all the information we need to know, it reduces our actual experiences of real life. I think tea is an opportunity for parents and their children, for example, to share real experiences and opinions, and perhaps foster more intergenerational conversation.

To be honest, I think tea is so much better for the body. I've been to some of the famous tea and coffee shops here in Tokyo and tried their new products, but for some people, it's hard to detach tea from its orthodox and staid image. I recommend having a meal of *chameshi*, which is rice prepared with tea instead of water, and represents a return to a more simple lifestyle and way of communication.

Beyond this, many companies are using *matcha* or *houjicha* in new styles of Japanese sweets, for instance. But I still think drinking real tea—tea that has actual leaves that you can watch float and sink in the water as it quietly brews—is still best for us.

> *If man has no tea in him, he is incapable of understanding truth and beauty.*
> — JAPANESE PROVERB

NATURAL TEAS

I think the most important thing for me to do is to have actual face-to-face encounters with my customers and get to know them as people. As I talk to them and listen to their feedback, I can respond to their tastes and recommend products to them. That's the most important thing for my business.

In Japan, we have many sayings from Sen no Rikyu and the tea ceremony. One of Sen no Rikyu's most famous sayings is *"wakeiseijaku"*. This refers not only to the peaceful and pure encounters between people and nature and the respectful, but also to the simple and quiet spirit that the tea ceremony provides. This idea of simplicity and quietude fits the spirit of Japan quite nicely, and takes tea beyond simply being a drink to a point where it is a window into our inner selves.

I think the psychological difference between the words *tea* and *cha* is quite large. I think there are chances for changes towards world peace in both cultures. I hope that we can use the good elements from both cultures to work toward peace. Any type of tea is fine—we use different temperatures of water for different types of tea in Japan—but as long as it's a type of tea that allows you to relax and calm your spirit, and perhaps encourage conversation, I think it's great.

No matter what type of beverage you drink, coffee or tea, they all contain caffeine. So it would be nice if no matter what the drink or country, it would be able to calm the drinker and foster harmony and peace among people. This *yamacha* is tea that grows wildly in the mountains that we process in the same way tea was processed before automation. It is said that before tea seeds from China were brought to Japan, some twelve hundred years ago, there were wild tea bushes growing here. Since the plants regenerate themselves when the seed falls from the bush, the tea plants are very old. There is a tea tree near a shrine that dates back to that period, twelve centuries ago.

Let us rise up and be thankful, for if we didn't learn a lot today, at least we learned a little, and if we didn't learn a little, at least we didn't get sick, and if we got sick, at least we didn't die; so, let us all be thankful."

—BUDDHA

THE MEANING OF
TEA

THE FIFTH CUP
FRANCE

. . . [tea] has cleansed every atom of my being . . .

—LU TONG

Around five thousand years ago, the news spread across China that a certain plant possessed curious powers beyond its ability to slake one's thirst. Legends soon spread about its wondrous medicinal powers, which could heal the heart, cleanse the blood, increase endurance, aid concentration, and heighten energy. Eventually, the tea plant was credited with a multitude of virtues, the famed "22,000 benefits." Among them was its power as a medicine for a wide range of maladies and concerns.

These benefits did not grace the European continent until around 1610 when the first boxes of tea were delivered to the docks of Holland and France. By 1648, it was being regularly sold in the markets of Paris, where it was soon "praised as a panacea" and used regularly by many famous authors, including Racine. But interest soon faded as the aristocracy became suspicious of the brew from the East. Soon after, the desire for tea was surpassed by the fad for coffee.

In this context, the two chapters that comprise two chapters that comprise Part 5: "France" offer us intriguing perspectives from the land of the coffee-fueled café life. The first comes from the French improvisational artist Pierre Sernet, who provides us with a vivid description of a few of the hundreds of sites around the world, from the Giza pyramids to the Great Wall of China, where he has performed virtually the same tea ceremonies as those of sensei Enriko—but in a transparent wooden cube the exact size of a traditional teahouse. His travels have taught him that people the world over have associations with the teahouse. For centuries, teahouses have teemed with travelers, doctors, storytellers, musicians, dancers, chess players, lovers, poets, artists, and soldiers, serving as a refuge from the hurly-burly of the workaday world, a place outside of time. Sernet performs his rituals out of a deep belief that tea ceremony illustrates deep values shared by people everywhere. He reveals that the responses he has garnered from these performances share one important feature: a sense of profound peace while watching his ceremonies.

Following Sernet is the young French student Mathieu Perez. His interview begins with reflections about teapots, which he views as a powerful metaphor because a teapot is empty and we have no idea what is inside. Therefore, he says, we must fill it with our own curiosity. Tea is soothing and salubrious, he says, "a remedy because it is associated with fantasies of health."

The curative aspect of tea is perhaps its most lapidary, as evoked by the root meaning of remedy, from the Latin remedium, "that which heals again and again." Beyond its social virtues, such as companionship and aesthetic pleasure, tea has been credited as a remedy for everyday concerns, such as sluggishness, lassitude, fogginess, and lack of alertness and concentration. In fact, in one of the very first texts that mention tea, the *Shen Nong Herbal*, it is written, "Drinking it one can think quicker, sleep less, move lighter, and see clearer."

What these two brief but poignant chapters evoke is the power of creating our soulful life. These interviews are reminiscent of the book, *The Art of Good Living*, by the nature essayist Svevo Brooks. Modern life, he writes, is riddled with stress from an unprecedented amount of cultural change. What is required of us if we are to live with renewed vitality is a more balanced life, says Brooks, a few simple practices, such as closing our eyes, relaxing, contemplating, and committing to a gentler rhythm of life. All of these are techniques and qualities that are evoked by one of the soundest and most natural of daily practices, the sipping of a simple cup of tea.

—P. C.

CHAPTER NINETEEN
THE GUERILLA TEA MOVEMENT

WITH
PIERRE SERNET

PIERRE SERNET

We call a civilized man cultured and a cultured man civilized.
To transform what is primitive in us through the artifacts of
culture is the great human task.

—JOEL, DAVID, AND KARL SCHAPIRA, *The Book of Coffee and Tea*

Born in Paris and having studied art at the Ateliers du Carrousel of the Musée du Louvre, Sernet worked in photography for several years before moving to the United States, where he pursued a successful business career. His activities included the creation of the first, and what was to become the largest, fine-arts pricing database in the world—Artnet.com. Through a varied series of works, Sernet explores the contrasts and similarities that exist across nationalities, ethnicities, belief systems, and lifestyles. His pictures are intended to show that seemingly different and incompatible cultures, lifestyles, or people can cohabit together in harmony. Though he and his wife live in Manhattan, he has performed and exhibited in major galleries and museums across the globe.

PIERRE SERNET: I am French and I am a conceptual artist. My work has to do with the contrast of culture and environments. I try to show that while we may all look different and may behave differently or have different activities or ways of thinking, we are, in fact, similar in many ways. Therefore, we should be more accepting of the cultures of other people. I try to show this through a series of Japanese tea ceremonies that reveal the similarities in different nationalities.

The Guerilla Tearoom is in this series and is sometimes called One. I set up a virtual and transparent cube with twelve pieces of wood, which is approximately six by six by eight feet, and represents the tearoom. It includes all that you would expect to find in a traditional Japanese tea ceremony room, which is the futo, the kettle, the brazier, the mizosachi, the water containers, the different tea bowls, the sweets, the flower arrangements.

We've performed this ritual all over the world. We've done it in Times Square; in the middle of the Thar Desert; on the border of Pakistan and India; in the favelas of Rio; at the pyramids of Egypt; in Sudanese deserts; in France, Italy, Greece, Vietnam, Thailand, Laos, Cambodia, and of course, in Asia. We've performed it in Pachinko parlors, in concrete factories, and tea factories in Japan. And we've done it on the Great Wall of China and in Shanghai, where we were invited by the police for a little talk for a couple of hours. That's probably why it's called "Guerilla Tea."

THE FOUR ELEMENTS

Essentially, tea is about four things: harmony, respect, purity, and tranquility. In my "Guerilla tea" performance, I try to convey these same four principles or feelings to the guests, whoever they are, because tea ceremony is about sharing moments in time with them. The host tries to make it as tranquil, as respectful, as pure, and as harmonious as possible.

If we are inviting a monk in Thailand for tea or a peasant with his cows, or somebody on a gay beach, the idea is always the same. We bring these guests from whatever environment they are in and we simply serve them a bowl of tea in a very traditional Japanese tea ceremony.

The concept here that I am trying to convey is that the cube represents a virtual space in which I have my values, which are very close to tea values. However, the guests all have spiritual, religious, or philosophical values of their own. If I can see that my values in the tea environment are compatible with the values of Time Square or the middle of Grand Central Station, then by extension your values, whatever they may, religious, spiritual, philosophical, are compatible with mine.

🖎

All the treasures of the earth can't bring back one lost moment.

—FRENCH PROVERB

We have served tea in places like the Charles de Gaulle Airport in Paris, where people are rushing to catch their planes. Each setting always has an interesting story. At Charles de Gaulle, we had a bomb scare and the police actually detonated a bomb about hundred feet away from us. The funny thing was that the French security forces cordoned off the area around my tea hut and went away. For some strange reason, they felt that they should be more respectful of me, so they said I could stay there dressed in my kimono.

What is interesting is hearing from guests all around the world who tell me, "It's very strange, there was all this noise, people going by, people talking, crowds, and yet when we were having tea it was very peaceful."

Recently, I performed a tea ceremony for a senior executive of one of the largest corporations of the world, at his office in Times Square. We had interviewing cameras, a tremendous amount of lights, security people, and onlookers from Broadway. And yet he told me, "You know, Pierre, there is a strange aspect to this. Despite all this noise, it felt like it was just the two of us in your tearoom; it was very peaceful."

© 2008 Pierre Sernet. Mrs. Watanabe, Mt. Fuji, Japan, 2003.

Of course, the cube where I make tea is only these twelve pieces of wood put together. But it creates a psychological space, a unique cocoon, an environment or space unto itself. Sharing a bowl of tea inside the cube is an event where one hopes to communicate at a much higher level than if we were just making and serving tea. The traditional procedure enables a certain rhythm to be created between the guest and the host. The harmony and respect that is felt inside comes from the way tea is made by the host and shared with the guest. This is a very deliberate way of serving tea, and it seems to draw the guest into the old rhythm of tea ceremony.

ORIGINS

Originally, tea came from China where it was first used as a medicine. Later, it was brought to the public at large through monks and used in the equivalent of Zen meditation as a way of staying awake. While meditating, the monks needed to be very quiet and peaceful, and at the same time to be alert. Much later, tea was used in Japan by the warrior class as a way of sharing an important moment in time with guests. Eventually, tea became an important way to find out a little bit more about the character of one's guest, especially in business relationships.

In Japanese tea ceremony we happen to use tea, but we might as well be using coffee, as I often joke. Tea is not the important part of the ceremony, although tea is, of course, very different from coffee. What is important is the procedure of *sharing* with someone.

Most people don't know that in Japanese tea ceremony, the host often does not partake. Tea is given to the guest, but unless the guest asks the host to share a bowl of tea, which is fairly rare, the host will not partake. Essentially, this is a generous way for the host to show respect for the guest.

When you can't find peace within yourself, it's useless to seek it elsewhere.

—FRENCH SAYING

Strange as it may sound, having a tea at home with my wife, with somebody in the desert, or in the tea factory in Japan, is quite similar. The tea ceremony is really about sharing a moment in time with somebody. If it happens to be your wife, that's great. If it happens to be somebody you have never seen before, it's not much different in terms of the respect that is displayed by you as the host. Remember, the host is trying to bring harmony and tranquility by making and serving tea in a pure way.

Ironically, tea was used in the sixteenth century as a very strong diplomatic tool. Tea was often used to create a space for negotiations and meetings between rival factions. Tea was so powerful at the time that it was considered a privilege to give it to certain lords so that they could perform a ceremony.

I remember I made tea for a very old nun in Cambodia. I tried to think about it being my last cup of tea and her last cup of tea. So I tried to make the ceremony as special as possible.

ONE MOMENT, ONE TIME

People always ask me why tea ceremony is so strict, why it is so controlled. They say there is no sense of freedom in it. I think that's wrong. The reason for the etiquette is that it's important for the host and the guest to know what they are supposed to be doing. The ceremony allows you to do not only what is expected and obvious, if you will, but to do it until it becomes irrelevant, so you can communicate on a much higher spiritual level.

Many of my friends, and even some of my family members, say to me, "You have been studying seven years! Why do you have to study another ten or fifteen years?"

I explain to them that the ceremony is about far more than just making tea. Tea is the way you live your life. Everything you deal with in tea is meant to translate into your day-to-day life. If you think about all the religions and philosophies around the world, they are more or less saying the same thing. Your belief and practice must translate into day-to-day life.

There is a famous saying in Japan: *Ichigo ichie,* that essentially means "One moment, one time." We are having this moment speaking together, and we may have many meetings together, but this particular moment will never happen again. That's what tea is about, sharing that unique moment in time. When tea happens, it is a fleeting moment and it will never happen again, so it is a very important moment. This belief really stems from Buddhism, Zen Buddhism in particular, where you really have to live the instant. Don't live yesterday, don't live tomorrow—live now.

LIVING TEA

I don't think there is any difference in serving tea in Paris or in New York or in the middle of a temple in South America. The concept of tea as a way of life is basically about how you behave and how you act. We all have choices to make in life. We can make tea or we can sleep. To a large extent, one is responsible for what happens in one's life. Sometimes there are circumstances beyond our control, but otherwise, I think it all depends on your own decisions. *Everything depends on how you conduct your life.*

If you follow the principles of tea, I don't think it matters where you are. If I meet somebody in the middle of Rio or in Cairo or in Mykonos, it doesn't matter. That

> *The world is a dewdrop within a dewdrop.*
> *And yet, and yet . . .*
> —ISSA, JAPANESE POET, (1763-1828)

person and I will meet once and there is a high probability that we will never meet again. I will make a bowl of tea for that person probably only that one time. Hopefully, I will try and put the same amount of attention as I would for my wife or for somebody I have known for twenty years.

In the complex and active world that we live in, tea acts as a focusing and a directing tool. It doesn't mean you always will be focused, but tea certainly can act as a way to achieve better control and better knowledge of yourself in day-to-day life.

Tea is a very humbling study. Tea drinking can have a calming effect and heighten your sense of awareness or enable you to be more creative. The green tea that we use in Japanese tea ceremony has the equivalent of three or four espressos with a lot of caffeine. Does it keep you awake? For sure. Does it increase your awareness? I don't know. It used to keep monks awake and aware during meditation.

Just as life has different meanings for each individual, tea has different meanings. For me, tea certainly has a personal meaning. That's what I would like people to understand. Japanese tea ceremony is about respect and accepting other people's thinking and lifestyles. I have never heard of anyone going to war because they like blue or because they like pink. What's the difference if they like Allah or if they like Jesus?

Acceptance of others is the key. If tea can help bring acceptance around the world, that would be a great thing.

© 2008 Pierre Sernet. Rockefeller Center, New York, 2001.

WITH
MATHIEU PEREZ

MATHIEU PEREZ

Whether I am a tomb or a treasure depends on he who passes.
For me to speak or be silent / this rests on you alone.
Friend, do not enter without desire.

—PAUL VALERY'S INSCRIPTION, CHAILLOT THEATER, PARIS

Born in Paris in 1984, Mathieu Perez undertook a comprehensive humanities-based education with a focus on philosophy. Reading Swami Yogananda excited his curiosity about the common philosophical roots in the East and West. He also studied how the work of Pythagoras, Zarathustra, and the Buddha influenced Nietzsche's philosophy. He is involved in documentary photography because of its goal of awakening people about social issues. His interest in tea is not only for its taste but for its mystery, especially its lessons on how to take the time to live in the present, to "be here now." Currently, he is working on a project to help elderly people share and pass on their memories, around a cup of tea, to the younger generation.

MATHIEU PEREZ: The comparison between tea and coffee is primarily cultural more than it is a question of taste. For example, I'm French, and I grew up learning about coffee. Tea isn't really part of French culture, except maybe as a class marker. So, I think people who drink tea are often people who, for one thing, have had enough of coffee. But I also think there are people who want to rise in the social hierarchy, and who are trying to show that they have distinguished themselves from others by drinking tea.

There is also a certain ambiguity to tea. It is first of all a drink. But it has a lot of associations. There's profound symbolism linked to tea. Of course, there is the myth of the exotic, of Japan, Asia, and India. Drinking tea engages the imagination. But there's also the refinement of taste, and many people drink it because there's such a variety of different teas. The more teas you drink, the finer your palate gets, and you want more and more to leave behind the bitter taste of coffee.

Personally, I drink both tea and coffee. In the morning I have tea, but there's a simple explanation. It's because of my studies, which are really stressful. If I have coffee in the morning, I'm even more wound up. I'd start off the day completely stressed out, such that by nine-thirty, I'd be ready to explode. I discovered that psychologically, drinking tea is more soothing. It's curative to drink tea because you think you're calmer, even if it's an illusion. But it works.

The pot of tea is a beautiful metaphor, a symbol in common between Asia and the West. We all know the tea is in the pot, but we don't know what's in the pot, because it's closed. So there's a kind of secret that we have to unlock for ourselves. The metaphor of the teapot is also the metaphor for the curiosity one can have for other people, other cultures. Somehow, to love tea is also to love reaching out to others, to reach out to other cultures.

Make tea, not war.
—MONTY PYTHON
FLYING CIRCUS

On the other side of the Eiffel tower is the Trocadero Square and two theaters, one of which is the Palais Chaillot. On the façade of one there are quotations from Paul Valéry, a great French poet, and the lines are sublime expressions of what it means to keep a secret, and the meaning of desire.

Valéry's metaphor suggests that the tea phenomenon today is much more bound to Asian teas than North African teas, because the pot holds a secret. In Morocco, you only share tea within the family. I think you have to be initiated if you're going to appreciate what Moroccan tea is like. Either you're Muslim or you have traveled to Morocco. But the teapot is really the embodiment of this metaphor. The pot is a secret that stays in the family; it doesn't go anywhere.

What Paul Valéry wrote is remarkably intelligent, because what works with the pot of tea works perfectly with respect to other people. The metaphor is extremely poetic and it doesn't surprise me that the words come from a great poet. The pot of tea is an inherently altruistic impulse, whereas coffee is socially coded as a more individualistic drink. In the imagination, tea is always shared. Think of the ritual involved. Tea is also associated with specific times of day. Tea brings

"Many years had elapsed during which nothing of Combray, save what was comprised in the theatre and the drama of my going to bed there, had any existence for me, when one day in winter, on my return home, my mother, seeing that I was cold, offered me some tea, a thing I did not ordinarily take. I declined at first, and then, for no particular reason, changed my mind. She sent for one of those squat, plump little cakes called "petites madeleines," which look as though they had been molded in the fluted valve of a scallop shell. And soon, mechanically, dispirited after a dreary day with the prospect of a depressing morrow, I raised to my lips a spoonful of the tea in which I had soaked a morsel of the cake. No sooner had the warm liquid mixed with the crumbs touched my palate than a shudder ran through me and I stopped, intent upon the extraordinary thing that was happening to me. An exquisite pleasure had invaded my senses, something isolated, detached, with no suggestion of its origin. And at once the vicissitudes of life had become indifferent to me, its disasters innocuous, its brevity illusory—this new sensation having had on me the effect which love has of filling me with a precious essence; or rather this essence was not in me—it was me. I had ceased now to feel mediocre, contingent, mortal. Whence could it have come to me, this all-powerful joy? I sensed that it was connected with the taste of the tea and the cake, but that it infinitely transcended those savors, could, no, indeed, be of the same nature. Whence did it come? What did it mean? How could I seize and apprehend it?"

—FROM *In Search of Times Lost*, BY MARCEL PROUST, 1922

people together. Tea is not drunk alone. Among the Touareg, in Africa, tea brings communities together.

Finally, it seems obvious that tea functions as a kind of escape from stress. It's amazing to see, in the modern world, how spirituality is making a comeback. So it's not surprising that tea, which is in some way a material expression of spirituality, should make such a comeback in France. This trend is beyond just fashion, beyond the shifts of fads. Since tea is clearly a way to withdraw from the stresses of life and from the city, it is like bringing a breath of country air to the city. Especially when you become a connoisseur of tea and appreciate its many different tastes. Then it is really a very interesting phenomenon.

In contrast, coffee has a reputation in cities for stress. But even if people really like coffee, tea offers a way to break with the city, break with stress, even to purify themselves. If you think about it, it's surprising how these days, coffee is associated with cigarettes, with the city, stress, with pollution, whereas tea is considered much more salubrious, more soothing, more purifying. You drink tea to cleanse yourself, empty yourself, because you believe it is definitely a remedy. In this sense, tea is associated with fantasies of healthiness.

For years, you saw women who were sexy when they smoked cigarettes, drank whiskey, and drank coffee. Now that we live in a society that's seeking a remedy for stress, it would appear that tea possesses sexual qualities. It is fun to ask such a question, because sexiness is in the attitude, not in the drink. A woman can be just as sexy drinking orange juice as she can be sexy drinking tea. It's all in how you see it; that's what makes something sexy.

No doubt about it, tea is more a part of British culture than of French culture. When you think of Britain, you think of bowler hats, suits, and tea. In North Africa, especially in Morocco, the metaphor is tea as a secret. And in France, tea is more of a fashion, something people seek out to free them from the bonds of daily life.

THE MEANING OF
TEA

THE SIXTH CUP
ENGLAND AND IRELAND

The sixth lifted me higher to kinship with the immortals . . .

—Lu Tong

In 1657, a broadside was published by Garraway's Coffee House, in London, that listed tea's many attributes and touted its many "medical virtues," including: "Headache, Stone, Gravel, Dropsy, Scurvy, Sleepiness, Loss of Memory, Looseness or Gripping of the Guts, Heavy Dreams and Collick proceeding from Wind . . ."

England's ardent belief in the powers of tea has scarcely waned in the ensuing centuries. What Cecil Porter of Gemini News Service wrote about tea in turn-of-the-century England still holds true: "Tea is much more than a mere drink in Britain. It is solace, a mystique, an art, a way of life, almost a religion . . . it has become the life-blood of the nation."

For nearly four centuries this "tea phrensy," as the mass affection has been called, has been a point of pride throughout the British Isles, imbuing everyday life with a sense of continuity, order, and pleasure.

In Part 6, we explore the nature of the unique relationship to tea that pervades England and Ireland. In chapter 21, the London silversmith, Steven Linden, describes the almost numinous properties of silver, as used in English tea ceremonies. Linden also explains tea as a tradition that has the capacity to bring charm and joy back to a world caught up in "rushing around." For Linden, English tea represents a kind of panacea for the falling apart of cultural norms. Moreover, enjoying "a cuppa tea" provides a much needed opportunity for the sheer pleasure of having a chat with "your fellow man."

Chapter 22 is devoted to the tea drinking habits of the Irish. Eilish and Robert Flood are effusive in their descriptions of the relationship between tea and talk in Irish society. "Conversation with the tea is," says Robert, "just as important as the tea." Having one's cup of tea provides "a moment of peace and refreshment." His mother, Eilish, counters with the insight that tea offers a chance to "gather your thoughts" and make time for "inspirational thoughts" to come to you.

Michelle Kelly, owner of a Dublin café with the unlikely name of the Budda Bag, suggests that tea is a supreme tool for helping her customers rejuvenate and simply enjoy life more, which she suggests is a healthy alternative for the suddenly frenetic pace of life in the land of "The Celtic Tiger."

Each picture tells a story, as the song goes, and every story needs tension to give it meaning. For our story we introduce the raconteur and musician Earl Okin, who provides us with the spirit of the contrary warrior. With a playful but biting sense of satire, Okin provides a foil for all the lofty praise raining down on tea in his English homeland. For him, tea is a kind of necessary indulgence, a rather namby-pamby lukewarm drink that satisfies the thirst and keeps the population sedated. His satirical comments allow us to laugh at the affectations of some tea drinkers, and by extension any behavior that takes itself too seriously. Paradoxically, his barbed comments also allow us to come full circle, as it were, to the period in the 17th century when tea was first introduced to the West and often drew antipathy from many quarters. His suspicion of so-called experts is also reminiscent of the widespread doubts in Europe when tea first arrived from the romanticized Orient with a reputation for elixir-like powers.

—P. C.

Chapter Twenty-One
The True Way of Tea

WITH
STEVEN LINDEN

STEVEN LINDEN

He was born with a silver spoon in his mouth.

—ENGLISH PROVERB

In 1959, the Linden family acquired the London Silver Vaults. At age sixteen, Steven Linden started working there. "From the start, I loved being surrounded by beautiful antique silver from the past three hundred years," he says. "I meet customers from all over the world—from famous film stars to politicians, pop stars and even royalty." As the business grew, Linden took a particular interest in the story of each piece of silver. The British hallmark tells the whole story: which city it is made in, the purity of the silver, the year it was made, and silversmith who crafted it. Today, the London Silver Vaults provide a unique treasure trove of all items related to tea—tea sets, bachelor teapots, tea strainers, tea caddies, tea kettles, teaspoons, and even a mote spoon to release the leaf from the inside of the tea spout.

A Very Nice Pasttime

Steven Linden: Tea is not just a product. It's a ritual, a tradition.

There are many people who say that silver is the only product that one should use for pouring and making tea. Now whether that's a myth or whether it's true is up to the individual, but many of our clients would swear by it. They would say that porcelain is an inferior teapot to use compared to silver. One thing that is true is that the pouring process through the spout of silver is much more functional, I believe, than through china. Silver also keeps the tea hotter for longer. That's a very important point, of course. You don't want cold tea. I think anyone who has ever drunk tea will agree with me there.

As far as the actual process of drinking tea goes, some would say it's a way of life for certain people. Certainly, in Japan tea is a whole tradition. Everywhere in the world the actual tea ceremony is more than just having a cup of tea. It is a ritual, which many people actually study. I believe that the ritual of taking tea is actually a very nice pasttime, especially these days when life is so fast.

We should probably all get more involved in tea. You can enjoy having a nice cup of tea and maybe have a meal with it. Having tea means you can sit down with friends and have a chat. It's a very nice ritual, which really most of us who use the modern teabag have completely cast aside. I believe it's a great shame. To true tea lovers, a teabag is a disgrace, and they would never have it in their home.

I also believe that people who enjoy the ceremony of tea would enjoy making it as much as they do drinking it, because it doesn't actually take that much longer. You only need to use fresh tea. You pour it in a pot and use a type of tea strainer. This is a very clever and ingenious product because, actually, you tip it to one side and then use your teapot to pour your tea through. Then you tip it back again so that all the drops go into the bowl. It only takes a few moments, as opposed to a teabag.

> *Only the spoon knows what is stirring the pot.*
> —Italian proverb

Then there are tea caddy spoons. Very important. Very, very important. Many people today are used to using teabags. But in times gone by—and still today—fresh tea is portioned out with a tea caddy spoon. This beautifully decorative spoon would have been used for one portion of tea for guests. It is hand-engraved and hand-pierced, and holds an exact portion of tea. As time went by, people used tea caddies of this form, which had pull-off lids. So you would pour out your tea into your pot and then you'd have an exact measure.

One example is a tea caddy made in 1911 in the town of Sheffield; it is sterling silver. If we go into more modern times, the tea ceremony is still very much in use. Many fine hotels in London have a beautiful served tea featuring many types of tea from all over the world. They serve tea as they used to many decades ago, with lovely sandwiches and cakes. It's a very nice experience.

Coffee has become increasingly popular in Britain over the past ten or twenty years, whereas we used to be known as a tea-drinking nation. Now we drink, I reckon, as much coffee as we do tea. To a certain extent, coffee has taken over as a fifty-fifty split in popularity. But I still think Britain is known for tea and it always will be, because we still have that tradition, and a lot of people still enjoy the beverage. But because of modern times and rushing around so much, tea drinking has changed enormously. The teabag, alas, is used more and more. People really haven't got the time that they used to have to sit down and enjoy a calm and quiet, relaxing time for tea, as in earlier days. Hopefully, one day they will again.

Unfortunately, in our modern society, we're all looking for the fast-paced life and how to make things easier for ourselves. However, I think the invention of the teabag has actually destroyed the ritual of drinking tea. But, I'm finding a lot of people are going back to old rituals, becoming nostalgic about the past. Most people think of their childhood with fond memories. If we go back in time to how things used to be, it can be a pleasant memory. In fact, recently I read that vinyl records, which were almost completely out of production, have

suddenly come back into fashion again. After so many changes, things go backward and change to the way things used to be.

Tea is one of those things that people don't enjoy in the way they used to, because they've chosen to use teabags for convenience. But I think eventually people will stop and look back and think, "We're missing out here. We really should go back to the way it was." English tea ceremony is a charming part of our past, and so some people think, "Well, why not? Why not do it again?"

I remember as a child we used to invite our family over for Christmas and other special occasions. Tea was a special part of those reunions, something that we all enjoyed. We sat down and talked to each other over tea. That intimacy is why I think tea will always be served.

Unfortunately, a lot of the younger generation do not even know about the original ceremony. They don't know what a good cup of tea tastes like. That's a great shame. Hopefully, one day they will all experience a decent cup of tea. If they do, I believe they will never go back to teabags.

WITH
Eilish & Robert Flood, Michelle Kelly,
Val Gannon & Stephen Hutchinson,
& John O'Byrne

ROBERT FLOOD: My great-great-great grandfather used to have a pub and grocery business. They imported tea into Ireland through wholesalers, which they sold over the counter to the public in weights of a quarter or half-pound or ounces in teabags with the family business label embossed on it. They blended together different teas.

Recently, I was talking to a friend about family tea businesses and he said his family in Donegal used to hide their money in tea boxes. They kept these boxes as an investment, instead of having cash. So tea was very important in our Irish families. It was a viable commodity, so valuable it was rationed during the war years.

He who comes with a story to you brings two away from you.

—IRISH PROVERB

In our guesthouse, there is no tea in the rooms because we don't want our guests trying to make tea and spilling it. That means our tea-making facilities are the first thing on their minds, and we say to them that there is lots of tea downstairs, in the controlled environment of the kitchen. So they come down to our dining room and have tea and scones. Other guests bring their own biscuits in anticipation of tea and conversation. This is because the conversation with tea is almost just as important as the tea itself.

In this sense, what tea is about is a moment of peace and refreshment. It is about taking time to stop your busy day, sitting down and relaxing with your cup of tea and not getting up off the seat. This is hard not to do in this business. But it is important to just switch off and go over your thoughts and enjoy your tea.

EILISH FLOOD: Tea time is time to gather your thoughts. It's contemplative time. If you want to figure out something you are going to do during the day, first you have to sit down with a cup of tea and clear your mind.

ROBERT: A tea-time moment is time to relax and watch the world go by from the window.

EILISH: For me, it is definitely a time to relax and to gather my wits about what I have planned for the day.

ROBERT: Between here and Newgrange [the megalithic site north of Dublin, shown below], there are many little farmhouses with little old ladies who love making tea for friends and strangers. They will drag you off the road just to find out everything about you. They want to chat about what's what, what you're doing, everything about you. *They don't want your money; they just want your conversation.* The Irish community is very outgoing, with a lot of conversations and discussions, not only over alcohol but over tea. Traditionally, alcohol would also be an important part of Irish life, another way to free the Irish spirit from its oppression. In the past, the family would come together for

a meal in the evening and have their tea and talk about everything that happened that day and about any visitors who had come around. There wouldn't have been any television at the time, which is an important point. There would have just been radio at home. And before radio there was just conversation, stories, tales, and *seanachies,* who were the people who told the old stories. Storytellers and musicians would have been playing in pubs or bars. But around family houses and gatherings at a large farm or estate, Irish people came together around the fireplace where they could keep warm together and talk about daily life, chatting and planning their next day over tea.

In our family there is a portrait of my great-great-grandfather and his wife, Catherine, with their two tea chests, which would have held many different kinds of tea. I still have those tea chests, which had been stored in my uncle's garage. My father-in-law, from Spain, has relacquered them and now they are lovely. During the famine of the 1840s, some people even survived on tea. Their money would have gone to tea maybe sooner than meat. You see, we Irish need our tea.

> *When I makes tea, I*
> *makes tea, as old*
> *mother Grogan said.*
> *And when I makes*
> *water I makes water.*
> *By Jove, it is tea,*
> *Haines said.*
>
> —JAMES JOYCE, *Ulysses*

EILISH: Even today, the first question you will hear from somebody welcoming you into their house is, "Would you like a cup of tea?" I even ask my children that when they come visit me. Or they might tell me, "Mom, put the kettle on!" It's always about the kettle being on for tea. Tea is a conversation piece and it breaks that initial reserve between people. When you sit down with your cup of tea, everybody relaxes. Tea has an amazing effect on people. It's not just that the liquid gets into your blood stream so fast that it relaxes you; it has to be psychological as well. It must be the mere mention of something that can relax you—the mention of "a cup of tea"—has the effect of calming a person. You are welcoming a guest into your home and you're saying, "Would you like a cup of tea?" This is a very friendly custom.

I think it's a time to opt out of the rat race we are caught up in. Nowadays, people are sitting at their desks and in front of their computers rather than relaxing in a chair with a cup of tea. They have less leisure time, and this has effected the amount of tea they might drink. They are working too hard to leave their computers and put on the kettle for tea. I think that we need to go back to the days of contemplation, which is away from the busy world we all live in. We need to take time out for those silent moments of meditation. This isn't a waste of time; it isn't laziness to just sit and look into space. It's important for the whole psyche.

Clearly, if we don't stop and think, we are not going to have any inspirational thoughts. But to do this, I think that we need to reeducate ourselves on how to get the best out of our lives in those valuable moments with tea. Thinking with a cup of tea is a nice thing to do for yourself.

MICHELLE KELLY

For the Irish, tea is a big family beverage at breakfast, lunch, and supper. Everyone has a cup of tea. The first thing Irish people do when guests come to visit is to ask them, "Would you like a cup of tea?"

The meaning of tea for me is a day in the life. Tea in the morning, tea at tea break, tea in the evening time. But also "t" is the twentieth

letter of the alphabet, which is also my age. "T" also stands for Taurus, and that's my birth sign. I love to dance, and my favorite dance is the "tango." My favorite food would be "tapas" with loads of red wine. So "t" is everywhere in my life. I suppose if anyone likes "t," it's me.

My favorite things to take with my tea would be toast in the morning with loads of marmalade, then for tea break it would be a snack bar or a biscuit with a lovely cup of tea. At lunchtime, a sandwich and a slice of cake goes well with a cup of tea; and at tea time, scrambled eggs with a big pot of tea.

We love drinking tea here in Dublin, in the Budda Bag Shop. Around eleven o'clock, one of us goes next door to the great café, and they do a wide range of teas. Everyday we have something different. We order all the different types of tea next door. But we all have our favorites; Chamomile is mine, for it relaxes me. I'm so busy here in the Budda Bag Shop, it's nice to take some time out and just enjoy the lovely flavors, tastes, aromas. It relaxes me. My favorite kind of music when I drink tea is classical, because tea calms me down, so I don't think I would be listening to heavy metal.

The philosophy of the Budda Bag Shop is: relax, kill time, and have fun. Even though we have the Buddha statues behind us, we are not Buddhist. The Budda Bag is not a religious concept. We just like to have fun. It's a place where everyone can come, young and old, and chill out.

If the Buddha were working here in the shop, he would prop himself up on the biggest Budda bag—which we call "MegaBudda"—and he'd sit there and chant all day long. I think the Buddha would drink a lot of herbal teas. He'd attract a very big crowd. The real Buddha would welcome you anytime you visited. The Budda Bag speaks for itself because of its ultimate comfort.

I take me tea very strong, with three or four sugars. I like to savor tea till the last drop. I have one cup in the morning and then I wait for my tea break and have another cup, which rejuvenates me so I can go back to work. But my best cup of tea of the day must be my last cup, late at night, in bed, watching TV. I drink a lot of herbal tea, but my favorite is our great Irish breakfast. That's the best tea for me.

VAL GANNON AND STEPHEN HUTCHINSON

VAL GANNON: Here at the Budda Bag Shop, I'll tell you the story of my first encounters with tea. When I was growing up, I used to drink tea with my half-cousins who were all big tea drinkers. We had big mugs of tea to start the day, and whoever had the most sugar was kind of cooler. One time I said to one cousin, "How many sugars do you have?" He said, "I have seven." He drank it, and then it was my turn for him to see how many sugars. I said, "Eight" just to beat him. When I had eight sugars in my tea, I got sick. I've hated tea ever since, though it's more of an indifference.

STEPHEN HUTCHINSON: My parents never let me have enough sugar in tea, so I never drank it.

VAL: He was a hyper-child! Me? I don't really experience tea. I don't know what the hype is about. It's just water with a kind of grass in it, just a little leaf in it.

STEPHEN: My family are big tea drinkers, my granny especially. Both my parents drink herbal teas and stuff like that, and I don't like them cause they smell like tobacco. That's my story.

STEPHEN: I think drunk people in Ireland don't drink tea very much now. It's come down. It seems like a grannyish type of thing to do.

VAL: In Ireland, too, no one drinks tea with saucers and a cup. We all use mugs.

STEPHEN: My granny uses mugs. It's a country thing. In the west, it's all the old people who drink tea—*loads* of tea. They all do.

STEPHEN: Where is tea grown? China—isn't it?

VAL: Yeah—but is it a tree?

STEPHEN: No, it's a plant.

VAL: Well, it's "like all the tea in China." That's a famous phrase.

STEPHEN: We have herbal tea in my house called Gun Powder from China.

VAL: Gunpowder wasn't invented in China.

STEPHEN: No, that wasn't my point. It's green tea.

VAL: Tea means just sort of a social scene.

STEPHEN: When we become old, will we drink tea?

VAL: It's just a social thing. Whenever someone comes to your house, you bring them in and you put on the kettle. And usually you reach out for the teabag rather than the coffee.

VAL: No, tea is losing its appeal.

STEPHEN: They need to have some young people advertising it.

VAL: A bit of Ronaldino or something, to make it cool.

SKATEBOARDERS ON STREET IN LONDON

My perfect cup of tea would be made by my mother, and with sugar in it. A bright, coppery, puddle color from down where my mom lives.

Tea means an excuse to eat food such as cake and biscuits. Tea also probably makes you think of colonialism. Everyone knows there is a massive economic force behind that—the British Empire. I was up in Darjeeling recently, and I saw the fields where I actually stayed in the old planters club. Fundamentally, I think tea is a great excuse for stopping what you are doing and taking time; it's the alternative to cigarettes.

The perfect cup of tea depends on when you are drinking it. First thing in the morning, really, first thing in the morning, that's the perfect cup of tea before the world starts and before you start doing any work. A cup of tea first thing in the morning kind of kicks you out and you're relaxed. Tea brings a memory of being at me granny's. She was a great tea person and used to love the sugar in the tea.

JOHN O'BYRNE

The English take everything too seriously. Irish people are a lot more relaxed about things. For example, the English take tea more as a formality. I get the impression from English people that tea has to be served in a certain kind of cup and drunk in a certain kind of way. If I go back in time, I can remember walking into Bewley's Tea Shoppe, on Grafton Street, here in Dublin—where I'm a maintenance man at Trinity College—where everyone was very informal, compared to England. I can also remember when I was a lad that people used to drink tea out of jam jars. Actually, a lot of people won't remember glass jam jars and milk bottles, but we did have them. And tea out of a glass, especially out of a jam jar or a milk bottle, tastes excellent.

MAN ON THE STREET

Does tea have a meaning beyond tea? Not for me. I think tea is a simple, enjoyable drink. It shouldn't be made any more complicated than what it is, just an enjoyable drink. I don't think it has any deep meaning beyond that. I think tea is just simply tea, and you shouldn't try making any more of it than what it is.

CHAPTER TWENTY-THREE

IT'S ALL VERY COMPLICATED

WITH
EARL OKIN

EARL OKIN

Tea's proper use is to amuse the idle, and relax the studious,
and dilute the full meals of those who cannot use exercise,
and will not use abstinence.

—DR. SAMUEL JOHNSON

B orn in London in 1947, Earl Okin is a poet, singer, musician, comedian, and obsessive record collector. He has been playing guitar and singing professionally since he was twelve years old when he appeared on a BBC-TV talent show. Since then he has written hit songs for Cilla Black and Georgie Fame, penned jazz criticism, and appeared at numerous music and comedy venues, such as the Edinburgh Fringe Festival. A self-described "Cat in Spats," has opened for the likes of Van Morrison, Paul McCartney and Wings, Billy Connolly and Jasper Carrott. His most recent album is "Musical Genius and Sex Symbol," recorded at the Kings Head Comedy Club in London.

EARL OKIN: The problem here is that I'm totally incapable of being able to describe tea, good, bad, or otherwise. I remember being offered a cup when I was about five or six years old and thinking it was totally revolting, and making a sort of inward contract with myself to never, ever drink the awful stuff again. I've kept to that ever since, and that was fifty years ago.

Now, tea, of course, goes back a long, long, long, long time, ever since we English started getting Chinese tea. The Indian tea came later. Then there were coffeehouses. *It's all very complicated.* There's a big, big history, and it's particularly involved when England ran India. I'm sure that was the heyday of it all. A great load of ridiculous paraphernalia grew up around tea. There was the tradition about how one should make the perfect cup, and another tradition for warming the pot, and one for standing on your head naked in the garden at night. Who knows what it was all about? *It's all very complicated.*

There was a time when tea was taken really seriously. As I say, tea was surrounded by all these ridiculous sorts of traditions about the right way to do this and that. You know how it is when people get to be an expert in something. They go, "Oh, no. You have to do it this way—and that way is wrong." And you say, "But you see, I don't like it that way. It tastes horrible." And they say, "We don't care. That's the way you have to have it. England is the only place where you can have a real tea. It's the only place. Nowhere else."

They all carried on like that.

All this sort of nonsense builds up. It's really just probably an excuse for making more money off somebody. These days, there are things that would probably make these people turn in their grave because now, there's something called instant tea that's even got the milk included. This is all white powder, a sort of beige color, because it's the dark tea mixed with dried milk. All you have to do is take a flat teaspoon and measure it out and then put it in the pot and then pour boiling water on it and—*zonk*—tea! My mum, who drank tea a lot, said it's actually a very good cup of tea.

There was a time when tea was a really expensive commodity. You kept it in a little tea cubby, in a special lead-lined wooden box, and, oh, it cost a fortune. Now it's instant tea, and you shove it in a cup or use teabags.

Coffee is a completely different drink. In London, in the eighteenth century, there were coffeehouses where journalism started. Dr. Johnson and all those literary people hung out in these coffeehouses, which must have been a bit like pubs. There was a lot of smoking with those long pipes and smoke everywhere, and there was old-fashioned coffee, like the strong Turkish type that was served in little cups without handles and without milk. They sat there for hours and hours and drank this really strong coffee until their brains buzzed. You could probably get an internal sort of combustion going on. These places were great centers of political unrest and sedition, where writers started producing newssheets. That's how the first newspaper got started. All this was slightly suspect, of course. If the wrong people caught you drinking coffee, it was rather like the McCarthy era: "Oh, he drinks coffee. He's probably a commie."

So some people have rather snobby attitudes about tea and coffee, and it's the same with beer. It's got to be real ale, poured in a certain way. You've got to hang upside down from the banister to drink it or it's got to be a certain temperature, and if it's not right, you're a complete moron or a Philistine and you have no brain cells at all. Simply because . . . you've not drunk the drink . . . the way they think you ought to. It's very strange.

Recently, I did have tea for the very first time in ages. I was stuck in Shanghai doing some cabaret shows, and tried some green tea, which is a completely different thing altogether. I could bear that. It's the typical English tea that I really don't like. I don't think I'd want to drink green tea all the time. I did not hate it; mainly it's a different taste. It was a novelty. But I personally don't care how the tea arrives, because I'm not usually going to drink it anyway.

One's taste changes over the years. I don't hate English tea—it is just too flavorless. It's such a wimpy flavor, sort of namby-pamby. *Nothingy.*

I like tastes that take you by the throat. When I order a curry, I order a *vindaloo*, the sort of curry where you go into an Indian restaurant, and the waiter says, "You know what you're ordering, sir?"

Those are the sort of flavors that I like. So tea is, you could say, delicate. I just think it's flavorless, like drinking warm tepid water with something in it that you can't quite identify. There are people who swear by it. I do, too, but it's a different sort of swearing.

Tea is not a sexy drink. It's associated with workmen having a break from hard work in hot weather having a "cuppa." And it's associated with rather over-posh ladies with delicate china, talking to each other, complaining about their husbands. Sexy is not what it is, although, really, it comes from India and ought to be very exotic. But it's become the everyday experience, and you don't think of it as being exotic or exciting. Whereas coffee you associate with either Africa or South America, truly exotic places. Hot climates. Exciting things going on. What we don't even know about. Coffee, it's sexy, yes, a sexier drink, I think.

TEA MUSIC

I'm not aware of the great jazz musicians drinking tea, other than with the other meaning of the word *tea*. The only tea that I associate with Duke Ellington would be a T-bone steak, but that's also a whole different thing. They were coffee drinkers, and they went to diners on the road. Whereas in England, we were singing nice little songs: "I like a nice cup of tea with my dinner. I want a nice cup of tea with my tea." That was our popular music. That's the difference between coffee and tea; that sums it all up. I think that proves the superiority of coffee. Just that song alone, you know?

Of course, the most famous tea song of all is "Tea for Two." Then Art Tatum did this amazing piano version of "Tea for Two," which defined what jazz piano was. Fats Waller was dethroned as a result of that recording. It's absolutely unbelievable, a famous song. Of course, if you're a jazz musician, if you're a trumpeter, you'll sound like the ducks and swans if you do that for too long.

There was a phenomenon in England for a long time called the tea dance. This was rather polite dance music, you know? Not too jazzy. A little bit of rhythm. As long as one didn't have to move one's lower regions too much, because who knows where that could lead?

The tea dance was held about five o'clock. There would be a little dance band, a group in the corner. You would possibly go to the Ritz Hotel or somewhere like that. The band played this sort of gentle dance music, and you would have a cup of tea, then possibly have a little dance? Yes? Possibly with your husband; possibly not. One doesn't know. I don't want to go into these things. It was a very polite thing. And it was all over by six o'clock. *It was all very complicated.*

So you would go home to hubby and nobody would know. You would just unruffle the clothes. It was a tea dance. Perfectly right. Very British. No sex at all. No suggestion of that sort of thing. You know, we don't talk. No, no. And it was very British. Very tea. That's your tea dance. That went on for a long time. Then people discovered rock 'n' roll, which coincided with the reappearance of coffee bars, and so the tea dance came to an end. One of the earliest rock'n'roll stars in England was a gentleman called Tommy Steele. He and some other peo-

To the People in Tea, South Dakota—

If you're going to have your town called Tea, the very least you should do is to study how to make a real teahouse, either Japanese or Chinese. I don't mind which one. Or you make it a little bit more refined than an old-fashioned English teahouse, where you drink tea not out of these rather revolting mugs. You should use a proper china teacup with a proper spoon. Standards are really dropping off in this country. And with your tea you should have, of course, a scone, yes? And on the scone you should have, of course, proper double Devon cream, available, strangely enough, in Devon and Cornwall. I can't describe how wonderful double Devon cream is. A cream tea in Devon is like a kiss. If you could import it from there, it would really put your town on the map. Then you would really be Tea! You could have proper china with the silver teapot. That's what you should have. That's what you want for Tea, South Dakota. It would change your entire world. People would flock there by the hundreds and hundreds. But let's not overdo it. If I were to serenade you, I'd sing: "Tea for Two," wouldn't I? Yes, that's what I would do.

ple were discovered in the West End in a little place called The Two Eyes Coffee Bar. Obviously, coffee really was something that led to licentious behavior.

Coffee is guilty of a lot of things, whereas tea is a safe drink. You won't get parents saying: "Now, now, little Billy, I don't want to hear that you've been out drinking tea! I don't want to hear that at all. If I hear that, I'll be very upset with you. No tea! You understand?" Right.

No, no. That's no good.

It used to be the same with tea. You had this whole list of different teas: Earl Grey, Duke of West, God knows what else. Now coffee is like that. There's always going to be tea tasters out there, just like there are wine tasters, who will take a sip of tea and spit it out. Then they order their brand. There's always somebody who's tried to tell you that they're the expert.

It's all very complicated.

THE MEANING OF
TEA

THE SEVENTH CUP
TAIWAN

The seventh is the utmost I can drink . . .

—LU TONG

Over the course of tea's long and venerable history, its reputed powers have been condensed and compressed into innumerable proverbs, folk sayings, maxims, such as "A hasty man drinks his tea with a fork," "Tea is drunk to forget the din of the world," and "If someone has no tea in him, he is incapable of understanding truth and beauty."

But not just any random amount of tea will do, as we've learned from Lu Tong's beloved "Song of Tea." There appears to be about as many versions of advice about the accumulative effects of drinking tea as there are species of tea plant. The Tang Dynasty tea master Jiaoran said, "One sip dispels sleepiness and thoughts got clear and active; second sip refreshes my mind like fine raindrops descending on dust; third sip brings enlightenment and worries evaporate without much ado." Similarly, the psychologist Robert A. Johnson once told me over a pot of Pu-erh: "The Chinese sages say the seventh cup of tea takes you to where you belong. It's the true drink."

With these descriptions of the myriad virtues of tea we return to where this book began, which is the realm of one of the most sublime benefits of all—the sense of *transport*. As described in the last line of Lu Tong's poem, the patient drinker is carried away by the final sip of tea by virtue of the taste, the beauty, the ceremony. No more is needed or required. You are, as the sages promise, where you belong. You have come back to where you started before you began your tea journey, a place of utter simplicity and serenity. And yet you have been transformed.

All told, these acclaimed benefits reinforce the claims for renewal, as proclaimed in the heralded "Song of Tea" poem. Each of these interviews brings to mind the recurrent theme of calm or peace, or what Arthur Waley, the scholar of Chinese studies, called quietism. His memorable image for this serene state of mind was the ability to enter a birdcage without setting the birds to start singing.

The final section of *The Meaning of Tea* encapsulates many of the lessons and much of the wisdom that lies at the bottom of the proverbial tea cup. In The Seventh Cup we travel to Taiwan, where we encounter eight individuals who share their knowledge and love for the rich range of teas that flourish on their island.

In chapter 24, Lu Lu-Feng, manager of the Wu Lin Tea Farm in Taiwan, seems to embody the attributes of Shen Nung, the Divine Cultivator, "the first to till the earth and to give the gift of tea to man." Mr. Lu describes himself as being in awe of the "gift" that nature has provided human beings, as well as a sense of gratitude for the spirit of tea and of his great fortune at being able to share tea with people around the world. Moreover, he says tea "brings back our humanity." Following Lu Lu-Feng is a third generation tea grower, Feng Ming-Zhong, who reflects on what he calls the "deeper meaning" of tea by describing how it allows him to appreciate life at a higher level. Tea has medicinal value and social benefits and provides us with far more than ordinary beverages. If you pay proper attention and respect, he says, tea can help you "cultivate your character . . . [tea touches] your true nature." To achieve this, he points out that we need to allow tea to teach us how to slow down, appreciate life, and be humble.

In chapter 25, we learn about the meaning of tea through the work of two master tea craftsmen, Zeng Cai-Wan and Lin Chun-Han. They reveal how their practice roots them in the reality of the earth itself. Zeng Cai-Wan describes the purpose of using accessories as a means to "elevate the symbolism" of the tea ceremony. Lin Chun-Han regards the purpose of using bamboo as a way to release "the spirits of tea." Together, they reflect the attitude of their fellow tea masters who believe that it is human touch that infuses tea with character. They remind us of the power of tea aesthetics: the mud of the earth that goes into their teapots, the intricate joints of bamboo, both of which bring out the soul of tea.

Our subject is approached more philosophically in chapter 26. Lin Jin-Xing's tea is best understood as a natural expression of the yin-yang forces of nature. With a poetic flourish that would make Lu Tong proud, Lin describes the source of the taste of tea as being a fusion of the fog, sunshine, soil, and human care. When all these factors converge, he says, "You feel a vastness in your spirit." To fourth-generation tea grower Wei Li-Yun, there is also a considerable "vastness" to tea, but it has to do with the intricate web of connections between her

family, the land, the plants, and the government assistance that is helping her produce organic tea. Her pride is great as she describes her family's efforts to produce the special flavors that make her tea famous all
over the world. "Tea is like life," she concludes. "If you don't drink tea,
you're not healthy."

In chapter 27, martial arts master Wu Sheng-Ben brings a unique
insight into the restorative powers of tea when he recommends people
focus on their heart when they drink it. For him, health benefits are primary; he emphasizes how it reduces the risk of diabetes, brings a sheen
to the skin, and rejuvenates the drinker by way of its detoxifying properties. Mr. Wu insists that tea drinking also encourages friendship
because it calms the spirits and lessens the tendency toward anger in
human interactions, which he feels is the most important of all its benefits. For music professor Lin Ku-Fang, tea isn't an isolated drink, but
a confluence of nature, art, and friendship. When conducted properly,
tea allows people to reveal their true natures. For tea grower Chang Fu-
Chin, tea is a life path he chose to honor his ancestors. In turn, he
believes that tea is a gift that he will pass down to future generations.
But it is *more* than tradition, he reveals; it is also hard work, which
requires time, observation, and a calm state of mind.

To fifth generation Taiwanese tea master Lin Zi-Pei, the essence of
tea is its ability to remind us of the possibility of spiritual comfort in a
highly stressful modern world. His interview in chapter 28 describes his
fear that people nowadays are moving so quickly that unless they
remember to practice tea, they will surely forget to slow down and
relieve their own anxieties. Beyond the health benefits, Mr. Lin suggests
that in the business end of tea one must constantly recall the greater
reason for selling it, which he feels is to help others relax body, mind,
and soul. For teahouse owner Tu Ying-Ming, tea represents a life-
change. He moved from the countryside to the city to ease the hard
work of his own life. Soon after, he realized that the urban dwellers
around him were coming to his shop to "adjust their body and soul."
And from Chuang Hsiu-Mei's perspective, tea isn't a luxury but a
necessity, and more, a symbol of respect for your ancestors. In tea, she
sees a powerful metaphor for living the good life: one must "boil
water" to bring out the savors, the rich qualities of our existence.

Creating and sharing tea, she concludes, may help us maintain our friendships, as well as our health.

The final chapter of the book brings us full steam into the modern world by featuring the story of the invention of bubble tea by the Taiwanese tea entrepreneur Lin Hsiu-Hui. Her disappointment is palpable as she describes the loss of affection for the ancient beverage; this was partly what spurred her on to invention, which she describes as her revival of fond childhood memories of tapioca balls. Her "secret recipe" has proved to be enormously popular around the world, bringing together a beloved tradition and a clever innovation, which has given her what she calls "a sense of value and purpose."

By drinking the right number of cups of the right tea with the right companions, these voices from Taiwan's tea world remind us, we might finally fathom for ourselves the meaning of tea, and eventually, the meaning of our own unique lives. Many a tea master has argued that they are one and the same.

—P. C.

WITH
Lu Lu-Feng & Feng Ming-Zhong

LU LU-FENG

Better to be deprived of food for three days than tea for one.

—CHINESE PROVERB

For the past eight years, Lu Lu-Feng has managed the Wu-Ling Tea Farm, which is located in Xue-Ba National Park of Taiwan. His gratitude for a life in tea shines through in this interview. He says, "This life-changing experience has enabled me to gain good health and spiritual awareness. I have had the good fortune of being guided in my profession by Chui-Feng Chiu, the Director of the Taiwan Tea Improvement Organization, who so graciously shared his knowledge and experience." He is particulary proud of the Wu-Ling Snow Summit Tea planted high in the mountains, at an altitude of over two thousand meters.

LU LU-FENG: Tea is my life. I've devoted my life to tea. Tea and my life have become one. I must have tea every day. I cannot live without tea. I feel funny and uncomfortable if I don't come across tea during the day. This morning I drank tea, as I always do. I must drink it after I get up every morning. After I drink tea, I feel fully awake. It is hard to count how many cups of tea I drink every day. But I drink it in the morning, afternoon, and night. If I didn't drink tea before I went to bed, I wouldn't be able to fall asleep.

Drinking a cup of tea daily will surely starve the apothecary.

—CHINESE PROVERB

I also drink tea according to the weather and how I feel. Tea tastes different in different weather. If it's hot, I like to drink lightly roasted tea because it's lighter and more aromatic. In the winter, I drink medium roasted tea because it's more soothing and I won't feel as cold. In any season tea makes me feel good.

I think tea is something very natural, and it's good that it's been brought to civilized society where a lot of things have gone wrong. When life is too busy and bustling, you miss the human touch. With tea, you can bring some humanity back to society. Tea won't bring chaos. It's good for your mental health. Some people need religion; others need tea to interact with other people.

But you must use your heart to really experience tea. When I drink good tea, I use my heart to smell the aroma. When I inhale tea it goes right into my soul. For a tea to be very good, you need the right combination of heaven, earth, and man. Sometimes it takes years for you to come across a very good tea. I feel very fortunate, as I've already come across it four times since I've been working in tea. It's so rare. Some people never come across a good tea in their lifetime. When I come across a good tea, I have a memory of it for many years. For a long time afterward, I remember that tea. So I am satisfied with my life. I am very lucky.

TEA MANUFACTURING

We grow many different kinds of tea at the Wu-Ling Farm, including Taiwanese Tea Number Twelve, Jin Shuen. This is a strain of tea that was developed here in Taiwan. At first it was planted at a low and mid-elevation. Then we brought it here to the mountains and made some experiments. The result was very special. It was different from everywhere else because of the higher elevation over here. The milky flavor decreased, but if it's too strong, it's easy for the taste to be overpowering and too strong on the stomach. We think we improved it by letting the leaves mature longer and grow thicker so the milky flavor would be reduced. We wanted to improve the quality, so we fermented it longer, but then the milky flavor was gone, and it tasted like regular Oolong. Even the tea experts couldn't tell the difference. But when they saw the leaves they realized it was Jin Shuen.

The environment in Taiwan has changed quite a bit. What we need to do now is protect it. That's why we've been trying to improve our tea manufacturing and management process. We've worked toward using organic methods, including water and soil conservation. That's why our tea trees are so tall. The roots grow deep, and the deeper the roots, the better the soil and water retention. If it rains, there won't be landslides. We used to tend vegetable patches, but now we've turned to afforestation, to leave a better environment for the next generation.

In my years working in tea there's been a lot of heartbreak and much learning experience. We didn't learn anything about the environment in the recent past, but we have to. Managing the farm used to mean getting rid of the insects and weeds. But now it's a lot more interesting with our new environmental awareness. Insects are living things, too. So wouldn't it be better if we can coexist? Isn't this better for society and for the environment and better for the planet?

There are many types of teas: green tea, lightly roasted tea, half-roasted, and fully roasted. We've discovered that when we're making tea we must control the temperature of the water, because different temperatures make different flavors. You can taste the difference. That's how you get the *essence* of the tea.

TEA AND HEALTH

If you want to be healthy, you must have a healthy body. It doesn't matter if you take a lot of supplements. As long as you've got a healthy body, you can naturally absorb nutrients. It's the same thing for tea

trees. Tea leaves are like human beings; they're alive. Don't just look at a tea plant as a bunch of leaves—it's a living thing. For tea trees to be healthy, you've got to have good soil. In order to have good soil, you need organic fertilizers. You don't need to add chemical fertilizers. If you do, the quality of the soil will deteriorate and acidify.

The reason our tea trees have grown to such heights is due to our good soil. If your soil isn't good enough, it doesn't matter what kind of fertilizers you add. The trees won't be able to absorb them. The most important thing is for the trees to become strong so they won't need chemical fertilizers.

Let your workings remain a mystery. Just show people the results.

—Tao Te Ching, Translated by Stephen Mitchell

When you're taking care of tea, it's like you're caring for a child. The tea tree goes through different stages, like a child who needs different types of milk at different ages of life. Tea trees need nutrients for each stage and weather and season. You must provide for that. There's no formula. When parents have several children, they all have different personalities, receive different education. Likewise, tea trees respond to the way you take care of them and educate them. If a tea tree grows a little bigger, you need to give it more nutrients and you need to see how it grows in order to take care of it.

Tea has emotions, too. In different temperatures, climates, and environment, their needs are completely different. Tea trees need water to survive. Without water, they won't survive. People need water, too. Without water we can't survive. Tea trees need sunshine, air, and water. It's the same for human beings. We need sunshine, air, and water. Without those things, we won't be able to survive. Nature has given gifts to mankind, but mankind also needs to take care of nature. Our way is to bring nature's tea to people.

The wise man, who by watchfulness conquers thoughtlessness is as one who, free from sorrows, ascends to the palace of wisdom.

—BUDDHA (C. 563–483 BCE) TRANSLATED BY JUAN MASCARO

The more civilized we are, the faster the pace of life we live. We have cell phones, computers, and a lot of other things that make us move so fast that it's easy to lose the sense of direction. Everyone has a lot of stress. So I think it's important for people to take time to drink a cup of tea. Drinking tea can relieve your mental and physical stress. After you've quieted down, you won't feel as much pressure. Your thoughts will change.

So take a tea break to plan your life. Taking time for tea takes you on a longer journey. You can experience spiritual growth. Tea is an excellent drink. It's more than a beverage. Tea can give you spiritual hope.

-+->-<-+-

FENG MING-ZHONG

My family has been growing tea for three generations, from my grand-father to my father and me. My grandfather was a tea master at the Tea Institute during the Japanese Occupation period. After that, he was hired by an exporting company that sent him up into the mountains to collect tea from various sources to sell to Southeast Asia customers.

During the 1960s, the export situation met a lot of obstacles. We then turned to the domestic wholesale market. I joined the business in 1982, but I wasn't too enthusiastic at first. I've come to know what's so special about tea, like Bao Zhong from our area. In the simplest terms, it has the classic five characteristics of fine tea: It's fragrant, strong, pure, rich, and beautiful. After I learned about its processing, I realized that tea has a *deeper meaning*. It allows me to enjoy life at a different, more elevated level. So that's why I've carried on the tradition.

Superior tea comes from high mountains.

—OLD CHINESE SAYING

Bao Zhong tea has been in Ping Lin for about a hundred and fifty years. At first, people relied on its production for a living. Then when its exportation began, the price became higher. The Council of Agriculture began to promote it as an export of high economic value, and its production became highly developed. During the 1950s and 1960s, the export of tea to Southeast Asia and overseas reached its peak. Because of that, a lot of tea farmers made much more money. My grandfather's time—from the twenties through the forties up until before his death, in 1980—was the height of tea export. Since then, Bao Zhong tea has fed many more families.

Under these beneficial circumstances, I came into the business and have come to learn about its production and development.

TAIWANESE TEA SALES HISTORICALLY

In such a good export environment, many tea farms developed across Taiwan. As for Bao Zhong tea, it has a very fatal weakness. It is easily damaged both in the production and consumption process. If you don't pay careful attention to the storage of the tea, it's very easy to lose its freshness. It's prone to absorb other flavors. Bao Zhong is wrapped, so it's easy to damage the leaves. Overall, the tea is very loose. In the distribution process, it's easy to damage the tea, which in turn lowers the salability in stores.

Over the years, Bao Zhong's market share has been steadily declining. At once it was 60 to 70 percent of the market, but now it's about less than 4 percent. That's a big difference. What's comforting is that from the decline in export to fewer sales directly to consumers we've gained a little more of the market. Tea farmers are still working very hard, so the share now is about 8 to 10 percent. As a result, farmers raised the quality of the tea—and the higher the quality, the more enjoyment for consumers.

In terms of the local government's agricultural policies, they've continued to promote Bao Zhong tea. From pest prevention to advocating technical advancements and market development in Japan, Europe, and even on mainland China, they've continued to support the farmers. For those of us exporting tea, the government has helped us develop the overseas market. Everyone is working very hard in this field.

THE GREAT REVITALIZER

For tea producers or those who appreciate tea, it's more than just a drink to quench thirst. The tradition passed down from our ancestors says tea can also help us adjust our physical well-being. It can help you cultivate your character, simplify your life, or let you touch upon your true nature.

For example, country folks like to store some well-dried tea at the Buddhist altar. It's a very simple method by just wrapping the tea in brown paper. Each year, they leave a bag for medicinal purposes. Although there's no proof of its effectiveness, it's what the ancestors left us. For a stomachache, you grab a handful of tea and stir fry it with some salt, then drink it with some hot water. It doesn't matter what ailment; you'd probably feel better within twenty or thirty minutes. If you catch a cold and feel nauseated, have a migraine headache, or cramps during menstruation, you should take a 500-cc cup of hot tea with a teaspoon of brown sugar. You can relieve the headache or cramps within thirty minutes.

How very noble! One who finds no satori in the lightning flash.
—BASHO (1644–1694)
TRANSLATED BY SAM HAMILL

I've taught this trick to the heads of corporations when they had a terrible headache after a hard day's work and couldn't eat or even take a nap. Soon after they drank this beverage, their headaches were gone because tea reduces congestion in the head.

TEA AND FRIENDSHIP

Tea shortens the distance between people. Whenever we have friends over, it's very natural to have tea. That's the way it is for us in the countryside. It's common nowadays that people are busy. But the elderly tell you to go make some tea anyway. Don't get so stressed out—go make a nice hot cup of tea! It can help you settle down and think. It's the same thing for ordained Buddhists. The first order of things is to have a cup of tea. Then they observe your attitude toward tea. The purpose is for you to observe yourself through tea. After your mind settles down, you can think about why you're there. At the same time, you

should be grateful for having that cup of tea. The earth has produced so many things, among them is this wonderful gift of tea. We should be grateful for this gift.

ECOLOGICAL CONCERNS

The relationship between tea and water is a very close one. Without water, you can't make tea. With good water, you can make good tea. But in modern society, it's not very easy to find it. If you were to make tea with very good mineral water, you might as well use twice-boiled tap water, with which you can also get very good results. Twice-boiled just means you add a cup of cold water to boiling water and let it boil a second time. It helps purify the water.

But when you don't have any water, you can still use tea by just chewing the leaves. If you chew about ten grams of tea a day, it can help quench thirst and start bowel movements. It's good for your overall health even if you don't have water. You can still use this action to cleanse your palate and help your digestive system.

Tea can be appreciated for its aroma and taste. The feeling you get from drinking tea is also very important. They say facts about tea only need to account for 30 percent—the rest of the 70 percent is your imagination. To truly appreciate the flavor of tea, you need to observe its colors, smell its fragrance, and taste its flavor. If your mind isn't calm, it's hard to appreciate the flavor. Once you're calm, you can taste its flavor, layer by layer.

If you pay deep attention while you're drinking tea, you can even tell when the tea was made, whether in the morning, noon, or afternoon, on a rainy day or an extremely dry, sunny day. Their flavors are very different. By the same token, you need to know how the tea was made.

A thousand moutains,
ten thousand streams.
Where can we meet
again?

—KUAN HSIU (832-912)
TRANSLATED BY
J. P. SEATON

Environmental pollution has already begun affecting the growth of tea in a very negative way. This is the undeniable truth. But this kind of challenge can be overcome in a small area of the tea gardens. We can make adjustments in the way we manage the crops. In Ping Lin, we only use organic fertilizers 90–95 percent of the time. We also plant trees to preserve the land water.

In my opinion, tea is more than just a drink. It teaches me to be more humble. It teaches me how to interact with people. I've been able to make friends through tea. In this process, I've learned how to respect people.

Through tea, you can learn a lot more about nature and about the things between heaven and earth. You can also say that tea is the basis of the ideal in Chinese philosophy in which heaven and earth and human beings are united. In learning how to be humble, you can improve your life.

For example, when you get up in the morning, a cup of tea will help you clear your mind and eyes. I drink a lot because I know the benefits. It clears my mind, clears any barriers. Every morning I make a pot of tea that I drink slowly by myself. I let my mind wake up and then start planning the day and eventually start working with a clear mind. After lunch, I gargle with tea. Sometimes friends come over and I have more tea. When we drink with others we shorten the distance between people.

Tea gives you a pause and allows you think. Many things can be done over a cup or a pot of tea, so you can plan your day and go through the day with ease. If you're stressed out, it's like what we say in Taiwanese, you still have to wait, even if you're in a big hurry. If you slow down, you can see and think through a lot of details. But if you're stressed and nervous, you can't see or think clearly. At that moment, you should have a nice cup of Bao Zhong tea to help clear your mind.

As life becomes more technologically advanced, it also becomes more compressed. But human life is finite. You can live to either fifty or one hundred. But you still end up in the coffin. Why not give your life a little leeway? Some space? What's the best way to do this? By drinking some tea to help you decompress and relax. It doesn't do any good for you to be in a great hurry and continue on a hasty journey to the end.

So stop and a drink a fragrant cup of tea and let your mind settle along the way. It can help you think clearly as to your next step in life.

WITH
ZENG CAI-WAN & LIN CHUN-HAN

ZENG CAI-WAN

When we look at things in light of Tao, nothing is best, nothing is worst.
Each thing, seen in its own light, stands out in its own way.

—CHUANG TZU (FOURTH CENTURY BCE)

Zeng Cai-Wan was born in 1931, in Ying-Ge, a small town
in Taiwan noted for its ceramics. "I began my apprentice-
ship in pottery-making at the age of thirteen and I have
been working in this art ever since," he says. In the 1980s, when
the Chinese Kung Fu (gongfu) style of tea became popular in
Taiwan, he started to create teapots that would be in harmony
with their unique contents. Since then, Zeng has pursued an
intense study of the history of teapots in order to match the shape
of his own ceramics with the taste and fragrance of Taiwan's rich
range of teas. He has recently exhibited his work in South Korea,
by invitation.

THE SOUL OF THE TEAPOT

ZENG CAI-WAN: People call me Master A Ban. Why? It's because I make teapots. No one else used the pottery wheel in Taiwan when I was younger and apprenticing, but I did. So people started calling me a Ban Master. I began because I was interested in drinking tea. I started learning about teapots because they are needed to complement the tea.

I started learning pottery-making when I was about thirteen years old. But I wasn't learning how to just make teapots. I was learning how to make figures and vats. Everyone used ceramic for all kinds of pots, to make figures and flower vases, and all sorts of other things. Everyone had been using ceramic for making teapots. But times changed, methods changed, and different materials came to be used, like plastics and aluminum. At that time, teapots in Taiwan were made from molds, by the injection method. Toward the end, I made them from a pottery wheel, which had one benefit. When you work the clay by injection, it's very dense. That's not too good for making tea. If you were to pull clay from the wheel, it would be finer and have little pores. The tea you would make from that clay would be good.

For me, what is different about making pottery from the wheel is that my customers now give me designs to work from. The teapots are made to their specifications—quality, size, and to type. We are creating pots for the *spirit of the tea,* so we make the shape that they want until they're satisfied. If we hand the customer the final product and they're not satisfied, we make it again.

There is one unique characteristic of a teapot made from the wheel. The potter will never be able to make another one exactly the same. So in the end, those people who like tea and teapots like to say, "I've bought a teapot from so-and-so." They realize they will never find another one that's the same. That knowledge makes them happy. They know the teapot will become a collector's item.

So for light tea, we make a light pot, and for regular tea like Oolong, we make it so the pot gives you an aftertaste. A customer also needs to choose the shape of the pot. Some people choose for aesthetic reasons; others for functionality. In my experience, most people choose what's practical.

Why is that? When people come to me to buy a teapot, they want it for making good tea. If they choose a shape primarily for aesthetic reasons, they won't be able to use it to make good tea. So that wouldn't be very meaningful. There are also customers who come to me to buy teapots who are even more professional or knowledgable about tea than I am.

That's for the functional pots. As for the prettier pots, if the leaves can't extend while they're steeping, then they're useless. From ancient times, some people have liked big teapots, the kind with the big belly. Only now do we make strange shapes for aesthetic purposes. But it's the practical ones that are useful so they can just make good tea. Sometimes those who come for custom-made pots are more expert than we are. We just know how to make them; they know what to choose. They choose how the water comes out, how tight the lids are, and the shape of the handle. Taking time to make a good cup of tea means you first need to take time to make a good teapot. Whatever you do, there's a long and involved process. To do it well, you need to make things together. For a good teapot, you need clay from the right place along with right temperature to go with a certain kind of tea. That's how you make good tea.

My regret is that we don't make much money from this craft. We make just enough profit to make a living, which is some comfort. Today, people are indeed very busy, they really don't have the time for tea. I have some friends who say they really don't have the time—yet they love to drink tea. Even so, they will still make tea at least once a day. Other people have the interest in tea. They don't know anything. Why would they bother to make tea? Well, some might believe that drinking tea might refine their character, but it is more than that. Tea is very good for your circulation and can expel toxins, which means it is excellent for your health.

It's very easy to talk about all this now, but when I was learning it was hard work. I didn't sell a single pot for three years. Now it's not so bad making teapots. People finally like them!

ART DESIGNS

A teapot has its own life. I'm very happy with a pot when it has a spirit of its own. Then I won't sell it; I keep it on the shelf. When customers come here and choose their designs, they already have ideas as to size and what it should look like. As a potter who uses a wheel, I can ask them to come and look at the results. If they're happy with it, then they'll buy it. If they're not happy, we redo it.

Sometimes a customer offers a lot of money to buy a teapot from someone else. But the owner won't sell. The offer can go higher and higher, but he just won't sell. After all, if that teapot is his prized possession and if he loves tea and loves making tea with it, why would he sell it?

If your teapot has a flaw, you can cover it up with floral designs. But with smooth pots you can see all the details, so a repair will be very obvious. Smooth teapots are harder to make. That's why teapots have their own spirits, lives, and feelings. That's why people treasure teapots.

THE HEART OF THE TEAPOT

Those of us who value teapots have two ways of thinking about them. One is that someone is deeply interested in tea, and that's why he collects teapots. But nowadays, there are those who don't drink tea but nevertheless collect teapots as antiques. Things from the past are considered antique, but you wouldn't make tea from a teapot from the Ming Dynasty or Ching Dynasty, because those pots aren't for making tea. They're strictly collector's items.

Collectors might admire a teapot for the year it was made or for its historical period. Their way of thinking differs from someone who makes and drinks tea. I believe tea drinkers have a better way of thinking. But for some collectors, once they place a teapot on display, it is frozen. Happily, however, both tea drinkers and collectors are satisfied with my teapots.

THE TAO OF TEA

Chado is the Japanese ceremony. You kneel on the tatami and use all sorts of tea equipment. The fastest you will be served your cup of tea will be after thirty to forty minutes. The Japanese do not make tea only to drink, but for the sake of the ceremony as well.

In Taiwan, when we make tea, it's not really chado, but it's not solely for the consumption of tea either. You could actually say it's the art of tea. We study the techniques on how to make good tea, such as the tea from a certain mountain that needs a certain temperature, and which kind of teapots are used, and how much time is required. That's the art of tea, and in Taiwan, we are amazing tea drinkers.

In Korea, tea drinkers are more like the Japanese. I went there recently and I discovered that some of them really liked tea but they have fewer ceremonies than the Japanese to receive and welcome special guests. It's not like that in Taiwan. In Taiwan, when good friends visit, we make good tea, and with great care. We pay attention to sanitation in every feature of the ceremony so our guests are assured that the teacups are clean. We wash the cups with hot water first and then we make the tea. For us, the purpose is not the ceremony; the purpose is the drinking of the tea.

Sometimes when I have guests over in the morning they stay all day, often until more guests join us. We talk and drink tea until the evening, and tell stories, discuss various interests, and exchange ideas. We talk about finding the right type of teapot for a certain tea, but not about spending a lot of money for one. If it were just about money, a tea ceremony would be less interesting. My guests want to discuss many things all day and all night.

The way I drink tea nowadays is not cheap. I don't just drink any tea; I buy special ones in two seasons every year—spring and winter—from Lu Gu. In terms of how much I drink, it's hard to say. When guests come over, we talk and drink tea. We don't just use one set of leaves, for after a while, the tea would become tasteless. If it's tasteless then why are we drinking it? So sometimes we change the tea so we can savor it more.

You can say that drinking tea is a cultural custom for the Chinese and that the Tao is very deep. But our Taiwanese tea is also very deep. It's not just casual. Our art of tea is very deep. Each has its merits. That's the way it is.

> *Vast indeed is the Ultimate Tao . . . Taken as a pattern by a hundred kings. Transmitted by generations of sages, it is the ancestor of all doctrines, the mystery beyond mysteries.*
>
> —MING DYNASTY

LIN CHUN-HAN

Among my earliest childhood memories are the times when I was helping out with chores at the family farm. My first recollection of tea is of my parents making a huge teapot and bringing it out into the fields so everyone could quench their thirst.

When the quality of life in Taiwan changed and improved, so did the demand for the quality of tea and the techniques behind the making and manufacturing of it. During this period, more refined blends appeared that expressed the art of tea.

Currently, I design and make bamboo art, including tea equipment. I'd like to see bamboo play a more important role in the art of tea. I want to let consumers who are tea lovers appreciate this material and look at it from a different perspective. By doing so, we can elevate the level of both the art and the culture of tea.

The art of tea is a very important part of our native Taiwanese culture. There are lots of different types of equipment for tea. But teapots made of bamboo are not as common. From my many years working with bamboo, I've realized that it is an excellent material to use for teapots. I've taken advantage of its natural design to create the accessories of tea consumption.

Besides ceramics and metal that have been widely used, I've chosen a material that is highly popular. By using bamboo, I would like to elevate the ambience of tea drinking. But the main reason why I use bamboo is my desire to elevate the symbolism of accessories. Usually, people drink tea to reduce tiredness or to adjust their physical and mental states. When we use a natural material, such as bamboo, it raises the level of enjoyment.

All conversations done, in emptiness, sensing a strange fragrance.

—WANG CHANG-LING, CHINESE POET (698–756)

Even if you don't have a teapot, you can just take a little pinch of tea and put it in your mouth. Don't break the tea leaves; just chew lightly, then spit them out. It's OK to swallow, too. Use your mouth as a teapot! It's even better when you're hiking—very pleasant from morning to night.

THE NATURE OF BAMBOO

Besides the teapot, there are cups, picks, and funnels that are used to practice the art of tea. These items are usually made of ceramic, metal, and bamboo. But bamboo already plays a very important role as the pick that gets the leaves out of the pot or the funnel from the can. Now we're developing bamboo cups; I've even made some bamboo teapots that were well received on the market. People find bamboo materials helpful in creating a mood when serving tea.

In tea culture, bamboo has been associated with being humble because it is simply hollow inside. Its height symbolizes sophistication.

I've worked in bamboo for about sixteen years, and have come into contact with many types of bamboo materials. If you wish to express the art of tea by using a tall bamboo pole to make a teapot, it is quite difficult to work with. But you can do it if you assemble the different parts, like the body of the teapot, the spout, the handle, and the cap. You need to be highly familiar with bamboo to find the right part. When you've assembled everything from zero, you'll be able to see the spirit of bamboo in a work of art. Every teapot has its own story.

To accommodate the atmosphere of drinking tea, there's no better material than bamboo. Bamboo is a natural and very easy material to work with. When I was a student, I spent about ten years studying forestry, so I do have some knowledge of the different types of trees. It was then that I realized bamboo's characteristics are very unique from those of other trees. Characteristically, what is special about bamboo is the space between the joints. Besides using the individual joints, you can adapt your processing methods to create various styles. For teapots, you can use the space between those two joints as the body. If you simply use a bamboo tube as a teapot, it will seem rough and ordinary.

But it was only after I'd come into contact with different types of bamboo materials that I realized they can be assembled to form a work of art. The height of bamboo can reach about twenty meters and has a number of joints. In between the joints there is a hollow space that is very suitable to turn into a container, such as a cup. The material you need for this is very simple. You only need a bottom and a tube around it and then it can be used to drink from. This just happens to match the natural design of the bamboo with all its joints. Being so, it's very suitable to make cups out of bamboo.

This bamboo I painted a long time ago. Now you want me do another? Impossible! When the sparrow grows old, it becomes a clam in the sea. You ask it to turn back into a sparrow, But how can it fly again?
—HSU WEI, PAINTER, CALLIGRAPHER (1521-1592)

The process to make a cup is very simple. First, we retain the outer feature of the bamboo, then we smooth the rim. If we decorate the cup a little more, we can add to its value.

If we don't varnish the bamboo, a natural aroma is released when you pour tea into it, and it increases with the temperature of the water. The aroma from the tea and the aroma from the bamboo make a very pleasing and natural combination. When you add tea to bamboo, you get a very soothing result.

BAMBOO TEA POTS

Many years ago, I thought it would be nice to design my own teapots to increase my pleasure when drinking tea. For a teapot, we take two joints to make the basic round shape for its body. If we find a fitting handle, it'll add to the value of the pot. The material we use is from bamboo roots. With the handle, the cap, and the spout pieced together, it becomes a very complete teapot. Then we finish it with lacquer taken from lacquer trees, a natural substance to protect the outer layer so that the teapot feels very warm and soothing. This helps set the mood for having tea.

Strange how a teapot can represent at the same time the comforts of solitude and the pleasures of company.

—ANONYMOUS

For my teapots, I choose a very natural material and glaze it in lacquer, so the resulting vessel won't cause any side effects to health or the environment. The ability to integrate this into the art of tea for me is a great enjoyment in life, the ultimate for me.

WITH
LIN JIN-XING & WEI LI-YUN

Lin Jin-Xing

Its liquor is like the sweetest dew from heaven.
—Lu Yu, *The Classic of Tea*

Lin still lives in Yi-Lan County, in Taiwan, where he was born and grew up surrounded by fields of Su-Xin tea in this agricultural countryside. "I believe that is why I have a special connection with tea," he says. After retiring from business he wanted to share his peaceful life in his small village. So he built a new house in traditional Chinese style, with an adjoining traditional teahouse. "I am pleased to offer visitors an exceptional bed-and-breakfast experience," he declares, "as well as the feeling of harmony in this environment, while savoring the flavors and friendship of tea."

LIN JIN-XING: Our ancestors were very wise. The wisdom we get from the *I-Ching (The Book of Change)* distinguishes between yin and yang. We only choose spring and winter tea because at the beginning of winter the sun is considered to be on the yang cycle. By summertime the yin cycle begins. What we get is tea from the yang cycle. We believe that during the beginning of winter, the yang rises, and in the beginning of summer, the yin rises. After summer begins, yin chi begins to flow. That is why we drink yang tea.

Traditionally, the fields and the mountains are masculine. This refers to the yin and yang of Chinese culture. Tea leaves actually grow on top of the trees. You pluck the leaves and steep them in water. This is yang. The yin part is the fog. When you integrate the tree and the fog, it's the combination of yin and yang. The tea you make from that is the best. The best place to grow tea is where you have water, fog, and sunshine. If you look across a tea field, you look up into the mountains and you see mist or fog. This is what we mean when we say drinking tea is the integration of the sky and the earth.

When I drink tea, I am conscious of peace. The cool breath of Heaven rises in my sleeves, and blows my cares away.
—LU TONG, TANG DYNASTY

Taiwanese tea has been classified as spring, summer, fall, and winter.

In general, most people drink spring and winter teas. Very few people drink summer and fall teas. Spring teas absorb the best from the earth; the same thing with winter teas. After the beginning of winter, there's a lot of fog, both up in the mountains and down in the fields. That humidity is the best for our health and for tea.

And as a poet said, there's a connection between the vapors, the fog, and the cup. The tea absorbs the fog from the earth, the extract of the earth. It absorbs sunshine and fog. The tea that we make contains this sunshine and fog. What we drink is the extract, only the best from nature. Another reason we believe tea is very beneficial to human beings is because it is based on the design of the human body. When we pick up a cup of tea and smell it, our brain detects the aroma. We can identify it as good aroma or familiar aroma. We let our brain feel it.

*Fill your bowl to the brim and it will spill. Keep sharpening
your knife and it will blunt. Chase after money and security
and your heart will never unclench. Care about people's approval
and you will be their prisoner. Do your work, then step back.
The only path to serenity.*
—THE I-CHING: THE BOOK OF CHANGE

Then when we drink it we let our taste buds savor the sharpness and sweetness of the tea. That reaches the highest level of tea drinking. To do that we need a combination of both good water and good tea leaves.

We can also make a distinction between a good tea and bad tea from the color and the feeling you get from the taste. If the water is good, you feel very pleasant and brisk when you drink it. When you drink tea, you can imagine yourself to be in a very idyllic place. Tea makes you feel excellent. You feel a vastness in your spirit. You feel that your soul has opened up. You feel very carefree. You almost feel like a god.

THE CONNECTION BETWEEN HEAVEN, EARTH, AND MAN

Technique in making tea is also very important. When you have good tea leaves and good water but your technique is bad, the tea you make won't be any good.

When we talk about good tea, we need a good climate for the leaves to absorb; we need good water; and we also need good technique. Only then can you make good tea.

In ancient times, in the *I-Ching*, our ancestors talked about heaven, earth, and man. Heaven refers to climate. Earth refers to the tea produced from the land. Man refers to how good you make the tea. With good tea you need good water; without good water, you won't be able to make good tea. You need the combination of all three elements to reach the ultimate state, which is the level of heaven-earth-man. When we talk about that level, we also differentiate between yin and yang. The ancients say things don't deepen in yin, and in yang things don't grow.

Thus, we need to combine yin and yang to get the best results, the ideal situation for tea drinking. This is called the *tao* or *the way of tea*.

THE PURPOSE FOR DRINKING TEA

Tea can help you stay alert. I drink over 1000 cc of tea every day. If I don't drink tea, I feel a little strange, like the time I was abroad and it wasn't convenient to drink tea. If I'm at home, I usually drink tea, but it isn't like drinking other beverages. But again, it depends on the weather.

If there is a purpose to drinking tea, it is to reach the state of forgetting—a state where you can let go of everything around you. When you pick up a cup and smell the tea, your mind becomes empty. After your mind is empty, you drink. When your taste buds savor the tea, your body becomes very light. It's not the same as drinking in gulps when you're thirsty. After drinking a cup of tea, you feel like you're floating free from stress. You feel like you are in a very peaceful place. You feel confident and accomplished. And when you feel all these things, you have become a real part of the environment and you have reached a higher state of being. We drink so that we feel one with the tea. In tea, that's the ultimate enjoyment. That's it.

> *Tea is drunk to forget the din of the world.*
> —TIEN YIHENG

From a seed to a sprout to a tea tree growing between heaven and earth; now we can talk about what can be grown from tea. We can stir fry the leaves and eat them like a vegetable or make tea from them. As for the seeds, you can extract oil from them. You get seeds from the flower, and you can extract oil from the seeds. The oil is very good for our bodies. The entire tea tree is a treasure.

Some people like to drink alcohol. Some people like to smoke. Some people like to drink coffee. Some people like to drink tea. If you want to think deeply about something, have a cup of tea by yourself. It will help you calm down and understand how you should proceed with your life.

It's the same thing when going to paint a painting. If you have random thoughts on your mind, it's difficult to come up with a good painting. When you pick up a brush to finish a work, you must let go until you're weightless, until you've forgotten yourself. Only then can you make a good work of art.

Let me say something else about making tea. I have a fishpond, so there's the sound of water around us. When I hear the sound of water while making tea, my heart becomes even calmer. When it's quiet I can reach a better state of being. This also happens with tea and music, tea and ancient poetry. When I drink tea, I like to play some zither music, which loosens me up. This is how music and tea can be melded into one.

For our Chinese people, this is our way, or the tao of tea. It's a combination of climate, tea leaves, water, and technique. People in ancient times named four classics: lute, chess, calligraphy, and painting *(chin, chi, shu, hua)*. But you can't do any of these without tea. Scholars from ancient times must have reached this level. Some scholars knew how to play musical instruments. Some were poets. Some were painters. These ancient people would not use alcohol. They drank tea. They wouldn't perform any of these classical arts without tea.

> *The valley spirit not dying is called the mysterious female. The opening of the mysterious female is called the root of heaven and earth.*
>
> — TAO TE CHING

Today people drink many different teas. Some favor green tea. Some drink Pu-Er tea. Nowadays, most people like to drink tea that's aromatic. The richer the smell, the better the tea. The higher amount of chlorophyll, the harder it is to fall asleep, because it stimulates you. So people drink Pu-Er tea to avoid that. The type of tea you drink affects the way you feel. When you drink good tea, you have that lasting sweet flavor in your mouth and throat. You feel very pleasant and happy.

We live in an industrialized country where tea leaves absorb the sunshine and air. When the rain comes down or fog descends, it affects the growth and the quality of our tea. If the tea field's location is good, it will not be affected by the industrial pollution. But my view is that if you have a good tea, you don't need to put other ingredients into it. If it is an authentic spring or winter tea, the growers wouldn't add other things.

This is why we must choose teas from good locations. When we drink tea, we must choose it from different places that give us different kinds of feelings. To make a good tea, you must use your heart.

WEI LI-YUN

I care not a jot for immortality, but only for the taste of tea.

—LU TONG

I came to the East Coast in 1973 because of the Council of Agriculture. The council said it was a very poor region, but if we could plant crops of high economic yield, the farmers' lives would improve.

My family lives in Longtan, Taoyuan. We farm tea over there. We've been working in tea for four generations. The government wanted us to help promote tea in this area. Out of curiosity, we came here after two days of travel. Transportation was very inconvenient back then.

Afterward, the government was very diligent in promoting tea. Tea shoots were free, so my husband felt a sense of mission, that he had to succeed in promoting this tea. He told the farmers to plant the tea and said that they could rest assured that he wouldn't leave them, that he would work alongside them. So he worked very hard and didn't dare to think about leaving.

At first we thought we'd go home to Longtan after we succeeded. But people over here in Wu Hou were so nice we gradually settled down. This place slowly developed into a tourist spot. The government established a model farming village. The place had no water at first. People used to live up in the mountains or in the valleys where there was water. But then we got tap water and a model village developed.

In 1979, Li Chung-Tao, then chairman of the Council of Agriculture, came and visited the site and thought we were doing well. He named it Tien He Tea. Everyone worked very hard on it. At this point, we're promoting organic tea. Everyone's working in this direction. Our family runs a model organic farm. We use organic fertilizers and organic methods to promote the Tien He tea because it is so good for the soil. The tea produced from soil that isn't fertilized with chemicals is sweeter. As for pest control, we don't use pesticides either. We use pests' natural enemies; we raise insects to eat other insects. So we don't use pesticides or chemical fertilizers on our tea.

Green lacewing ("chao ling") is the tea aphids' natural enemy. We use green lacewings to get rid of aphids, to prevent them from eating our tea shoots. The quantity that we produce is less than those sprayed with pesticides, but the quality is a lot better. After being bitten by insects, the flavors are different. Sometimes we want insects to bite the leaves on purpose. Those that we leave for insects to bite on we call Honey Flavor Black Tea. After the insects have bitten the leaf, it has a sweet honey taste. By using organic methods, nontoxic methods, the tea is sweeter. If everyone could work this way, we could harmonize with nature.

Let me introduce the different types of tea we produce. We dry our white tea in the shade after we pluck a bud with a leaf. Then we roast it in very low temperature and it becomes a very light, but very sweet, tea. We cook our green tea in steam. This is rich in Vitamin C. You need very fresh tea to steam and produce a tea with a little flavor of seaweed. Our Oolong tea has two leaves to every bud. It's fermented very slowly. After the leaves are plucked, they are wilted three times and then reshaped. The aroma becomes very fragrant, and we stop the fermentation process, which gives the tea a special flavor.

The processing of Wu Yi is very similar to that of Oolong. After the tea is finished, we roast it again. The temperature depends on how well done we want the tea to be. The tea is very smooth, different from Oolong.

Taiwan's black tea is a combination of mountain tea and a Burmese tea. It's called Taiwanese No. 18 Red Jade. This has a little hint of cinnamon, a little bit of mint. It tastes completely different from regular black tea, and is very good for health.

In addition to tea, I drink water. But I mainly drink tea, so I'm very healthy. The first thing I do every morning is drink tea. After that, I exercise. Then I come back and have breakfast and feed the fish in my fish tank. When you're happy, you should drink a lighter tea. When you're unhappy, you should make a strong tea. It will make you feel better and quench your thirst.

Life is meant for happiness.
Life is full of ups and downs;
Sunshine comes and goes;
Then why such fuss and bustle?
Let's live for happiness . . .
Make a delicious brew,
Then taste the joys
Of Lu Tong's seven bowls
Of famous Yang-Hsien tea!
—TEA MASTER CHANG TIEH-CHUN

THE IMPORTANCE OF TEA

Tea is the most important thing in my life. When I was young, my family was in education. I was a teacher. Then I married my husband, who came from a fourth-generation family of tea farmers. After getting to know tea, it became very important to me. The desire to watch the tea trees grow slowly and to grow different teas comes from a belief that everyone should be able to drink good tea. If it is a good strain, then we put all our effort into it, and we try it out for ourselves. If we don't like it, we let it go. If it is an excellent strain, then we—our three children and my husband and I—will try to preserve it. We also like to share our knowledge with everyone. We tell people we've planted this strain for several years. Let's all plant it.

Nowadays, I use the organic method. We grow grass in between the tea, so there won't be weeds and no need to spray chemicals. As for the tea leaves, we raise insects to eat other insects. Although the quantity won't be a lot, it will be very good. Tea production is very hard work. The tea you pick in the morning must be done before the next morning. When you're blending tea, you have to do it once every hour on the hour. When you're blending, you won't be able to sleep at night. If you sleep, the tea leaves go bad. You have to smell it to see if you can stop the fermentation. Everyone needs to work hard to try the tea to see if it's overfermented or not fermented enough. Everyone wants to make a very good tea because the following day the entire family will taste your tea. We use little cups to taste it. Sometimes we say you fermented it too long, you probably fell asleep, or it's not aromatic. But if you pay careful attention, you can make very good tea.

To be a tea man or tea woman is to doctor one's mind. Cultivation of immediate responses to the Here and Now by means of the tea art leads gently to a more permanent awareness.

—JOHN BLOFELD, "THE CHINESE ART OF TEA"

In our family, tea is a very important crop. Tea is like life. If you don't drink tea, you're not healthy. So in our family, we don't drink water, we drink tea. We make a huge pot of tea, which is our water for the day and drink as much as we can.

My son, Yeh Pu-Kuang, will carry on our tea tradition; he's the captain here. He's the tea captain. I hope tea will be passed down for generations. I hope we can keep promoting Tien He tea from Wu Hou. As the leader, my son works very hard in hopes of improving the tea. I also hope he produces some organic tea so everyone can drink healthful tea. I drank tea when I was pregnant and I drank tea after I gave birth. I even used tea leaves to bathe him!

WITH
WU SHENG-BEN, LIN KU-FANG & CHANG FU-CHIN

WU SHENG-BEN

This evening sky may bring snow. Come enjoy a cup with me.
—PO CHU-I, CHINESE POET, (772–846), TRANSLATED BY SAM HAMILL

Seen here on his rooftop at tea time, Wu Sheng-Ben is a Hakka from Hsin Chu, originally the land of the aboriginal people of Taiwan. He has been studying tea for over forty years, during which time he has helped create the history of Yu Lan Tea. When he began to cultivate tea, the land was neglected, wild, and heavily forested. But the virgin soil was rich enough for the tea plants to flourish. "When I was young," he says, "I didn't understand a thing about tea growing, but because I had an agricultural high school education, I easily learned and became skilled."

WU SHENG-BEN: The origin of the name for our tea is interesting. The president of Taiwan, Lee Teng-Hui himself coined the name. Upon drinking it, he proclaimed our tea's aroma to be like Yu Lan's flowers, so he named it Yu Lan Tea.

During the time Mr. Chen Ting-Nan was governor it was possible for individuals to join the Tea Grower's Association. So small villages could grow excellent tea. As a result, the tea market opened up and the lives of villagers were improved. When Governor Chen special ordered our tea as a retirement gift for his workers, many other government agencies and corporations were inspired to purchase their tea from us.

During this early period, our women workers here didn't know how to draw or pour tea properly. They invited tea masters to come and teach them the proper tea skills. After the women learned to draw tea properly they were able to make truly quality tea for our customers. Our price dramatically rose from one to ten to one hundred dollars per kilogram. This was a time when our manufacturing business was growing.

When Mr. Chiang Ching-Kuo, over in Dong Ding, touted the health benefits of tea, the price for Yu Lan Tea went up from thirty to three hundred dollars. After a while, everyone learned the news that this old mountain was growing good tea. The rate for our tea leaves kept increasing up to thousands of dollars. Of course, the farmers' lives also improved while everyone was making a profit.

It quenches thirst. It lessens the desire for sleep. It gladdens the heart.

—SHEN NUNG, 2737 BCE

In the ensuing race to produce good tea, more and more people joined in on the clamor, which was similar to the recent spring tea competition when so many different growers won awards. Overall, our success illustrates that the soil and climate here are good, and so by the grace of nature we are able to make excellent tea.

When drinking tea you should focus on your heart. When you think of the word *tea*, the word *heart* should also come to mind. Ask yourself, "Is this astringent? Is it aromatic? Is there a rhythm in the flavor?" These considerations are important. For those who don't understand these aspects, it is like a cow drinking tea. They will probably drink a big cup in one gulp. However, people who understand tea drink tea differently—slowly and mindfully.

When former President Lee Teng-Hui coined our product's name, he gave the first cup to the first lady. After he toasted her, he lightly inhaled the aroma of the second cup and drank it with a deep purpose. Then he said, "This Jin-Xuan tea is excellent. Its fragrance can be compared to a flower's."

CHALLENGES

As I have said, in recent years there has been a heavy traffic increase in our tea business. Not only people from Taiwan buy more tea from us, but more and more tea lovers from Japan, Korea, and the United States flock here looking for the best tea. Many foreign visitors want to drink good tea and don't haggle about price. We always give them a fair deal, because all of us here are honest. Recently, some Chinese-Americans and Chinese-Canadians visited us and drank our Yu Lan tea and said how great it was. They invited us to come to America and Canada to grow tea.

When our guests ask why our tea leaves are so superior, I tell them the reason is that our native tea gardens are at medium-altitude, which is a climate that is not too cold and not too hot. If the weather gets warm early, the tea will bud early, and the leaves will be thin. Of course, only thick-leaf tea will have rhythm in the flavor. Temperature variances here also mean the picking season runs later. The quality of our water is also excellent. It is not chalky and does not contain iron. We don't use wet ground to grow tea. I have high regard for the safety and quality of water. I hope all tea farmers will abide by and stick to this principle. Furthermore, the climate, topsoil, and thermal balance are suitable. Good water and good soil determine if the quality of tea will be good.

Water and air pollution are problems that tea growers face alone. The current government proactively encourages the farming sector not to spray pesticides. Instead, we are encouraged to use appropriate fertilizers. If we want to plant a crop tomorrow, we first inform the farming sector assay office. Then we bring in some tea leaves, which they will test to verify that the leaves don't have pesticide residue. If you pass the test for five straight years, the government awards you a certificate that affirms you are a model tea grower. I have been elected to the list of Top Ten Exemplary Male Tea Farmers in our country, and my daughter has been selected to the Top Ten list for female growers of tea. From all these factors you can tell that Taiwan is a precious island. So our leaves are superior. As a result, our tea steeps better than other leaves.

HOW TO SAVOR TEA

During tea drinking, you should hold the cup with your palm facing up and toward yourself, with the back of your hand facing out—or else you are being discourteous. This drinking pose shows you have good manners.

When drinking tea, let it swirl and stop for a moment in your mouth so your nose also senses it. Then swallow the tea by letting it flow down your throat. The tea swirls in your mouth, allowing you to feel its astringency, and pushes its aroma to your nose. This way, you can taste the tea's complex flavor and slowly drink it, enjoying its sweetness and rhythm.

There is a saying about afternoon tea: "Drinking tea makes friends." This adage expresses my deepest feeling about tea. Tea drinkers are generous; their hearts are calm and collected. Many of the people who come here to drink tea have become my sincere friends, like brothers or like family to me. What I'm saying is that "tea people" are very genuine in their actions.

Drinking tea also helps maintain your body's nourishment. If you're very nervous or ready to yell at someone, your bad attitude makes you even more nervous. You will never interact well with other people. In society we shouldn't be nervous; we should be calm and collected. You need a firm understanding of your own heart. You should let this understanding show when you talk to others so the social atmosphere will be placid and people will take notice of you and concentrate on what you are saying.

If you treat your clientele this way, you will make your greatest friends. You can calm the storm brewing inside you by drinking a cup of tea so your "temper" will become "tempered" and you will settle down. If you do so, a certain breadth of mind will take over and you will not want to fight with anyone.

These skills are the real benefits of drinking tea. But they are very difficult to attain. Everyone should practice these skills. Everyone should drink tea as often as possible.

LIN KU-FANG

For some people who like to drink tea, it's just tea. But for me, a professor of music, drinking tea isn't simply the act itself. In Chinese culture, we say it has more than one dimension, just like music. It is far more. Tea can induce happiness. With different types of tea we can actually taste different moods and aspects of life. It is a confluence of art and the exchange of friendship. While meeting friends over tea, we make observations about life. What is revealed during the consumption of tea is something integral—*people reveal themselves*.

A person who is steeped in tea culture believes he cannot complete himself alone. He must have an exchange with another person, someone to reflect himself in order to complete his life. That is why we use the idea of the four seasons and the different stages in life to describe the dimensions of tea. Through this activity, I'm not only enjoying life, I'm also *observing* it.

Regarding the seasons and the weather, we can take it a step further and say that drinking a certain tea has to do with how you feel. We can choose a specific type of tea for a specific mood. When we're faced with a certain type of friends, we select the ideal tea to receive them. Tea reflects our overall concern for culture and the surrounding environment, and brings out our philosophical expressions.

CHANG FU-CHIN

There are three things that are all important to get the best flavor out
of your tea, namely the teapot, the water you use, and how you heat it.
In the tea world there is a saying that the pot is the father of tea,
the water is the mother of tea, and charcoal is the friend of tea.

—MASTER LAM KAM CHUEN, *The Way of Tea*

CHANG FU-CHIN: I come from a farming family. We farmed different kinds of crops on this land before. The reason that we have Tie Guan Yin here is because in 1980, the government made a big effort to promote it. Over a period of time, Tie Guan Yin covered most of this area. In 1980, many people now in their fifties and sixites were still young when they decided to plant a great quantity of Tie Guan Yin. That's why it became well-known throughout the world.

Gradually, as the tea workers began to age, the industry itself started to decline. That led to the current situation, which is more like tea tourism than an educational industry. We plant seeds and teach visitors about tea.

I chose this path after my military service because this tea way of life was passed down to us from our ancestors. We have the duty to pass it on to our children. That's our tradition. If we don't maintain what we have this generation, then we're not doing right by our next generation. Tie Guan Yin was brought over from China by our forefathers. It flourished over here in Taiwan. We shouldered a heavy responsibility to carry on. I believe I would be letting my ancestors down if I let this tea tradition die.

When I was young, around seventeen or eighteen, I wasn't paying as much attention as I am now to tea. When I started to have responsibilities, like feeding my kids, my interest in tea grew as well. The reason why I stayed is really because of the competitiveness of the outside world. By remaining here, I don't need to compete fiercely. I can just carry on what was passed to me. I can provide for my family this way. If I couldn't feed my family, then it's possible that we'd leave, too. But at least for now, society has treated me warmly. Maybe our children won't have the same interest in tea, but that's hard to say. Every year we have two tea competitions here in Mucha province. If we don't place in the competition, or show some accomplishment, then our reputation and profit will suffer. Eventually, I won't be able to feed my family and won't be able to work in this business anymore.

THE QUALITY OF LIFE

Today, we bring the tea baskets up the mountains. If we talk about tea farming, we have to talk about hard work. I get up around six or seven in the morning to start the prep work for our tea workers. We bring bamboo baskets up the mountains and make some tea. The pickers usually arrive around seven o'clock to pick the greens. We have four rounds throughout the day, from ten to noon, then at two and four in the afternoon, to pick up the tea greens to dry. The age of our three tea pickers—

"Among the kinds of teas, the bitter still excels the sweet, but among them all, these tastes can both be found; We know not indeed for whom they may be sweet or bitter; We've picked till the ends of our pearly fingers are quite marred."

—FROM *A Ballad on Picking Tea in the Gardens in Springtime* who we call *masters* because they are all elderly—adds up to over two hundred years. They're grandmothers and to be honest, we're a little worried. The land in Mucha is hilly. When the seniors go up these slopes, it's easy for them to fall, if they don't watch their steps carefully. So we feel we have a big responsibility for them. If your grandmother went to your backyard to pick tea, you'd worry about her, too.

A DAY IN THE LIFE OF THE PLANTATION

We're constantly learning as we're processing tea. The knowledge behind roasting Tie Guan Yin is very deep. Starting from our teenage years, up to our 20s and now 30s and 40s, we're learning all the time. The learning is endless. One year you can come up with a good tea, and then a decade or two later, you come up with an even better one.

When we're making tea, our state of mind is important. A good tea needs the right coordination of several steps like natural sunlight or indoor drying. I was recently telling a customer that if I had a fight with my wife today, the tea I would make wouldn't be any good, because if I'm in a state of anger or feeling down, my sense of smell and touch wouldn't be the same. When we're making tea our state of mind is important.

As for weather, I prefer to make tea on rainy days. As for the spring or fall teas, I like fall much better. As part of our education, we've served tea to all types of customers. Some customers go on and on about how awful our tea is but end up buying the most. What we say in Taiwanese is that the ones who criticize the products are often the most expert buyers. Only when you keep criticizing my tea do I have room to improve. On the other hand, if someone was going to come to give me pointers about tea, but kept complementing it, then it's over. The tea will remain at that level forever. However, if you can pinpoint the mistakes—either in your fertilization or drying—it's all very helpful. It's the same in life. In the process of making tea you come to see the meaning of life.

There are different steps, including drying and rolling, that will affect the overall quality of tea. The information we receive from the previous generation of tea masters will teach us well if we're humble. Most likely, those tea masters in their sixties and seventies won't teach you anything. The reason is that they guard their knowhow. They won't tell you what they know. How should I put this? They would probably pass their so-called secret knowledge on to their own children, but they won't teach it to you directly.

When we try to understand tea processing we need to look at the entire process. At Tie Guan Yin, the manufacturing is very important. When we encounter a problem during the roasting process, the elder master won't tell you that the fire is too high or whatever the problem is. But if you have the right intention, you'll observe and experience things on your own. If you roast the tea too long and it burns, he'll probably give you a hint. But you need to experience it yourself; you need to pay careful attention. We believe we've gotten good results if consumers validate our quality. Then we feel comforted. Therefore, we won't hesitate to produce the best tea.

ORGANIC TEA FARMING

Our generation has come to be concerned about the environment, which is very different from the time when we were little. About two-thirds of my tea is organic. We cannot choose our environment, but in my opinion, we can change it. In terms of tea, the land is something that was passed on from our ancestors. The soil at Mucha has already been acidified because it is an old tea-farming area. We started to change the soil into organic soil when I joined the farm associations in the 1990s. We used things like garlic and wood vinegar repellent to get rid of insects. About ten years ago, I started doing organic tea, because we cherish the environment we had when we were little and don't want to continue destroying it.

For example, tea leaves are most vulnerable when they're about ten days old, after they sprout. But we have a lot of bugs on our land and they act the same as humans. They eat to survive. However, we don't necessarily have to kill them; we just have to repel them. So we use an organic repellent, which won't kill the insects. It just gets rid of them. And we only need to use it once a week for three or four weeks.

In organic farming, this is the best method to change the soil. But for those of us farming around the city, it's unlikely for us to come up with organic fertilizer. The cost to grow tea is more than to buy it. For example, it costs a hundred dollars for twenty-five kilograms. The farm associations are promoting organic fertilizers, so there're some government subsidies in these organic fertilizers and it won't cost us a lot to use it. By now, a lot of consumers can accept the quality of tea that doesn't use insecticide. To be honest, the quality of the tea isn't as good, because it has a little flavor from the insects. But for health reasons, organic is much better.

Once you're surrounded by nature, you feel like you've been embraced by it. There are a lot of things that you can't find in the city. It's not something you can buy with money. Many things in nature require time and observation for you to experience and understand. If you have a chance to spend time in the mountains, you realize there are things in life you don't need to mind or argue over. Slowly, when you return to your office or when you're with your colleagues and friends, your mind will remain open and you won't mind so many things.

Today, everyone feels stress. At Tie Guan Yin we feel stress if our tea does not come out well. But if you change your surroundings, you change your mood. When you have tea with a couple of friends and they listen to you—even if you whine when you talk—your mind will automatically relax.

Of course, you can say that there are plenty of tea beverages in the city, but it's just not the same as the actual making and sharing of tea with friends here in the mountains. If you were to come up to the mountains and experience having tea here, I would say it would be much better for you.

Chapter Twenty-Eight
THE SPIRITUAL COMFORT OF TEA

WITH
LIN ZI-PEI, TU YING-MING & CHUANG HSIU-MEI

Lin Zi-pei

On the peaks of Mount Ling, a wondrous thing is gathered. It is tea.

—Tu Yu, Ode to Tea (Fourth-century bce)

L in Zi-Pei is a seventy-year-old tea farmer who lives in Lu Gu Village, Taiwan. He sells Dong Ding Oolong tea, which he makes according to traditional methods. He takes great pride in the uniqueness of his tea, which is half-fermented, using manual labor and wood coal to roast his tea. He says his quality is very different from others. "If you drink our tea, it will improve your health, because it is rich in minerals."

LIN ZI-PEI: My ancestors were tea farmers in the Dong Ding Mountains. After the Japanese occupation period, we hadn't yet developed Taiwanese tea. When Vice President Hsieh Tung-Ming came here for a visit he decided to develop tea. After he became president, Chiang Ching-Kuo, son of Chiang Kai-Shek, came to have tea with us and decided to promote our tea. That's how Taiwanese tea became so well-developed. It was through the good deeds of these two old men. Otherwise, the business wouldn't have been the same.

Our Dong Ding Oolong tea is considered a very fine tea, unlike anyone else's. After you drink it, the tea leaves a special taste in your mouth and makes you feel good. The reason is because of the excellent geographic location where it grows at a high altitude. Some mountains are higher; some are lower. The soil is yellow in color, like eggs. The airflow is good, and there is ample sunshine and there isn't any air pollution.

When we savor tea, we drink for the taste. The smaller the cup, the stronger the tea. If we drink from a big bowl, we drink just to quench our thirst. When you drink from a big bowl, you are just swallowing a liquid beverage. There's no meaning at all; there's no wisdom. When we drink our tea from a little cup, we smell the aroma and savor the aftertaste. That's all there is to drinking tea. Tea is there to adjust your mental and physical well-being. When you're feeling depressed and you drink some tea, you just feel better. This is a very important part of your leisure life.

From what enchanted Eden came thy leaves, That hide such subtle spirits of perfume? Did eyes preadamite first see the bloom, Luscious Nepenthe of the soul that grieves?

— "TEA," FRANCIS S. SALTUS, (1846–1889)

As for regular Oolong tea, there are many types. In Taiwan, we have Bao Zhong, black tea, and many other varieties. But Dong Ding Oolong tea is especially popular. Nowadays, not too many people produce half-fermented Dong Ding Oolong tea. It's very rare, because everyone now uses machines in the production process. But mechanical tea doesn't have the same quality. We use the sun to dry tea leaves and then use wood-burning coal to roast them. The resulting quality is a different flavor from that of everyone else's.

BODY AND SOUL

You drink tea to relax the body and soul. When you're very tired from working, make some tea and relieve your stress. It can take away your worries. It's something to *regulate your body and soul*. It doesn't matter how busy you are. If you can't make tea, you can suck on tea leaves. That's also very good for you. You won't get thirsty. Your digestive system will be very healthy. You don't need to eat other miscellaneous stuff. You can just put tea in your mouth then drink water. You don't need to make it according to strict rules. If you've used this tea for a long time, you'll live longer.

To use modern language, this is organic tea. I guarantee that there's nothing else involved. I firmly recommend that you drink tea everyday. If you have time to make tea, make a big cup. Drink it while you work, while you rest and at night.

As for manufacturing tea, it is easy as long as you have a conscience. If you don't think about creating a lot of wealth or making a lot of money, you can make very good tea. You don't need additives or other ingredients to add to the tea. To maintain the tradition of tea culture, you can make the best tea as long as you don't put profit above all else. Use your compassion to share good tea with people. Society has changed so much over the years that you must be determined in your beliefs.

Mr. Chiang Ching-Kuo once said to me, "You must preserve such good quality in your tea. Don't let it be lost." So I pass this wisdom to my son. If he carries on, the tea tradition will continue for another hundred years. It's like doing a good deed. Think of it that way. Don't think about profits first. Put all your efforts into your efforts. Maintain your standards.

We just need to be healthy, energetic and happy. Whenever you'd like to eat, drink a cup of tea. Relax your body and soul, quench your thirst the right way. You don't need to drink too many other things. As long as you're healthy, whatever you do you'll be happy. What you can't find in other food, you can find in our tea. This is one of the reasons why I'm so resolute. That's the way it is.

TEA EXPERIMENTS

Mainland Chinese tea and Taiwanese teas are unique because of our climate and altitude. Taiwan has an oceanic island climate. The tea it produces has the distinction of four seasons. The spring, summer, fall, and winter seasons all produce their own unique teas. Mainland China in general has two seasons. Their climate, altitude, soil, and method of making are different. The quality of their tea, according to my years of experience, can't compare with our tea.

As to the meaning of tea in my life, there's too much meaning already. I simply maintain my beliefs and make good tea for everyone to taste. That's all. I'm very satisfied. To actually achieve that goal now is quite difficult. Sometimes, we have even financial difficulty because we insist on using manual labor. But we can't make the best tea without strong determination. If we put profits first, then we couldn't go on making good tea like this. We must maintain our standards. So I've kept my beliefs through all these years in making the very best possible tea.

Those who don't know how to savor tea usually don't come to my place. The customers who come here are very high class, but it is not a question of whether they are rich or not. They know how to savor tea. They are interested in real tea. As long as they are interested in the real

thing and they have the spirit of research and would like a tea that's good for health, then they've come to the right place. They are seeking me out for the right reason That's the way it is.

THE ART OF MAKING TEA

Tea is extremely important to people from all backgrounds, because people everywhere in the world get thirsty. That's the first reason we drink tea. But when we drink tea, we must choose a good tea—we must not drink random tea. Good tea is a necessity, like rice, oil, wood, and vinegar.

Tea is still popular among ordinary people, but it seems like scientists have forgotten about it. Everyone is more into technology. That's where the money is. Profit is everything. In our entire town, I'm the only one who insists on doing it the old way, with coal from wood and manual labor. The old practices are uncommon nowadays. We've been doing it this way for over a hundred years. I'm the fifth generation. We carry on from the perspective of ordinary people, not from technology. It's an ordinary way of living.

I would very much like to see this way of tea carried on for another few decades—or a hundred years. But I don't think it will be. We are considered the sunset. Sunsets are wonderful, but soon it will be dusk. We've already reached the peak. It's possible that no one else has this determination to do this. This is it.

On earth, no feast lasts forever.
—CHINESE PROVERB

In our everyday life, we are usually in a rush, but we can get rid of some of the stress from all this haste. What I want to do is disseminate information in our culture that allows people to enjoy the good fortune of tea. That's my goal; that's why I insist on making good tea. When I accomplish that, I am satisfied.

People ask about the meaning of tea. Well, it can make you more alert. Tea inspires your mind and allows you live peacefully and make you happy. You won't be impatient. You'll come up with good ideas. You'll do good things. That's my feeling about tea. You can concentrate better. That's the great spiritual comfort you get from tea.

A Humorous Story About Tea

Chao-chou asked a newcomer monk. "Have you just come?"
"Yes," replied the monk. "Then have a cup of tea," said Chao-chou.
He said to another monk, "Have you come recently, too?"
"No," said the monk. "Then have a cup of tea," said Chao-chou.
The chief monk, Inju, said, "Why do you offer tea to a monk who has come
recently, and to one who hasn't, in just the same way?"
"Inju!" said Chao-chou. "Yes?" asked Inju.
"Have a cup of tea!" said Chao-chou.
—PARABLE ABOUT ZEN MASTER CHAO-CHOU TSUNG-SHEN (778–897)
BY PAUL REP, "ZEN FLESH, ZEN BONES"

MAKING DING DONG TEA WITH MR. LIN

When you make tea, you must select the right equipment. The best
teapot is made of ceramic, not porcelain. First, you warm up the pot
and then the teacups. After it's warm, you put in the tea leaves. Fill one-
fifth of the pot with tea leaves. Don't put in too much. You need to seal
the tea container, otherwise, moisture will get in. Rinse the leaves. Pour
out the water quickly and then put it back in. Let it steep for forty seconds. You can drink tea now—but don't drink the entire cup at once.
Take about six sips to taste the flavor. After you're done, you can smell
the aroma. Now you can put the cups back and have a second round.
Heat the pot. Wait another forty seconds. Make sure to inhale the tea
so the aroma goes into your stomach. You need to slurp the tea a little,
make some noise. Otherwise, you can't taste the tea. The next time, add
ten seconds, the third time, add ten more, and so on. You can continue
making tea up to twelve times, but extend the steeping ten seconds each
time. Remember, don't pour it from up high. We pour a bit at a time so
everyone gets a very even tea. The first three times you need only forty
seconds. After you finish drinking, then you add water. Then fill the
teapot with water until the next day or whenever you're finished with
work. Then drink it; that way is also very good. That's the way we've
been making tea since ancient times.

So we can taste the flavor and taste the spirit, we put our attention into this, and then we relax. We can't be impatient. That's the spirit of tea making. That's the tradition in our culture. This way of making tea calms you down and allows you to think. That's the reason behind it. There's no other reason. We sit down and very quietly have some tea. That's the way it is. Don't be afraid of wasting time by having tea this way. Our society is very stressful. Tea doesn't allow you to be impatient, like you're in a race. Tea gradually relaxes you. It relieves your body and soul.

TU YING-MING

Currently, I'm the owner of Taichung's Wu Wei Tsao Tang Teahouse in Taiwan. I drink tea three to five times a day. I start drinking tea after I get up in the morning, and I keep drinking tea the rest of the day, until I go to bed. My family has been drinking tea since my grandfather's generation. I was raised in that kind of environment. Naturally, tea became a big part of our lives. Then we came to work in the city. As we aged, we yearned for those scenes from our childhood. We came from the countryside and didn't have many resources; we had to work hard. Sometimes when I go home, my grandmother reminds me not to overwork and to slow down a little. So I decided to change our way of life and began to run this teahouse, which fits into this kind of thinking. We gradually

slowed down our very busy pace of life and hard work. Our way of life is now considered more leisurely and is closer to our dream life.

We built Wu Wei Tsao Tang mainly to create a very convenient corner for people living in the city. For Taichung people, they can turn around the corner and come here to adjust their body and soul. When we began the teahouse we wanted to retain a natural environment; we didn't adorn it too much. Gradually, it became more and more natural. I think drinking tea is definitely like a medicine. Tea helps you find the balance between your body and your heart.

CHUANG HSIU-MEI

When we were little, we drank tea as if it were water. Every morning when we got up, we would actually drink tea, whereas others might have a drink of water. We drink tea almost all the time. Because my family had a farm, what we saw were big teapots. Tea is a daily necessity. So it's very natural to drink tea everyday. Now that we're grown, we still drink tea everyday. It'd be weird without tea. It's not just a spirit, but it's a daily necessity. So drinking tea feels very pleasant.

In my memory, my parents worked hard in the fields. When we thought they looked tired, we quickly offered a big pot of tea. We'd bring the pot and serve them tea. That was to express our filial piety. And when their friends came over to visit, our parents would also ask us to serve tea to the elders. Then they would complement us. So tea was like a medium in teaching us how to behave. Another thing is when we pray to our ancestors, we also serve tea. It's not just a daily necessity. It's also a symbol of honoring your ancestors and of filial piety in our culture. Therefore, tea is very important to us.

Even though we drank tea as children, and still do as grownups, the meaning has changed. I think that it's related to life. Now, it seems like you need to boil the water. After the water has been boiled, then you get the aroma of tea. And in life, you also need to go through many ordeals, to become more at peace. Tea is more than just a daily necessity. It's a process that one must go through in life. Just as we boil water to bring out the rich flower of tea, there are things we must do to savor the richness of life.

When I get up in the morning, I start drinking tea. I also drink tea at noon and after I eat, and then in the evening, unless it's right before I go to sleep. So it feels like tea has been integrated into my life. It's like Westerners who drink coffee. But unlike coffee, tea does not affect our bone density. It's very pleasant to drink tea. It's not just very pleasant for your mind, but also for your body. It absorbs fatty acids. So it's good for beauty, skin, and losing weight. That's why I keep drinking tea. But I actually don't spend a lot of time drinking tea—at least not like those who are into the Tao of tea and take time to drink slowly. I make a pot of tea for work. I drink it whenever I'm thirsty or when I'm not feeling well. But I don't take a lot of time drinking it, so it has not affected my activities. On the other hand, it's given me pleasure and helped me become more efficient at work. We always get together over tea, and it has helped us maintain the friendship. Usually, when we get together with friends, we have tea. And then we talk about what's happening in our lives. We have a good time drinking tea and chatting, and it's very happy, and it makes us want to get together often.

In fact, tea may be responsible for our friendships lasting this long, so tea is very important to us.

WITH
LIN HSIU-HUI & KIDS AT THE TEA HOUSE

LIN HSIU-HUI

When I was a little girl, tea was hard to come by. When grownups had guests, we'd serve them wine. Only when special guests came by did we serve tea. I think it's a generational difference. That's the big change.

In 1984, I entered into the world of cold-tea beverages. I discovered a very delicious and rich milk tea. To this cold milk tea, I added tapioca balls. I developed this into what became known as bubble tea.

Nostalgia isn't what it used to be.

—PETER DE VRIES,
AMERICAN HUMORIST,
(1910–1993)

Why did I come up with this bubble tea? I invented it because it contains what I loved best from my childhood: tapioca balls. So bubble tea to me isn't simply a beverage; it also brings back nostalgic memories.

In the late 1980s, when I came into touch with cold milk tea, it was fun for me. It no longer tasted nasty. Instead, it was icy, cold, sweet, and delicious and especially suitable for Taiwan's summers. It seemed completely different from what I had tasted when I was a little girl. So I wanted to bring together the sweet memories of my favorite tapioca balls from my childhood with the latest wonderful innovations in the tea world, to bring together tradition and modernity. It made me feel like a very good tea maker.

In the beginning, it was just a secret recipe that I shared with my friends. At the end, in 1987, I registered the recipe and it became an official product that I could share with other friends of tea. That's when bubble tea officially went on the market.

Actually, I'm a country girl. My family sold vegetables at the local market. In my memory, tea was something you only served when guests came to visit. It was very hard to get good tea. Usually, the tea we made was fairly light farmer's tea, the lowest grade. But I didn't have many chances to drink tea because it wasn't something kids liked; it was hot and bitter, tart and nasty, and not very tasty.

Water makes life possible, tea brings nature to society.
—CHINESE SAYING

In the market where I grew up a bowl of tapioca balls cost only five cents. My mother often bought a bowl for my brother and me to share. They were very warm and they evoked soft and sweet feelings, which is why I think they became an important part of my childhood.

To me, the meaning of tea is very broad. Tea is at the core of my life. It has enriched me and given me a sense of value and purpose. I couldn't do without tea for a single day. It's very clear that I'm destined to share tea with a lot of people and mix a lot of drinks.

→>-<←

Kids at the Tea House

FRIEND #1: I like bubble tea more because it's chewy. There's nothing in traditional tea that you can chew on. There are bubbles in bubble tea. When you drink, you can suck them up, and that feels pretty good.

FRIEND #2: I like bubble tea because when you drink it, it's not as boring as traditional tea. You're not just drinking. I like the feeling of chewing on something.

FRIEND #3: My grandmother thinks it's not as healthy as the old tea. She thinks the bubbles aren't very healthy. But students are young and don't care about that. They enjoy the texture. When I drink bubble tea, I discuss things with my classmates. Then things won't be so serious. We can be very natural and enjoy ourselves. Discussions can be serious, but through bubble tea, we can enjoy our differences. My grandmother thinks that drinking sweet beverages is like drinking junk food, that sweet beverages are bad for your health, and young people shouldn't drink as many as we do. I think whoever invented bubble tea is pretty amazing.

FRIEND #2: What is a cool and sexy drink? Bubble tea! I think drinking bubble tea is really cool. Even when you can't finish your cup, you can still sit there and blow on the straw. The tapioca bubbles are like paint balls you can spit at your friends. So it's fun. With traditional tea, when you're done, you're done. I like bubble tea better. It's sweet, and young people prefer to eat sweet things. And the bubbles are chewy. When you eat them, it feels pretty neat. And with bubble tea, you can spit at your friends. So bubble tea is really cool. That's it. If my grandmother were to see me spit bubbles at people, she would probably think it's very dirty. She would probably insist on the traditional way of thinking. But she probably didn't have this kind of fun when she was our age. That's it. I think this is very cool. It reminds me of movies where they mix drinks and stir ice cubes. It feels very hip. I feel very handsome when I stir the bubbles. That's it.

It is more important to find out what you are giving to society than to ask what is the right means of livelihood.

—JIDDHU KRISHNAMURTI
(1895–1986)

FRIEND #1: A lot of people still drink "old folks" tea, hot tea in tiny cups. But I came into tea as a cold beverage. Drinking bubble tea is fun. Every time I come into contact with it I feel like a magician, because it keeps changing. I think the fun with bubble tea is endless.

Appendix A

A Nice Cup of Tea

George Orwell

Evening Standard, 12 January 1946

If you look up 'tea' in the first cookery book that comes to hand you will probably find that it is unmentioned; or at most you will find a few lines of sketchy instructions which give no ruling on several of the most important points.

This is curious, not only because tea is one of the main stays of civilization in this country, as well as in Eire, Australia and New Zealand, but because the best manner of making it is the subject of violent disputes.

When I look through my own recipe for the perfect cup of tea, I find no fewer than eleven outstanding points. On perhaps two of them there would be pretty general agreement, but at least four others are acutely controversial. Here are my own eleven rules, every one of which I regard as golden:

- First of all, one should use Indian or Ceylonese tea. China tea has virtues which are not to be despised nowadays—it is economical, and one can drink it without milk—but there is not much stimulation in it. One does not feel wiser, braver or more optimistic after drinking it. Anyone who has used that comforting phrase 'a nice cup of tea' invariably means Indian tea.

- Secondly, tea should be made in small quantities—that is, in a teapot. Tea out of an urn is always tasteless, while army tea, made in a cauldron, tastes of grease and whitewash. The teapot should be made of china or earthenware. Silver or Britanniaware teapots produce inferior tea and enamel pots are worse; though curiously enough a pewter teapot (a rarity nowadays) is not so bad.

- Thirdly, the pot should be warmed beforehand. This is better done by placing it on the hob than by the usual method of swilling it out with hot water.

- Fourthly, the tea should be strong. For a pot holding a quart, if you are going to fill it nearly to the brim, six heaped teaspoons would be about right. In a time of rationing, this is not an idea that can be realized on every day of the week, but I maintain that one strong cup of tea is better than twenty weak ones. All true tea lovers not only like their tea strong, but like it a little stronger with each year that passes—a fact which is recognized in the extra ration issued to old-age pensioners.

- Fifthly, the tea should be put straight into the pot. No strainers, muslin bags or other devices to imprison the tea. In some countries teapots are fitted with little dangling baskets under the spout to catch the stray leaves, which are supposed to be harmful. Actually one can swallow tea-leaves in considerable quantities without ill effect, and if the tea is not loose in the pot it never infuses properly.

- Sixthly, one should take the teapot to the kettle and not the other way about. The water should be actually boiling at the moment of impact, which means that one should keep it on the flame while one pours. Some people add that one should only use water that has been freshly brought to the boil, but I have never noticed that it makes any difference.

- Seventhly, after making the tea, one should stir it, or better, give the pot a good shake, afterwards allowing the leaves to settle.

- Eighthly, one should drink out of a good breakfast cup—that is, the cylindrical type of cup, not the flat, shallow type. The breakfast cup holds more, and with the other kind one's tea is always half cold before one has well started on it.

- Ninthly, one should pour the cream off the milk before using it for tea. Milk that is too creamy always gives tea a sickly taste.

- Tenthly, one should pour tea into the cup first. This is one of the most controversial points of all; indeed in every family in Britain there are probably two schools of thought on the subject. The milk-first school can bring forward some fairly strong arguments, but I maintain that my own argument is unanswerable. This is that, by putting the tea in first and stirring as one pours, one can exactly regulate the amount of milk whereas one is liable to put in too much milk if one does it the other way round.

- Lastly, tea—unless one is drinking it in the Russian style—should be drunk without sugar. I know very well that I am in a minority here. But still, how can you call yourself a true tealover if you destroy the flavour of your tea by putting sugar in it? It would be equally reasonable to put in pepper or salt. Tea is meant to be bitter, just as beer is meant to be bitter. If you sweeten it, you are no longer tasting the tea, you are merely tasting the sugar; you could make a very similar drink by dissolving sugar in plain hot water.

Some people would answer that they don't like tea in itself, that they only drink it in order to be warmed and stimulated, and they need sugar to take the taste away. To those misguided people I would say: Try drinking tea without sugar for, say, a fortnight and it is very unlikely that you will ever want to ruin your tea by sweetening it again.

These are not the only controversial points to arise in connexion with tea drinking, but they are sufficient to show how subtilized the whole business has become. There is also the mysterious social etiquette surrounding the teapot (why is it considered vulgar to drink out of your saucer, for instance?) and much might be written about the subsidiary uses of tealeaves, such as telling fortunes, predicting the arrival of visitors, feeding rabbits, healing burns and sweeping the carpet. It is worth paying attention to such details as warming the pot and using water that is really boiling, so as to make quite sure of wringing out of one's ration the twenty good, strong cups of that two ounces, properly handled, ought to represent.

Appendix B

Health Benefits

Pamela Yee

Pamela Yee, MD is board certified both in Internal Medicine and Holistic Medicine. She combines her medical training with evidence-based unconventional modalities for the treatment of a variety of conditions including, but not limited to, cancer, digestive distur-bances (IBS), chronic fatigue, fibromyalgia, infertility, rheumatologic and neurodegenerative disorders. Dr. Yee received her education at Barnard College at Columbia University and State University of New York at Stony Brook School of Medicine and trained in Internal Medicine at Santa Barbara Cottage Hospital in California where she also served as Chief Resident. She also completed a prestigious fellow-ship in Integrative Medicine at Beth Israel Medical Center in New York—only one of two such programs in the country. Her diverse train-ing also includes clinical hypnotherapy through the Milton H. Erickson Society for Psychotherapy and Hypnosis and as a medical acupunctur-ist trained through the UCLA School of Medicine. She currently main-tains a private practice in New York.

The apocryphal origin of tea dates back to 2737 BCE, when Emperor Shen Nung serendipitously discovered the joys of the beverage. Legend has it that a breeze blew some leaves into a boiling pot of water from a nearby *Camellia sinensis* tree, yielding a tasty brew. It is said that the Emperor noted its delightful qualities by saying, "It quenches thirst, it lessens the desire for sleep, and it gladdens and cheers the heart."

Throughout time, tea from *Camellia sinensis* has been observed to have a calming effect, despite the presence of methylxanthines (caffeine, theophylline, theobromine), which are known to have stimulating effects. Aside from a myriad of vitamins, minerals, and amino acids found in tea, the major amino acid, L-theanine, may be the reason for tea's calming effects. Interestingly, L-theanine is an amino acid than can only be found in the *Camellia sinensis* plant and in some mushrooms. Studies have indicated that this amino acid can have effects on mood modulation and on decreasing side effects of certain chemotherapy drugs. L-theanine's antianxiety effects are thought to be due to the increase in certain mood-enhancing neurotransmitters in the brain such as serotonin and GABA. In healthy volunteers, taking L-theanine subjectively seemed to induce a sense of tranquility while at baseline compared with alprazolam, a pharmaceutical anxiolytic. However, both agents were not helpful in an experimentally induced anxiety state. Though large clinical trials are lacking in this area, smaller studies suggest L-theanine, at a certain dosage, can affect alpha brain waves. These are the same brain waves that can be induced by meditation, creating a state of deep relaxation.

By trying to ascertain what particular single component may be responsible for tea's calming effects on mood, there is another perspective aside from scientific studies one could consider. Perhaps an examination into the cultural and spiritual aspects of tea in ancient and modern-day Asian countries can give us some insight. In China, tea making and tea drinking is an integral part of ritual and ceremony. Each region has its own tea ritual sometimes involving the commemoration of heroes, the memory of ancestors, or a celebration of marriage. Ritual can be a very strong meditative practice, though most of us think of meditation as sitting quietly in one spot either trying not to think or simply repeating a mantra. Jon Kabat-Zinn, one of the pivotal players bringing the concept of mindfulness into the mainstream medical field in the late 1970s, defines this idea of mindfulness medita-

> *Tea. Earl Grey. Hot. And whoever this "Earl Grey" fellow is, I'd like to have a word with him.*
>
> — JEAN-LUC PICARD, "STAR TREK: THE NEXT GENERATION

tion as a moment-to-moment nonjudgmental awareness. One does not necessarily need to sit to meditate. Meditation can be practiced while participating in all activities of life if done with moment-to-moment awareness. One example of participating in an activity that brings about a sense of peacefulness is the Japanese tea ceremony also known as Cha No Yu. The ceremony is designed to lead one into the present moment by participating in complete awareness during the ritual. Peacefulness can, indeed, be obtained through a bowl of tea.

STRESS AND ILLNESS

The foundation for the prevention of all chronic illness lies in our ability to eat well, exercise, and to manage stress. Stress is a known disruptor of health, affecting the immune and endocrine system and is a strong contributor to many chronic diseases. Stress itself is an enigmatic term, because it can be difficult for some to clearly define it or because one may not necessarily be aware of its presence, registering just as a general sense of unease. It can be thought of as what happens emotionally, mentally, and physiologically as a result of not being in a state of moment-to-moment awareness. It is when one is living either in the past or the future, but not in the present moment.

Most of us know we have stress and most of us are aware that we should have less of it, but in the end, most of us aren't sure really how to manage it. The key is management of stress, not the elimination of it. Scientifically speaking, the term *stress* is synonymous with the idea of fight or flight, a well-known evolutionary concept that has evolved with us for millions of years and it is how we and other animals have learned to survive. Bring your imagination to prehistoric times where you are gathering food in the woods for your family. Your attention is suddenly brought to the presence of a carnivorous animal eyeing you as it is also gathering food for the day for its own family. What happens biochemically in that moment of time is the sudden production of a cascade of hormones and neurotransmitters that are released in your body to enable you to either fight the animal or flee from the area. If you decide to fight, massive amounts of adrenaline are released, blood flows to your muscles for more power and is shunted away from the surface of your skin in preparation for an impending wound so your body will not excessively bleed. If you decide to take flight, your heart is now pumping faster to deliver more blood flow to your legs, your eyesight sharpens so that you can see even farther ahead, and all the secondary functions of your body, digestion, immunity, sexual function, close down temporarily as your body directs all of its energy in keeping you in one piece. Your mind is focused on one thing: staying alive. In the end, you somehow extricate yourself from the danger either by killing the animal or outrunning it. The biochemical cascade has turned off and you resume your usual state of relaxation and equilibrium.

Your reincarnation has brought you to present-day-twenty-first century and you have a family with two small children. By the time you get everyone fed and out of the house, you realize you forgot to feed yourself, so you grab a muffin and coffee to hopefully perk you up. You commute an hour and a half to work by car, bus, or subway either in full-on traffic, or being pushed by large and not-so-pleasant crowds. At work, you may be trying to meet a deadline, placating your boss, or dealing with the numerous variables that make work unharmonious. By the time you get home, you have to feed the family, maybe try and get a workout in, and finally collapse in a complete state of exhaustion. As soon as you lie in bed, however, insomnia ensues because of the constant mind chatter worrying about future events or events that have already occurred.

The cycle repeats the next day and the frantic life most of us lead is similar to the prehistoric cavemen except it continues twenty-four hours a day, seven days a week. There is no return to a state of relaxation and equilibrium, and over time, the consequences of this state of alert, fear, worry, and stress are emotional disorders, infertility, heart disease, possibly cancer, and many more maladies.

TEA FOR CANCER

Tea, in all of its forms—white, green, Oolong, and black—is undergoing intense research sponsored by leading prestigious places such as the National Cancer Institute, the Linus Pauling Institute, and many other research centers across the world for its potential benefit in both the prevention and treatment of cancer. Green tea is the most vigorously studied for its flavonoid content and a specific set of antioxidants known as catechins. These studies span laboratory, animal, and human clinical trials to determine the effectiveness and the mechanisms by which they help prevent or treat cancer. The research extends to many individual cancers, including colon, esophagus, lung, liver, breast, prostate, stomach, ovarian, bladder, leukemia, lymphoma, and skin. I have outlined them to the most relevant and recent evidence available.

PROSTATE CANCER

Much has been written in the way of the protective effects of tea, specifically green tea, for prevention of prostate cancer as shown in laboratory and epidemiological studies. It remains an area of considerable interest, because prostate cancer is the second most commonly diagnosed cancer in men. In China, where there is a lower incidence of prostate cancer, one study showed that green tea consumption was significantly associated with a decreased risk of prostate cancer, and its effects became more pronounced as the frequency, quantity, and duration of the tea drinking increased. Even more astounding was a recent human clinical trial showing that in men with an already diagnosed precancerous prostate condition, consumption of green tea could alter prostate cancer risk within just one year. These men, who already had a high risk for prostate cancer and statistically would have developed it in a year, actually did not when taking green tea extracts! This study has huge implications on populations that are prone to prostate cancer, such as those with a family history, those who are African-American, or those who are elderly.

BREAST CANCER

Because of the lower incidence of breast cancer in Asian countries, it is speculated that various dietary factors particular to those cultures, such as tea consumption, may play a large role in the prevention of breast cancer. As seen with other cancers, epidemiologic studies indicate a positive association between green tea consumption and a lower risk of breast cancer but it should be noted that some have also failed to show a decreased risk. The jury is still out, but theoretically speaking, the effects of tea on breast cancer prevention may have to do with an individual's metabolism and thus are genetically determined. What this means is that one woman's body uses the constituents of tea differently than the next and may or may not benefit from tea, depending on her genetic makeup. Studies, however, continue to be published examining the mechanisms by which tea has an effect on slowing down breast cancer in animals and laboratory research.

COLON CANCER

There are conflicting reports regarding the preventive effects of drinking green and black teas for colon cancer. There is some supporting evidence that flavonoids found in fruit and vegetables are associated with a lower risk of colon cancer, and one positive animal study showed that mice prone to the development of colonic tumors did not develop the amount of tumors expected when exposed to green and white teas. However, large epidemiological studies have failed to show that specific tea consumption is associated with a lower risk of colon cancer.

LUNG CANCER

Although smoking is the largest risk factor in the development of lung cancer, there are many who develop the condition without a history of cigarette smoking. This has been widely publicized with the recent death of Dana Reeves, which brings up the question of why some nonsmoking women seem more susceptible to lung cancer than their nonsmoking male counterparts. Science has not been able to tell us why, but it is speculated that the inhalation of passive smoke may have a more deleterious effect on women than men

The reputed preventive effects of green tea on lung cancer have been shown in laboratory, animal, and epidemiological studies. In a population-based study of women living in Shanghai, consumption of green tea among nonsmoking women was associated with a decreased risk of lung cancer. In Korea, coffee-drinking smokers compared with smokers drinking just two or three cups of green tea daily for six months appeared to have a decreased rate of DNA damage. The protection was even seen in the oral cells of smokers with the equivalent of five cups a day of green tea. Smoking-induced DNA damage appeared to decrease by the inhibition of cell growth and the promotion of apoptosis, or programmed cell death. In animal studies, groups of mice exposed to a carcinogen known to produce lung tumors were given different concentrations of green tea two days after exposure. The highest concentration of green tea extract reduced tumor burden by factors inhibiting a process known as angiogenesis, one of the mechanisms by which a tumor can grow and spread.

Aside from the prevention of lung cancer, a few studies have examined the role of green tea as a possible treatment for lung cancer, showing that tea compounds can alter and inhibit the growth and survival of lung cancer cells in the laboratory. A phase-one trial of green tea extract was completed at Memorial Sloan Kettering in New York, but failed to show that the extract as a single agent at a certain dose had any bearing on participants with advanced lung cancer. This is not surprising given the advanced state of disease and the use of green tea as the only method of treatment. Perhaps studies showing different dosing, an early stage of lung cancer, or a combination with conventional treatment may show different results in the future.

SKIN CANCER/AGING

White, green, and black teas have strong laboratory evidence supporting activity in protecting the skin when used orally and topically. Rapid aging of the skin can be attributed to sun damage from prolonged exposure. Tea's strong antioxidants may have an additional protective effect when given topically with sunscreens by preventing further oxidative damage by the sun. You may have already noticed tea in the new skin products emerging on the market. Skin cancer, a further result of that same oxidative damage from the sun, can be potentially modulated by green tea's effect on inhibiting cancer growth and preventing the new formation of blood vessels that cancers need in order to enlarge and spread. Interestingly, melanoma, one of the deadliest cancers, responds to the antitumor effects of one the most powerful catechins in green tea called

EGCG. EGCG was able to kill cancer cells while having no detrimental effect on normal cells; it may also prevent further spread of melanoma to other organs of the body and, when combined with chemotherapy, may increase survival time, the ultimate goal in cancer treatment.

CARDIOVASCULAR DISEASE

Drinking different types of teas may have a significant effect on your cardiovascular health and may be able to decrease the risk of heart attacks, stroke, and can potentially modulate important risk factors in heart disease such as blood pressure and cholesterol levels. Many of the studies looked at the use of both black and green teas. Some studies also suggest that the more tea you've consumed in the year prior to a heart attack, the less likely you are to die after a heart attack. One large study examined black tea drinkers without any history of heart attacks and showed that those drinking more than three cups a day of black tea had a 43 percent risk reduction in heart attacks and a 70 percent risk reduction in fatal heart attacks. These are impressive numbers that strongly suggest a protective effect of black tea on heart health.

But what about green tea? In one Japanese study looking at patients with proven coronary heart disease, those who drank at least one cup a day of green tea had a 42 percent risk reduction in heart attacks compared with non-green tea drinkers.

For stroke prevention, daily black tea consumption appeared to have a protective effect. Investigators also examined the individual effects of certain risk factors of cardiovascular disease, such as high blood pressure, high cholesterol, endothelial function (the inner lining of the blood vessels), and inflammation, and if tea had a direct effect on those parameters. Consuming at least four ounces of green or Oolong tea daily over the period of a year decreased the risk of developing high blood pressure than those who infrequently drank tea. The effects of tea on cholesterol are also favorable. It appears that it may be a combination of different flavonoids found in green and black teas that can reduce cholesterol with a significant reduction in bad cholesterol or LDL. Endothelial function is another important parameter of cardiovascular health. Atherosclerosis, a condition whereby plaques develop in the blood vessels, can impair the body's ability to relax or vasodilate these vessels effectively. Just a single dose of black tea had a significant effect on improving the endothelium and was able to restore blood flow after a high-fat meal, a known instigator of reduced endothelial function.

There is also growing data supporting the important role inflammation plays in the development of not only heart disease, but many chronic and debilitating conditions such as neurodegenerative diseases (Alzheimer's, multiple sclerosis, Parkinson's disease), cancer, and even obesity. *Time* magazine brought it to our attention when it highlighted the subject a few years ago calling it "The Secret Killer." Growing proof of the role of inflammation has prompted cardiologists and other astute physicians to routinely measure blood levels of inflammation as part of their evaluation. Though there may be many reasons for increased inflammation in the body, including genetics, a poor diet, and possible infectious bacteria and viruses, fighting inflammation begins with reducing consumption of foods that contribute to the problem and replacing them with foods that have natural antiinflammatory properties such as tea. Epidemiologic, laboratory, and animals studies have shown that components in white, black, Oolong and green teas inhibits a variety of pro-inflammatory substances in similar ways that aspirin works. As you can imagine, this has important implications in both treatment of certain diseases and the prevention of many chronic illnesses.

OSTEOPOROSIS AND BONE HEALTH

There is evidence that tea may help to build and strengthen bones and may protect against osteoporosis. Osteoporosis is a genetic and age-related condition that thins the bones leading to bone fractures and a shortened stature; it is generally measured by a Bone Mineral Density test. One study found that habitually drinking at least one cup of tea per day increased hip bone density by 6.2 percent compared with non drinkers. Bone density, however, does not equate to a lower fracture risk, and a prospective study showed that though there was an increase in bone density associated with tea drinking, it did not alter the fracture rate among postmenopausal women.

OBESITY

Alarming trends and statistics in the United States indicate that the prevalence of obesity is growing in epidemic proportions despite the abundance of diet foods and diet books. Sixty-five percent of Americans are either overweight or obese. If we continue this trend, it is estimated that in five years, four out of ten Americans will be obese—at least thirty pounds over a healthy weight. Obesity is a major risk factor in the development of diabetes, heart disease, certain cancers, and a whole host of other diseases. People spend millions on products that promise to help them shed pounds, but clearly, with the increasing obesity trend, something is not working. Most recently, green tea extracts have entered the multi-million dollar market of herbal supplements that promote weight loss. What evidence do we have that supports the use of green tea in weight loss? People in some Asian countries consume tea at the same frequency their American counterparts consume coffee, and obesity rates are comparatively much lower. Though diet and activity level can also account for the differences, many studies are under way to evaluate tea's role as a slimming aid.

Animal studies showed profound weight loss in rats injected with high concentrations of EGCG, the most studied green-tea catechin. The rats had a decrease in appetite and rapidly lost a significant amount of weight. This is an example of a study that is difficult to translate for humans concerning clinical uses for tea as a weight-loss aid, but more and more studies are examining tea's role through clinical trials. One small study found that a standardized supplement of EGCG given to moderately obese subjects for three months showed a modest decrease in body weight (4.6 percent) and waist circumference (4.5 percent). This preparation, marketed as AR25 or Exolise, has been recently linked with a case report of liver toxicity. A slightly more rigorous twelve-week double-blind study comparing daily ingestion of Oolong tea containing a normal amount of catechins compared with an Oolong tea containing a large dose of catechins showed that weight, body mass index, and subcutaneous fat were significantly lower in the catechin-enriched oolong. Like the herbal weight-loss remedies that predated green tea extracts, one such extract called Exolise has been removed from several European markets because of reports of liver toxicity. Exolise is an 80 percent ethanolic dry extract of green tea used in European weight-loss programs mentioned above. What is important to take away from this is that preparations and extracts of nonregulated herbal supplements may have unknown side effects, but this should not cause the consumer any alarm in enjoying the actual teas as beverages.

NEURODEGENERATIVE DISORDERS

DEMENTIA: Tea is being studied for the neuroprotective effects, and these effects have been demonstrated in various animal studies. It is thought that the production of inflammatory molecules called cytokines contribute to the development of a variety of cognitive and neurodegenerative diseases such as dementia and its most common form, Alzheimer's disease. Cytokines may directly act on neuron and glial cells in the central nervous system. The less-common form of dementia, known as vascular dementia, occurs as a result of decreased blood flow to the brain, most commonly due to a stroke. Alzheimer's disease is characterized by the deposition of certain plaques, "neurofibrillary tangles," and the loss of neurons in the brain. There is no known cause for the death of these neurons.

There is great hope that tea can play a role in modulating the risk and progression of dementia in its many forms. One animal study showed that giving EGCG to gerbils after reducing blood flow to one side of the brain (simulating the conditions of a stroke) seemed to have protective effects by the reduction of swelling and the decrease in the amount of infarcted or dead tissue seen. In other animal studies, mice were programmed to develop Alzheimer's. After several months of injections with EGCG, there was a dramatic 54 percent reduction in the plaques associated with the disease, suggesting that EGCG somehow interferes with the production of these beta-amyloid plaques. This has huge implications in both prevention and treatment of Alzheimer's disease. It will not be surprising to see upcoming clinical human trials utilizing components of tea in the disease.

MULTIPLE SCLEROSIS: Accumulating evidence suggests that oxidative stress may play a large role in the development of multiple sclerosis. To combat oxidative stress, the body uses its own antioxidants as well as utilizing them from exogenous sources (what we eat and drink). Several studies examine this phenomena and attempt to ascertain tea's antioxidant effects on multiple sclerosis animal models. EGCG, the main catechin or antioxidant in green and white teas, was found to limit severity of disease in one particular animal study. This devastating disease, striking young adults in their twenties and thirties is in need of better therapies. I expect to see more studies examining the potential of tea and its constituents in the treatment of multiple sclerosis.

Appendix C

Evidenced Based Medicinal Herbs

James A. 'Jim' Duke

James A. Duke (born 1929) is an American botanist. He is known for his numerous publications on botanical medicine, including the CRC Handbook of Medicinal Herbs. *He is notable for developing the Phytochemical and Ethnobotanical Databases at the USDA. He received his doctorate in botany from the University of North Carolina in 1961. He is the author of* Medicinal Plants of China *(1984) and* The Green Pharmacy *(1998).*[1]

TEA (Camellia sinensis (L.) Kuntze) ++

SYN.: Camellia thea Link; Camellia theifera Griff.; Thea assamica; Thea bohea L., Thea chinensis Sims; Thea cochinchinensis Lour.; Thea sinensis L. Thea viridis L. fide DEP

NOTES (GREEN OR BLACK TEA): Most people don't think twice when they hear chocolate called a spice, yet they'll balk if I call tea, coffee, cola, guarana and mate spices. Their main function in many lands is to spice up the world's most important beverage, water. Tea is probably the worlds most widely and frequently used beverage, after water, being a bit lower in caffeine than coffee. And we do think of tea in the same sense: "tea and spice" and "sugar and spice." It's hard for me not to include tea if I include chocolate in my admittedly broad spice concept. If I include those two, where do I draw the line among the others of the world's favorite caffeine-containing adulterants of water?

---

1. entry from Wikipedia

Alcazar at al (2007) say tea is one of the most popular and widely consumed beverages in the world with an estimated per capita worldwide consumption of 40 liters per year. Drying and roasting the leaves without fermentation produces green tea, oolong is further fermented a bit, black tea is fermented even more. White tea is unfermented new shoots with young leaves, sometimes shaded from the sun, perhaps etiolated. Pu-erh tea, from a special Yunnan variety, can be aged for years, involving some oxidation and fermentation. It is interesting how the white tea excels as far as free amines are concerned; the high for asparagine (11,090 ppm) making it 5th highest in the USDA database (http://www.ars-grin.gov/duke), and the second highest for alanine (2,090 ppm). The white tea had more alanine, arginine, asparagine, glutaminic acid, histidine, isoleucine, leucine, phenylalanine, serine, and theanine, than green, black, oolong or pu-erh. Since the white tea is based on partially etiolated shoots, I wonder but what etiolation leads to the freeing up of normally bound amino acids?

Tibetans make a paste or powder like cocoa by churning boiled brick tea with butter and salt. In his marvelous *Cornucopia*, Facciolo says of tea "Both the leaves and brewed tea add flavor to meat and fish dishes." Chinese sometimes boil eggs in leftover tea. Green tea powder or matcha is used in Japanese sweets. Burmese and Thai eat sour fermented leaves as a snack: bai-ming. Leaves are used to smoke duck flowers and made into tempura with the seed oil.

Eg., tea is very important to Buddhists, the priests believing it keeps them awake during meditation, yet relieves them of fatigue. I need to look into a sect I never heard of until I reviewed Hara's book on *Green Tea*. There is a religion known as teasim, an aesthetic cult founded on worship of the beautiful, the love of nature through simplicity of materials. Fond of such principles, I am less fond of the tea ceremonies, but see how both ceremony and tea could contribute to mental well being, of aestheticists, atheists, Buddhists, Catholics, deists, even evangelicals. I fear I am closer to teaism than theism. And editorially I feel if I capitalize one of the isms, I should capitalize all. Note how I speak of Green or Black tea. Even Linnaeus gave two scientific names to them in the second edition of his *Species plantarum*, Thea viridis and Thea bohea. Maybe there's something to Sumpio et al's (2006) title *Green tea, the "Asian paradox," and cardiovascular disease.*

Dr. Robert Bonakdar, MD, opened the Scripps Symposium: 5th Annual Natural Supplements: An Evidence-Based Update, with a lecture "Coffee, Tea or Chocolate". (Jan. 2008). Even after his talk, I was not sure why he put coffee first and chocolate last. I don't know which is healthier or which is unhealthier. But if caffeine can help Americans reduce their obesity with no harmful side effects, I believe these caffeinators, potentially loaded with side effects, do deserve a role among the top food pharmaceuticals. In preparing for a chapter listing the dozen most important food pharmaceuticals, I opted for the chicken way out and referred to them collectively as The Caffeinators, because there is a smouldering battle going on beteen cacao, coffee, tea and me: which one is most important, for which disease? One could easily devote a year to the subject and come out with an interesting book, but probably no definitive answer. There are a lot of good things about caffeine but like all chemicals it has its negatives as well. Here's the message I get from the newspapers in January of 2008: 200 mg caffeine or two cups of coffee a day can double the risk of miscarriage here in America. That's roughly equivalent to four cups of tea. So pregnant Americans might use tea if indeed they must "caffeinate." Though the tea plant contains more caffeine, the tea beverage contains less than the coffee beverage.

SLIM-SIP = a proposed weight-loss beverage?

I've enjoyed capsaicin, chicken essence and green tea, and I suspect the mix has some thermogenic slimming synergy. So here I sit, sipping on an encapsaicinated green tea chicken soup, in my geriatric approach to an afternoon pick-me-up. I won't call it a high afternoon tea, nor an afternoon tea high. The major antiobesity components of tea are catechins, caffeine, and theanine. These vary dramatically in pu-erh, black, oolong, and green teas. The MAM for tea and obesity is pretty impressive. Molecular mechanisms of fatty acid synthase gene suppression may rest with the tea polyphenols (EGCG, theaflavins).

According to Lee and Balick (2006), Americans consume 210 mg caffeine per day. Average Swede consumption is 400 mg/day. When Lee and Balick published, worldwide consumption of caffeine was put at 120,000 tons per year, or one caffeinated beverage per person per day. Over 60 species of plants manufacture caffeine. My USDA phytochemical database ranks tea leaves as the richest potential source of caffeine (to 9.3% ZMB), followed by guarana (to 7.6%), coffee (to 3.2%), yoko (to 2.7%), cola (to 2.5%), genipap (to 2.2%), mate (to 2.0%), and cacao (to 1.3%). Often when one methylxanthine is high, there is a compensatory lower figure for other methylxanthines. Though low in caffeine, chocolate can be very high in theobromine and surprisingly richer in theophylline than tea (which has only 4 ppm). But tea the leaf is my richest source of caffeine, unlike tea the beverage which is only about half as potent in caffeine as coffee the beverage. Figures I see in 2008 suggest about twice as much caffeine in beverage coffee as in beverage tea. Bonakdar cites tea as the 2nd most frequently consumed beverage in the world, after water, whereas Lee and Balick list coffee as second after water.

DOSAGES (GREEN OR BLACK TEA): One of the world's most widely distributed beverage plants: 1–2 tsp. dry lf/cup water 1–3 x/day; 50–100 mg green tea polyphenols; 100–200 mg StX (50% polyphenols); three 333 mg green tea capsules each containing 50 mg polyphenols/day; 240-400 mg polyphenols.

- Ayurvedics consider the leaves orexigenic and stomachic
- Chinese have eaten tea shoots for 2000 years to protect from eye ailments
- Orientals chew the leaves to combat garlic or onion breath
- Peruvians apply moist tea bags to inflamed eyes
- Peruvians take concentrated tea infusion for diarrhea
- Spaniards suggest tea or its extracts or caffeine to massage cellulite
- Yunani consider the herb cerebrotonic, depurative, detergent, diaphoretic, diuretic and resolvent, using for cardialgia, hemicrania, inflammation, ophthalmia, piles

DOWNSIDES (GREEN OR BLACK TEA): Class 2d Fermented black tea not recommended for excess or long term use. In excess can cause GI distress and nervous irritability (due to caffeine). All things in moderation.

Studies of Molinari et al (2006) add to previous reports of acute liver toxicity in individuals consuming green tea extract. Overdoses can cause fluorosis. Brewing time increases the fluoride content, more in black tea than other teas; 0.32–4.54 mg/l, 0.37–0.54mg/l for white tea. For adult and children tea drinkers consuming five cups of black tea per day, the intake of fluoride will be in the range of 8.0–303%, and 12–303% of the Safe and Adequate Daily Intake. Long-term exposure to large amounts of fluoride can lead to skeletal fluorosis. One woman who consumed the equivalent of 65 g/day tea leaves for 5 years exhibited liver dysfunction. Ascites and splenomegaly resolved after tea was discontinued. Pedersen, who does not cover conventional tea, says that peppermint leaf contains much astringent tannin that can damage the liver and intestine with prolonged use. Since the more widely used tea (Camellia sinensis) often contains twice as much tannin as peppermint, this recommendation should be doubly pertinent under tea, or maybe we should call these tannins by the more attractive names "OPCs, polyphenols and pycnogenols" and declare them useful antioxidant good guys instead of hepatotoxic bad guys.

Re: caffeine "Pregnant women should under no circumstances exceed a dosage of 300 mg/day (5 cups of tea spread out over the course of a day) ... Infants whose nursing mothers consume beverages containing caffeine could suffer from sleep disorders." Tea can interfere with uptake of several nutrients including iron and folic acid (negative effect of tea on iron status arises not only from polyphenols iron complexes but also from Al released in tea decoction.

EXTRACTS (GREEN OR BLACK TEA): At the 5th Scripps Symposium in San Diego (2008), Dr. Bonakdar noted that those who drank 5 or more cups a day had fewer deaths from heart diseases, cancer, and all causes. The intake of tea and flavonoids prevented ischemic heart disease. Daily intake of green or oolong tea (120 ml/day or more for a year) significantly lowered hypertension. A proprietary green tea formulation proved clinically to be safe and effective at preventing cold and flu symptoms, and at enhancing T cell function. Since this was an extract, I only scored it 1 in my evidence based scoring. But I would recommend green tea along with other cold preventives when cold and flu are going around. Green tea consumption may be effective to prevent future cardiovascular events in chronic smokers. Compared with

EGCG, ECG more effectively suppresses prostate cancer and epithelial ovarian cancer. Topical tea extracts (5%) were clinically more effective (81.3%) than Framycetin and Soframycin (72.2%) and oral Cephalexin (78.6%) against impetigo contagiosa (smears showed pure Staphylococcus or a mixture of S. aureus and Streptococccus pyrogenes). 1,500 ml daily of oolong tea with about 350 mg caffeine and 1,500 mg polyphenols, [unsweetened or sweetened with Stevia] may be an effective adjunct to oral hypoglycemic agents in type 2 diabetes. Tea's caffeine, epicatechin, epigallocatechin, diphenylamine, and theophylline are all associated with antidiabetic activity. Epigallocatechin even suppresses hepatic glucose production. The major antiobesity components are catechins, caffeine, and theanine. These vary dramatically in pu-erh, black, oolong, and green teas.

Both the polyphenols (OPCs, tannins) and xanthines (caffeine, theobromine, theophylline) have their good and bad side. As a major source of the major COX-2 Inhibitor ([+]-catechin), this might be viewed by enthusiasts as another herbal miracle aspirin. Muroi and Kubo (1993) demonstrated synergies for antibacterial activity in compounds from tea (Camellia sinensis): ". . . green tea extract is effective in the prevention of dental caries because of the antibacterial activity of flavor compounds together with the antiplaque activity of polyphenols . . . Synergism was found in the combination of sesquiterpene hydrocarbons (delta-cadinene and beta-caryophyllene) with indole; their bactericidal activities increased from 128-fold to 256-fold . . . the combination of 25 ug/mL delta-cadinene and 400 ug/mL indole reduced the number of viable {bacterial} cells at any stage of growth." Translation: The mixture ("herbal shotgun") of three bactericidal compounds that might help prevent plaque was more than 100 times more potent than the isolated individual compounds ("magic bullet"). And then there is the natural fluoride. (130-160 ppm if we can believe the herbal PDR). Unique to tea, theanine is a "kind of amino acid constituting more than half of the amino acids in tea," according to Hara. Theanine antagonizes the stimulus of caffeine while "vitalizing . . . brain neurons." I think Hara may be exaggerating when he says "Major catechins in tea are also unique to tea." Many of them occur in other woody species in other plant families. By 2001, more than 600 aroma compounds had been identified in tea. But green tea catechins at 10 ppm have antioxidant capacity comparable to Vit. E (specifically dl-alpha-tocopherol) at 200 ppm. EGC>EGCg>EC>ECg>BHA> Vit. E. EGCg was synergic citric-, malic- and tartaric acids tocopherol. Green tea catechins (specifically Polyphenon 60 with 64% catechins) were 13 times more radical scavenging than pinebark OPC's and 10 times more than grapeseed OPC's.*

CAMELLIA SINENSIS (L.) KUNTZE
"TEA"

ACETIC-ACID
ACETONE LF PAN
ACETOPHENONE
2-ACETYL-FURAN LF PAN
2-ACETYL-PYRIDINE LF PAN
2-ACETYL-PYRROLE
ADENINE LF AYL
ALANINE 20-2,090 LF X17595106
ALKALOIDS 10,000-50,000 LF KC2
ALLANTOIC-ACID PL PAN
ALLANTOIN PL PAN
ALUMINUM 690 LF
AMINO-ACIDS 40,000-53,000 LF PCF-I:102
ALPHA-AMINOBUTYRIC-ACID
2-AMINO-5-(N-ETHYL-CARBOXAMIDO)-PEN-
TANOIC-ACID 120 LF PAN
AMMONIA(NH3) 400 LF PAN
ALPHA-AMYRIN TR OI (SD) PAN
BETA-AMYRIN 76 OI (SD) PAN
ANGELIC-ACID
ANILINE LF PAN
`ANTHOCYANIDIN LF CHA
APIGENIN LF WO3
`APIGENIN-5-O-ALPHA-L-RHAMNOSYL-(1-
>4),6"ACETYL-BETA-D-GLUCOSIDE LF WO3
`APIGENIN-5-O-ALPHA-L-RHAMNOSYL-(1->4)-
BETA-D-GLUCOSIDE LF WO3
2-O-BETA-1-ARABINOPYRANOSIDE-MYOINOSI-
TOL 4,000 LF PAN
2-O-(BETA-1-ARABINOPYRANOSYL)-MYOINOSI-
TOL 4,000 LF PAN
ARGININE 0-2,740 LF X17595106

ASCORBIC-ACID LF
8-C-ASCORBYL-EPIGALLOCATECHIN-3-O-GAL-
LATE 11 LF PAN
ASPARAGIC-ACID
ASPARAGINE 0-11,090 LF X17595106
`ASPARTIC-ACID 30-2,330 LF X17595106
ASSAMICAIN-A 58 LF PAN
ASSAMICAIN-B 77 LF PAN
ASSAMICAIN-C 34 LF PAN
ASTRAGALIN LF PAN
AVENASTEROL SD CCO
BARRIGENOL-R1 LF WO3
BARRINGTOGENOL-C LF
BENZALDEHYDE 2,100-2,300 SH PAN
BENZOIC-ACID LF
BENZOAXAZOLE LF PAN
BENZYL-ACETATE LF
BENZYL-ALCOHOL 1-160 LF PAN X16719518
BENZYL-ALCOHOL 900-1,400 SH PAN
BENZYL-BUTYRATE LF PAN
BENZYL-ETHYL-KETONE LF PAN
`BENZYL(TETRA-O-ACETYL)-BETA-D-GLUCOPY-
RANOSIDE LF WO3
`BISFLAVONOLS LF CHA
BRASSICASTEROL SD PAN
BRASSINOLIDE 0.0000046 LF PAN
BRASSINONE 0.000002 LF PAN
BUTYRALDEHYDE LF
3-N-BUTYL-PYRIDINE LF PAN
4-N-BUTYL-QUINOLINE LF PAN
BUTYRIC-ACID
BUTYROSPERMOL SD PAN

---

* Dr. Duke's chapter was submitted with references, often with more than one reference per word, using the same abbreviations and approaches to his extensive citations as covered in his recent Duke's *Handbook of Medicinal Plants of the Bible* (CRC, 2008) and Duke's *Handbook of Medicinal Plants of Latin America* (CRC, 2008). To shorten this chapterlet, we have deleted all references. Dr. Duke's chapter may soon be updated and published in Duke's *Handbook of Medicinal Plants*, with an explanation of and guide to the references. Stay tuned.

DELTA-CADINENE LF JAF41:1102
CAFFEIC-ACID LF CHA JLS58:142
CAFFEINE 3,810-93,000 LF AYL JBH WO3
CAFFEINE 38,100-47,900 SH PAN
CALCIUM 327-2,456 LF CRC WOI
CAMELLIAGENIN-A LF
CAMELLIAGENIN-D PL JSG
CAMELLIANIN-A LF WO3
CAMELLIANIN-B LF WO3
`CAMELLIASIDE-A SD WO3
`CAMELLIASIDE-B SD WO3
`CAMELLIASIDE-C SD WO3
CAMPESTEROL SD PAN
CAPROALDEHYDE LF
CAPROIC-ACID LF
CAPRYLLIC-ACID
CARBOHYDRATES 536,000-590,000 LF CRC
BETA-CAROTENE 27-84 LF CRC
CARVACROL LF CRC(FNS)
BETA-CARYOPHYLLENE LF JAF41:1102
CASTASTERONE 0.1 LF PAN
`CATECHINS 150,000-200,000 (-300,000) LF CHA
(+)-CATECHIN 85-12,700 LF PAN CHA
`(-)- CATECHIN PL CHA
D,L-CATECHIN 2,664 LF
CATECHIN-(4-ALPHA-8)-EPIGALLOCATECHIN 12-
45 LF PAN
CATECHIN-(4-ALPHA-8)-EPIGALLOCATECHIN-3-
GALLATE LF PAN
CATECHINS 100,000-250,000 LF PHR
CATECHOL-TANNINS 100,000-200,000 LF BIS
CHLOROGENIC-ACID LF JBH PAN
CHLOROPHYLL 5,000 LF PCF-I:102
CHONDRILLASTEROL SD PAN
CINNAMIC-ACID LF CHA
CITRAL-ALPHA LF
CITRONELLOL LF
COPPER 20 LF
N-P-COUMAROYL-GLUTAMIC-ACID LF PAN
P-COUMARYLQUININC-ACID
M-CRESOL LF CRC(FNS)
O-CRESOL LF CRC(FNS)
P-CRESOL LF CRC(FNS)
CRYPTOXANTHIN LF
BETA-CYCLOCITRAL 800-1,000 SH PAN
CYCLOHEXANONES LF LAF
CYSTEINE LF
CYSTINE LF
BETA-DAMASCENONE LF PAN
ALPHA-DAMASCONE LF PAN
BETA-DAMASCONE LF PAN
DAMMARADIENOL 30 OI (SD) PAN
DECA-TRANS-2-CIS-4-DIENE-1-AL LF PAN
DECA-TRANS-2-EN-1-AL LF PAN
DEGALLOYL-THEASINENSIN-F 1-2 LF PAN
`5-DEHYDROQUINIC-ACID LF CHA
`5-DEHYDROQUINIC-ACID LF CHA
5-DEHYDROSHIKIMIC-ACID LF CHA
5-DEHYDROSHIKIMIC-ACID-REDUCTASE

DEHYDROVOMIFOLIOL LF PAN
`DELPHINIDIN LF CHA
`3-DEOXY-D-ARABINO-HIPPURONIC-ACID-7-
PHOSPHATE LF CHA
DEXTRIN LF
1,3-DIACETYL-BENZENE LF PAN
1,4-DIACETYL-BENZENE LF PAN
6,8-DI-C-BETA-D-ARABINOPYRANOSYL-API-
GENIN 20 LF PAN
M-DIGALLIC-ACID LF
DIHYDROACTINIDIOLIDE LF PAN
1',2'-DIHYDRO-1',2'-EPOXY-BETA-IONONE LF PAN
ALPHA-DIHYDROERGOSTEROL LF
DIHYDROKAEMPFEROL SH PAN
1',2'-DIHYDROXY-1',2'-THREO-BETA-IONONE LF
PAN
22,23-DIHYDROSPINASTEROL SD CCO
22,23-DIHYDROSPINASTERONE SD CCO
3,4-DIMETHOXY-ACETOPHENONE LF PAN
2,4-DIMETHYL-ACETOPHENONE LF PAN
N,N-DIMETHYL-BENZYLAMINE LF PAN
3,5-DIMETHYL-2-ETHYL-PYRAZINE LF PAN
3,6-DIMETHYL-2-ETHYL-PYRAZINE LF PAN
2,5-DIMETHYL-4-ETHYL-THIAZOLE LF PAN
3-(S)-7-DIMETHYL-OCTA-1,5-DIEN-3,7-DIOL LF
PAN
3-(S)-7-DIMETHYL-OCTA-1,5,7-TRIEN-3-OL LF PAN
2,4-DIMETHYL-PROPIOPHENONE LF PAN
2,3-DIMETHYL-PYRAZINE LF PAN
2,5-DIMETHYL-PYRAZINE LF PAN
2,6-DIMETHYL-PYRAZINE LF PAN
2,5-DIMETHYL-PYRIDINE LF PAN
2,6-DIMETHYL-PYRIDINE LF PAN
2,4-DIMETHYL-QUINOLINE LF PAN
2,6-DIMETHYL-QUINOLINE LF PAN
4,8-DIMETHYL-QUINOLINE LF PAN
DIMETHYL-SULFIDE LF LAF
2,4-DIMETHYL-THIAZOLE LF PAN
2,5-DIMETHYL-THIAZOLE LF PAN
6,10-DIMETHYL-UNDECAN-2-ONE LF PAN
DIMETHYLXANTHINE LF AYL
DIPHENYLAMINE 130-11,700 LF PAN
N-1-DOTRIACONTANOL LF CCO
EO 30-10,000 LF HHB WOI PAN
(-)-EPIAFZELECHIN 6 LF PAN
EPIAFZELECHIN-3-O-GALLATE 10-11 LF PAN
(-)-EPIAFZELECHIN-3-O-GALLATE 37 LF PAN
EPIAFZELECHIN-3-O-GALLATE-(4-BETA-6)-EPI-
GALLOCATECHIN-3-O-GALLATE 5-6 LF PAN
EPICATECHIN 149-21,250 LF AYL PAN CHA WOI
(+)-EPICATECHIN PL CHA
(-)-EPICATECHIN PL CHA
EPICATECHIN-3,5-DI-O-GALLATE 4 LF PAN
EPICATECHIN-EPIGALLOCATECHIN-(4-BETA-8)-3-
O-GALLOYL 50 LF PAN
EPICATECHIN-GALLATE 5,417-44,000 LF PAN PCF-
I:102 JAF51:2837
(-)-EPICATECHIN-GALLATE 12,400-16,600 LF PAN
CHA

EPICATECHIN-3-O-GALLATE 20 LF PAN
(-)-EPICATECHIN-3-O-GALLATE 3,077-3,188 LF PAN
EPICATECHIN-3-O-GALLATE-(4-BETA-6)EPIGAL-
LOCATECHIN-3-O-GALLATE 6 LF PAN
EPICATECHIN-3-O-GALLATE-(4-BETA-8)EPIGAL-
LOCATECHIN-3-O-GALLATE 4 LF PAN
EPICATECHIN-3-O-P-HYDROXY-BENZOATE 4 LF
PAN
EPICATECHIN-3-O(3-O-METHYL)-GALLATE 71 LF
PAN
(-)-EPICATECHIN-3-O(3-O-METHYL)-GALLATE 962
LF PAN
EPICATECHIN-(4-BETA-8)EPIGALLOCATECHIN-3-
O-GALLATE 21 LF PAN
EPICATECHIN-3-(3-O-METHYLGALLATE) 47 LF PAN
EPICATECHIN-3-O-(4-O-METHYL)-GALLATE 16 LF
PAN
1-EPICATECHIN-GALLATE 8,000-16,650 LF AYL
WOI PCF-I:102
EPICATECHOL SH PAN
EPICATECHOL-GALLATE SH PAN
(-)-EPIGALLOCATECHIN 862-39,000 LF PAN CHA
PCF-I:102
EPIGALLOCATECHIN-3-O-P-CAFFEOATE 2 LF PAN
(-)-EPIGALLOCATECHIN-3-O-CINNAMATE 13 LF
PAN
EPIGALLOCATECHIN-3-O-P-COUMARATE 83 LF PAN
(-)EPIGALLOCATECHIN-3-O-P-COUMARATE 38 LF
PAN
EPIGALLOCATECHIN-(4BETA->8)-EPICATECHIN-3-
O-GALLATE 28 LF JBH PAN
EPIGALLOCATECHIN-3,3'-DI-O-GALLATE 3 LF
PAN
(-)-EPIGALLOCATECHIN-3,3'-DI-O-GALLATE 9 LF
PAN
EPIGALLOCATECHIN-3,5-DI-O-GALLATE 10 LF
PAN
EPIGALLOCATECHIN-3,4'-DI-O-GALLATE 3 LF PAN
(-)-EPIGALLOCATECHIN-3,4'-DI-O-GALLATE 9 LF
PAN
(-)-EPIGALLOCATECHIN-GALLATE 16,600-54,300
LF JBH PAN CHA PCF-I:102 JAF51:2837
EPIGALLOCATECHIN-3-O-GALLATE 224 LF PAN
(-)-EPIGALLOCATECHIN-3-O-GALLATE 7,140-8,718
LF PAN
EPIGALLOCATECHIN-3-O-GALLATE-(4-BETA-6)-
EPICATECHIN-3-O-GALLATE 4 LF PAN
EPIGALLOCATECHIN-3-O-GALLATE-(4-BETA-8)-
EPICATECHIN-3-O-GALLATE 44 LF PAN
EPIGALLOCATECHIN-3-(3-O-METHYL-GALLATE)
197 LF PAN
(-)EPIGALLOCATECHIN-3-O(3-O-METHYL-GAL-
LATE) LF JAF51:510;
(-)-EPIGALLOCATECHIN-3-O-(4-O-
METHYL)GALLATE: LF JAF51:510;
EPIGALLOCATECHOL-GALLATE SH PAN
EPITHEAFLAGALLIN 6-74 LF PAN
EPITHEAFLAGALLIN-3-O-GALLATE 17-46 LF PAN
EPITHEAFLAVIC-ACID LF PAN

EPITHEAFLAVIC-ACID-GALLATE LF PAN
6,7-EPOXY-DIHYDROTHEASPIRANE LF PAN
ERUCIC-ACID SD PAN
ETHER LF
N-ETHYL-ACETAMIDE LF PAN
ETHYL-ACETATE LF PAN
P-ETHYL-ACETOPHENONE LF PAN
ETHYLAMINE LF CHA
N-ETHYL-ANILINE LF PAN
24-ETHYL-BRASSINONE LF PAN
24(S)-ETHYL-BRASSINONE 0.0000005 LF PAN
4-ETHYL-7,11-DIMETHYL-DODECA-TRANS-2-
TRANS-6,10-TRIENE-1-AL LF PAN
2-ETHYL-HEXAN-1-OL LF PAN
4-ETHYLGUAIACOL LF CRC(FNS)
ETHYL-OCTANOATE LF PAN
ETHYL-PHENYLACETATE LF PAN
N-ETHYL-PROPIONAMIDE LF PAN
P-ETHYL-PROPIOPHENONE LF PAN
2-ETHYL-PYRIDINE LF PAN
ETHYL-PYRAZINE LF PAN
EUGENOL FR PAN
EUPHOL SD PAN
TRANS,TRANS-ALPHA-FARNESENE LF PAN
FARNESOL LF PAN
FAT 20,000-165,000 LF AYL CRC
FIBER 87,000-300,000 LF AYL CRC PCF-I:102
FLAVAN-3-OL-GALLATES LF CHA
FLAVAN-3-OLS LF CHA
FLAVONOIDS 1,490 LF JAF49:3106
FLAVONOL-GLYCOSIDES 500-4,400 LF PCF-I:102
FLAVONOLS 400 LF PCF-I:102
FLORATHEASAPONIN-A FL X18176066
FLORATHEASAPONIN-B FL X18176066
FLORATHEASAPONIN-C FL X18176066
FLORATHEASAPONIN-D FL X17409555
FLORATHEASAPONIN-E FL X17409555
FLORATHEASAPONIN-F FL X17409555
FLORATHEASAPONIN-G FL X17409555
FLORATHEASAPONIN-H FL X17409555
FLORATHEASAPONIN-I FL X17409555
FLUORIDE 130-188 (-2000) LF PAN PHR (CHA)
FOLIATHEASAPONIN-I LF X17268104
FOLIATHEASAPONIN-II LF X17268104
FOLIATHEASAPONIN-III LF X17268104
FOLIATHEASAPONIN-IV LF X17268104
FOLIATHEASAPONIN-V LF X17268104
FURFURAL LF WO3
FURFURYL-ALCOHOL LF AYL
GADOLEIC-ACID SD PAN
GALEGINE LF WOI
GALLIC-ACID LF PAN CHA
DL-GALLOCATECHIN 12,876 LF WOI
L-GALLOCATECHIN 25,974 LF WOI
GALLOCATECHIN-(4-ALPHA-8)-EPICATECHIN 8-
37 LF PAN
L-GALLOCATECHIN-GALLATE 79,920 LF CHA WOI
(-)-GALLOCATECHIN-GALLATE 1,880 LF PAN CHA
JAF51:2837

4-GALLOCATECHOL LF BIS PAN
1-O-GALLOYL-4,6-(S)-HEXAHYDROXY-DIPHE-
  NOYL-BETA-D-GLUCOSE 16 LF PAN
1-ALPHA-O-GALLOYL-4,6-(S)-HEXAHYDROXY-
  DIPHENOYL-BETA-D-GLUCOSE 30 LF PAN
GERANIAL LF LAF
TRANS-GERANIC-ACID LF PAN
GERANIOL 2-2,546 LF JAF41:1102 X16719518
GERANIOL 800-1,200 SH LF PAN
GERANIOL-BETA-D-GLUCOPYRANOSIDE SH PAN
`GERANYL-BETA-D-GLUCOSIDE LF WO3
GERMANICOL 25 OI (SD) PAN
BETA-GLUCOGALLIN 28 LF PAN
-GLUCOPYRANOSIDE SD WO3 X16608214
GLUCOTHEASAPONIN SD PAN
`GLUTAMIC-ACID 20-2,860 LF CHA X17595106
GLUTAMINE LF `X17595106
GLYCINE LF
GUAIACOL LF CRC(FNS)
GUM LF
HEPTANAL LF
HEPTAN-1-AL 200-300 LF PAN
HEPTAN-2-ONE SH PAN
HEPTA-2-TRANS-EN-1-AL LF PAN
HEPTA-TRANS-2-TRANSDIEN-4-1-AL 600-1,000 SH
  PAN
N-HEXADECANE LF PAN
HEXAN-1-AL 5,500-10,300 SH PAN
N-HEXANOL LF
ALPHA-BETA-HEXENAL LF
HEX-TRANS-2-CIS-4-DIEN-1-AL LF PAN
HEX-CIS-3-EN-1-AL 370 LF PAN
HEX-TRANS-2-EN-1-AL 1-2,548 LF PAN
HEX-TRANS-2-EN-1-AL 20,900-31,000 SH PAN
HEX-TRANS-2-EN-1-OL 400-600 SH
HEX-CIS-3-EN-1-OL 1-1,500 LF PAN
HEX-CIS-3-EN-1-OL 900-1,300 SH PAN
HEX-CIS-3-EN-1-OL-ACETATE LF PAN
HEX-CIS-3-EN-1-OL-BUTYRATE LF PAN
HEX-CIS-3-EN-1-OL-CAPROATE LF PAN
HEX-CIS-3-EN-1-OL-HEXANOATE 200-300 SH PAN
BETA-GAMMA-HEXENOL LF
HEXENOIC-ACID LF
HEX-TRANS-3-ENYL-ACETATE LF PAN
HEX-TRANS-3-ENYL-BUTYRATE LF PAN
HEX-CIS-3-ENYL-HEX-TRANS-2-ENONATE LF PAN
HEX-TRANS-3-ENYL-HEX-CIS-3-ENONATE LF
  PAN
HEX-CIS-3-ENYL-FORMATE LF PAN
HEX-TRANS-2-ENYL-FORMATE LF PAN
HEX-TRANS-2-ENYL-HEXANOATE LF PAN
HEX-TRANS-3-ENYL-METHYL-BUTYRATE LF PAN
HEX-CIS-3-ENYL-PROPIONATE LF PAN
HEX-TRANS-2-ENYL-PROPIONATE LF PAN
HEX-TRANS-3-ENYL-PROPIONATE LF PAN
HEXOIC-ACID LF
HEXYL-ACETATE LF WO3
N-HEXYL-ALCOHOL LF
HEXYL-BUTYRATE LF PAN

HEXYL-FORMATE LF PAN
HEXYL-PHENYLACETATE LF PAN
HISTIDINE 0-3,110 LF X17595106
6-HYDROXY-DIHYDROTHEASPIRANE LF PAN
2-HYDROXY-2,6,6-TRIMETHYLCYCLOHEXYLI-
  DEN-1-ACETOLACTONE LF
HYPEROSIDE LF PAN
HYPOXANTHINE
INDOLE LF PAN JAF41:1102
INOSITOL LF LF
ALPHA-IONONE 300-500 SH PAN
BETA-IONONE TR-31 LF PAN JAF41:1102 PAN
BETA-IONONE 1,700-2,900 SH PAN
IRON 189-1,500 LF CRC WOI
ISOAMYL-ACETATE LF
ISOAMYL-ALCOHOL LF
ISOBUTYL-ALCOHOL LF
ISOBUTYRALDEHYDE LF
ISOCAPRONIC-ACID
`ISOLEUCINE 30-1,660 LF X17595106
5-ISOPROPYL-HEPTAN-2-ONE LF PAN
ISOQUERCITRIN 1,820 LF PAN PCF-I:102
ISOSCHAFTOSIDE LF BIS
`ISOTHEASAPONIN-B1 LF X16808937
`ISOTHEASAPONIN-B2 LF X16808937
`ISOTHEASAPONIN-B3 LF X16808937
ISOTHEFLAVIN LF
ISOVALERALDEHYDE LF
ISOVITEXIN LF
CIS-JASMONE TR-20 LF PAN JAF41:1102
CIS-JASMONENE LF
JASMONIC-ACID FL PAN
JASMONIC-ACID-METHYL-ESTER LF PAN
KAEMPFERITRIN LF PAN
KAEMPFEROL 120-1,700 LF JLS58:142 PCF-I:102
  JAF49:3106
`KAEMPFEROL-3-O[2-O-BETA-D-GALACTOPYRA-
  NOSYL-6-O-ALPHA-L-RHAMNOPYRANOSYL-
  BETA-D
KAEMPFEROL-3-GALACTOSIDE LF JAF48:1657
`KAEMPFEROL-3-O-BETA-D-GALACTOPYRA-
  NOSYL-(1->2)-BETA-D-GLUCOPYRANOSIDE SD
  WO3
KAEMPFEROL-3-GLUCOSIDE LF JAF48:1657
KAEMPFEROL-3-GLUCOSYL(1->3)-RHAMNO-
  SYL(1->6)GALACTOSIDE 700-1,330 LF JLS58:142
  PCF-I:102
KAEMPFEROL 3-GLUCOSYLRHAMNOSYLGALAC-
  TOSIDE LF JAF48:1657
KAEMPFEROL-3-O-RHAMNODIGLUCOSIDE SH
  PAN
`KAEMPFEROL-3-O-[BETA-D-GLUCOPYRANOSYL-
  (1->3)ALPHA-L-RHAMNOPYRANOSYL-(1-.6-
  BETA-D-GLUCOPYRANOSIDE SH WO3
KAEMPFEROL-3-RHAMNOGLUCOSIDE 4,300 LF
  PAN PCF-I:102
KAEMPFEROL 3-RHAMNOSIDE LF JAF48:1657,
KAEMPFEROL-3-RUTINOSIDE 1,010 LF PCF-I:102
KAEMPFEROL-3-O-BETA-D-RUTINOSIDE LF

KAEMPFEROL-3-TRIGLUCOSIDE LF
`KAEMPFEROL-3-O-[2-O-BETA-D-XYLOPYRA-
NOSYL-6-O-ALPHA-L-RHAMNOPYRANOSYL-
BETA-D-GLUCOPYRANOSIDE SD WO3 X16608214
6-KETO-28-HOMOBRASSINOLIDE LF PAN
6-KETO-28-NORBRASSINOLIDE LF PAN
LAURIC-ACID SD PAN
`LEUCINE 20-1,340 LF X17595106
LEUCINE LF
LIGNIN 65,000 LF PCF-I:102
LINALOL 6-1,984 LF JAF41:1102 X16719518
LINALOL 4,000-10,300 SH PAN
CIS-LINALOLOXIDE 600-1,600 SH PAN
TRANS-LINALOLOXIDE 2-423 LF PAN
TRANS-LINALOLOXIDE 1,500-4,300 SH PAN
CIS-3-HEXENOL LF X16719518
`LINALOOL-OXIDES LF X16719518
LINOLEIC-ACID SD PAN
LOLIOLIDE LF PAN
LUPEOL SD PAN
LUTEIN LF
LYCOPENE LF
LYSINE LF `X17595106
MAGNESIUM 2,200 LF
MALIC-ACID LF
MANGANESE 1,200 LF
MESOINOSITOL
`METHIONINE LF X17595106
4-METHOXY-BENZALDEHYDE LF PAN
3-METHOXY-PYRIDINE LF PAN
METHYLAMINE 50 LF PAN
N-METHYL-ANILINE LF PAN
2-METHYL-BENZALDEHYDE LF PAN
2-METHYL-BENZOTHIAZOLE LF PAN
5-METHYLCYTOSINE LF
METHYL-TRANS-DIHYDROJASMONATE LF PAN
24-METHYLENE-DAMMARENOL TR OI (SD) PAN
METHYLETHYLKETONE LF
2-METHYL-5-ETHYL-PYRIDINE LF PAN
2-METHYL-6-ETHYL-PYRIDINE LF PAN
5-METHYL-2-ETHYL-PYRAZINE LF PAN
6-METHYL-2-ETHYL-PYRAZINE LF PAN
2-METHYL-5-ETHYL-PYRIDINE LF PAN
2-METHYL-6-ETHYL-PYRIDINE LF PAN
2-METHYL-HEPT.2-EN-6-ONE LF PHR
4-METHYL-HEX-5-EN-4-OLIDE LF PAN
24-METHYLLATHOSTEROL SD
METHYL-MERCAPTAN LF
S-METHYL-METHIONINE 70-245 LF PAN
METHYL-OCTANOATE LF PAN
5-METHYL-2-PHENYL-HEX-2-1-AL LF PAN
4-METHYL-2-PHENYL-PENT-2-EN-1-AL LF PAN
METHYL-PYRAZINE LF PAN
2-METHYL-PYRIDINE LF PAN
3-METHYL-PYRIDINE LF PAN
4-METHYL-PYRIDINE LF PAN
2-METHYL-QUINOLINE LF PAN
6-METHYL-QUINOLINE LF PAN
METHYL-SALICYLATE LF `X16719518

5-METHYL-THIAZOLE LF PAN
METHYL-XANTHINES 35,000 LF PCF-I:102
MYRCENE LF PAN
MYRICETIN 200-500 LF PCF-I:102 JAF49:3106
MYRICETIN PL JBH JLS58:142
MYRICETIN-3-GALACTOSIDE LF JBH JAF48:1657
MYRICETIN-3-GLUCOSIDE LF JAF48:1657
MYRICETIN 3-RHAMNOSYLGLUCOSIDE LF
   JAF48:1657
MYRISTIC-ACID SD PAN
NARINGENIN SH PAN
NARINGENIN-FRUCTOSYL-GLUCOSIDE LF PAN
NEOCHLOROGENIC-ACID LF
NERAL LF PAN
NEROL LF
NEROLIDOL LF JAF41:1102 PAN
NEROLIDOL 800-1,200 SH PAN
NIACIN 46-76 LF
NICOTIFLORIN LF PAN
NICOTINIC-ACID LF
NONA-TRANS-2-CIS-4-DIEN-1-AL LF PAN
NONA-TRANS-2-CIS-6-DIEN-1-AL LF PAN
NONA-TRANS-2-TRANS-4-DIEN-1-AL LF PAN
NONA-TRANS-2-EN-1-AL LF PAN
NONAN-1-AL 400-600 SH PAN
NONAN-2-ONE LF PAN
28-NORBRASSINOLIDE LF PAN
CIS-BETA-OCIMENE LF
TRANS-BETA-OCIMENE LF
OCTA-TRANS-2-CIS-4-DIEN-1-AL LF PAN
OCTA-TRANS-2-TRANS-4-DIEN-1-AL LF PAN
1-OCTANOL LF JAF41:1102
OCTA-TRANS-3-CIS-5-DIEN-2-ONE LF PAN
OCT-TRANS-2-ENOIC-ACID SD PAN
OCTAN-2-ONE LF PAN
TRANS-2-OCTENAL LF
N-OCTYL-ALCOHOL LF
OLEIC-ACID SD PAN
OOLONGHOMOBISFLAVAN-A 11 LF PAN
OOLONGHOMOBISFLAVAN-B 7 LF PAN
OOLONGTHEANIN 2 LF PAN
OPC'S
OXALIC-ACID 2,192-10,000 LF PANWBB
3'-OXO-BETA-IONONE LF PAN
PALMITIC-ACID LF
PANTOTHENIC-ACID LF
PECTINS 65,000 LF WOI
PEDUNCULAGIN PL JBH
PENTAN-1-OL 600-1,100 SH PAN
`2,4,4`,6'-PENTAHYDROXY-CHALCONE LF CHA
PENT-CIS-3-EN-1-AL 2,100-2,300 SH PAN
PENT-1-EN-3-OL 2,100-2,300 SH PAN
PENT-CIS-2-EN-1-OL 1,000-1,400 SH PAN
PHENOL LF PAN
PHENOLS 50,000-270,000 LF AYL
PHENYLACETALDEHUDE 15,200-17,800 SH PAN
PHENYLACETIC-ACID 1,850-3,130 LF CHA
`PHENYLALANINE `20-2,180 LF CHA X17595106
2-PHENYLETHANOL LF PAN

2-PHENYLETHYL-ALCOHOL 1,000-1,300 SH PAN
2-PHENYLETHANOL LF X16719518
2-PHENYL-PYRIDINE LF PAN
3-PHENYL-PYRIDINE LF PAN
`PHENYLPYRUVIC-ACID LF CHA
PHOSPHORUS 3,200-4,150 LF CRC
PHYTOENE LF
PHYTOFLUENE LF
PHYTOSTEROLS 2,600-11,400 LF GAS
L-PIPECOLIC-ACID FR PAN
POLYPHENOLS 50,000-390,000 LF AYL BIS KC2
   PCF-I:102
POLYPHENOL-OXIDASE LF CHA
`POLYSACCHARIDES LF CHA
POTASSIUM 17,600
`PROANTHOCYANIDINS LF CHA
PROCYANIDIN-B-2 6 LF PAN
PROCYANIDIN-B-2-3,3'-DI-O-GALLATE 160 LF PAN
PROCYANIDIN-B-2-3'-O-GALLATE 167 LF PAN
PROCYANIDIN-B-3 6-11 LF PAN
PROCYANIDIN-B-4 13-47 LF PAN CHA
PROCYANIDIN-B-4-3'-O-GALLATE 141 LF PAN
PROCYANIDIN-B-5-3,3'-DI-O-GALLATE 141 LF PAN
PROCYANIDIN-C-1 3 LF PAN
PRODELPHINIDIN-A-2-3'-O-GALLATE 4 LF PAN
PRODELPHINIDIN-B-2-3,3'-DI-O-GALLATE 18 LF
   PAN
PRODELPHINIDIN-B-2-3'-O-GALLATE 18-238 LF PAN
PRODELPHINIDIN-B-4 10-57 LF PAN
PRODELPHINIDIN-B-4-3'-O-GALLATE 64 LF PAN
PRODELPHINIDIN-B-5-3,3'-DI-O-GALLATE 30 LF
   PAN
PROLINE LF
PROPIONALDEHYDE LF
PROPIONIC-ACID LF
3-N-PROPYL-QUINOLINE LF PAN
PROTEIN 150,000-283,000 LF CRC PCF-I:102
`PROTOCATECHUICACID LF CHA
PSEUDOTARAXASTEROL SD PAN
PYRIDINE LF PAN
PYRROL-2-METHYLKETONE
QUERCETIN 1,000-10,000 LF PAM JAF49:3106
QUERCETIN PL JLS58:142
QUERCETIN-FRUCTOSYL-GLUCOSIDE LF PAN
QUERCETIN 3-GALACTOSIDE LF JAF48:1657
QUERCETIN-3-O-BETA-D-GALACTOSIDE LF PAN
QUERCETIN-3-O-BETA-D-GLUCOSIDE LF PAN
QUERCETIN 3-GLUCOSIDE LF JAF48:1657
QUERCETIN 3-GLUCOSYLRHAMNOSYLGALAC-
   TOSIDE LF JAF48:1657
QUERCETIN-3-GLUCOSYL(1->3)-RHAMNOSYL(1-
   >6)GALACTOSIDE 760-1,000 LF PCF-I:102
QUERCETIN-3-O-RHAMNODIGLUCOSIDE 3,170
   LF PANPCF-I:102
QUERCETIN 3-GLUCOSYLRHAMNOSYLGLUCO-
   SIDE, LF JAF48:1657
QUERCETIN 3-RHAMNOSIDE LF JAF48:1657
QUERCETIN 3-RUTINOSIDE LF JAF48:1657
QUERCETIN-TRIGLUCOSIDE LF

QUERCIMERITRIN LF PAN
QUERCITRIN LF AYL
QUINIC-ACID LF PAN
QUINOLINE
O-QUINONE LF WOI
RIBOFLAVIN 8-12 LF CRC
RUTIN 1,200-1,580 LF AYL PANPCF-I:102
SAFRANAL LF PAN
SAFROLE LF PAN
SALICYLATES 5-65 LF JAD85:9501
SALICYLALDEHYDE LF
SALICYLIC-ACID LF
`SCOPOLETIN LF WO3
SERINE `20-3,250 LF X17595106
BETA-SESQUIPHELLANDRENE LF PAN
`SHIKIMIC-ACID LF CHA
SILICA 240 LF
BETA-SITOSTEROL 2,130-2,230 LF GAS
BETA-SITOSTEROL SD PAN
SODIUM 300-500 LF
ALPHA-SPINASTEROL LF CCO
ALPHA-SPINASTEROL-GENTIOBIOSIDE LF
SPINASTERONE LF CCO
STARCH 5,000 LF WOI
STEARIC-ACID SD PAN
DELTA-7-STIGMASTENOL LF CCO
STRICTININ 130 LF PAN
SULFUR 880 LF WOI
TANNIC-ACID 95,000-210,000 LF KC2 CHA
TANNINS 33,800-270,000 LF AYL PAN
TARAXEROL 20 OI (SD) MAP
TEASTERONE LF PAN
ALPHA-TERPINEOL 700-1,000 SH PAN
ALPHA-TERPINEOL LF JAF41:1102
4-TERPINEOL LF PAN
`2,4,4`,6-TETRAHYDROXY-CHALCONE-2-O-GLU-
   COSIDE LF CHA
2,6,10,14-TETRAMETHYL-PENTADECANE LF PAN
TETRAMETHYLPYRAZINE LF PAN
TETRAMETHYLTRIOXYPURINE LF
THEAFLAGALLIN 3-4 LF PAN
THEAFLAVIN 5-19 LF PAN CHA
THEAFLAVINS 1,800-`20,000 SH PANPCF-I:102
THEAFLAVIN-ACID LF
THEAFLAVIN-DIGALLATE 700-2,500 LF PAN CHA
   PCF-I:102
THEAFLAVIN-3-3'-DI-O-GALLATE 18-214 LF PAN
THEAFLAVIN-GALLATE-A 1,700-8,300 LF PCF-I:102
THEAFLAVIN-GALLATE-B 2,400-2,500 LF PCF-I:102
THEAFLAVIN-3-GALLATE LF
THEAFLAVIN-3-O-GALLATE 6-17 LF PAN
`THEAFLAVIN-3'-O-GALLATE 18-41LF PAN
`THEAFLAVIN-MONOGALLATE-A LF CHA
`THEAFLAVIN-MONOGALLATE-B LF CHA
THEANINE 5,777 CY PAN CHA
THEANINE `70-33,370 LF CHA `X17595106
THEANINE 4,560 SD PAN
THEANINE 63 SH PAN
THEANINE 35 ST PAN

THEAFLAVIN-MONOGALLATE LF PAN
THEAFLAVONIN LF CHA
THEAGALLININ LF CHA
THEARUBIGENS 17,000-`200,000 LF WO3 CHA
  PCF-I:102
THEARUBIGIN LF PAN
THEARUBIGIN 135,600-157,400 SH PAN
THEASAPONIN LF PAN
THEASAPONIN SD JBH
THEASAPONIN-A(1) SD X16499314
THEASAPONIN-A(2) SD X16499314
THEASAPONIN-A(3) SD X16499314
THEASAPONIN-A(4) SD X17202702
THEASAPONIN-A(5) SD X17202702
THEASAPONIN-C(1) SD X17202702
THEASAPONIN-E(8) SD X17202702
THEASAPONIN-E(9) SD X17202702
THEASAPONIN-F(1) SD X16499314
THEASAPONIN-F(2) SD X16499314
THEASAPONIN-F(3) SD X16499314
THEASAPONIN-G(1) SD X17202702
THEASAPONIN-H(1) SD X17202702
THEASINENSINS LF CHA
THEASINENSIN-A 3-48,718 LF JBH PAN CHA
THEASINENSIN-B 10-154 LF PAN CHA
THEASINENSIN-C 70 LF PAN CHA
THEASINENSIN-D 18 LF PAN CHA
THEASINENSIN-E 14 LF PAN CHA
THEASINENSIN-F 20 LF PAN CHA
THEASINENSIN-G 8 LF PAN CHA
THEASPIRANE LF PAN
THEASPIRONE LF PAN
THEIFERIN-A LF
THEIFERIN-B LF
THEOBROMINE 500-2,000 LF HHB JBH PANPHR
THEOGALLIN 6 LF PANJBH
THEOPHYLLINE 2-400 LF HHB JBH PHRR
THEOPHYLLINE SD PAN

THIAMIN 1-4 LF CRC
THREONINE `0-1,250 LF X17595106
THYMOL LF CRC(FNS)
TIRUCALLA-7,24-DIENOL SD
5-ALPHA-TIRUCALLA-7,24-DIEN-3-BETA-OL 12 OI
  (SD) PAN
TIRUCALLOL TR SD PAN
ALPHA-TOCOPHEROL 183-211 LF JAF49:3101
O-TOLUIDENE LF PAN
N-1-TRIACONTANOL LF CCO
TRICETIN SH PAN
TRICETINIDIN LF PAN
1,4,6-TRI-O-GALLOYL-GLUCOSE 5-10 LF PAN
1,2,4-TRIHYDROXY-BENZENE LF PAN
1,2,5-TRIHYDROXY-BENZENE LF PAN
1,3,4-TRIHYDROXY-BENZENE LF PAN
1,3,5-TRIHYDROXY-BENZENE LF PAN
`3,4,5-TRIHYDROXYCINNAMIC-ACID LF CHA
2,6,6-TRIMETHYL-CYCLOHEX-2-EN-1,4-DIONE LF
  PAN
2,6,6-TRIMETHYL-CYCLOHEX-2-EN-1-ONE LF PAN
TRIMETHYLPYRAZINE LF PAN
2,4,5-TRIMETHYL-THIAZOLE LF PAN
TYPHASTEROL LF PAN
TYROSINE 10-1,450 LF X17595106
UNDECA-TRANS-2-EN-1-AL LF PAN
UREA PL PAN
VALERIC-ACID LF
VALINE LF `X17595106
VICENIN-3 LF BIS
4-VINYL-PYRIDINE LF PAN
VITEXIN LF PAN
WATER 40,000-120,000 LF CRC
VIOLAXANTHIN LF
XANTHINE LF AYL KC2
O-XYLENOL LF CRC(FNS)
ZEAXANTHIN LF
ZINC 30 LF

BIOLOGICAL ACTIVITIES AND CHEMICALS FOR CARDIOPATHY/HEART PROBLEMS IN: CAMELLIA SINENSIS (L.) KUNTZE (THEACEAE) "TEA"

ACE-Inhibitor: (+)-catechin ; (+)-gallocatechin ; (-)-epi-catechin ; (-)-epicatechin-3-o-gallate ; (-)-epigallocate-chin ; (-)-epigallocatechin-3-o-gallate ; alpha-terpineol ; astragalin ; gallic-acid ; isoquercitrin ; isovitexin ; myrcene ; procyanidin-b-2-3,3'-di-o-gallate ; pro-cyanidin-b-3 ; procyanidin-b-5-3,3'-di-o-gallate ; quercitrin ; vitexin ; zinc
Antiaggregant: (+)-catechin ; (-)-epicatechin ; (-)-epigal-locatechin-gallate ; apigenin ; ascorbic-acid ; caffeic-acid ; epicatechin ; eugenol ; kaempferol ; ligustrazine ; magnesium ; menthol ; naringenin ; quercetin ; rutin ; safrole ; salicylates ; tetramethyl-pyrazine ; thymol

Antianginal: magnesium ; niacin ; tetramethyl-pyrazine
Antiarrhythmic: apigenin ; calcium ; magnesium ; potas-sium ; quercitrin ; vitexin
Antiarteriosclerotic: histidine ; linoleic-acid
Antiatherogenic: caffeic-acid ; opcs ; rutin
Antiatherosclerotic: ascorbic-acid ; calcium ; carvacrol ; chlorogenic-acid ; lutein ; magnesium ; malic-acid ; quercetin ; rutin ; thymol
Anticardiospasmic: thiamin
Anticoagulant: (+)-catechin
Anticoronary: beta-carotene ; lignin ; linoleic-acid ; magnesium ; zinc

Antiedemic: alpha-amyrin ; ascorbic-acid ; beta-amyrin ;
beta-damascenone ; beta-sitosterol ; caffeic-acid ;
eugenol ; linalool ; lupeol ; opcs ; quercitrin ; rutin ;
umbelliferone
Antihemorrhagic: ascorbic-acid ; quercitrin
Antihemorrhoidal: rutin ; tannic-acid
Antihypercholesterolemic: caffeic-acid ; chlorogenic-acid
; pantothenic-acid
Antihypertensive: arginine ; ascorbic-acid ; calcium ;
fiber ; magnesium ; polyphenols ; potassium ;
quercetin ; rutin ; tannin ; tetramethyl-pyrazine
Antiinflammatory: (+)-catechin ; (-)-epicatechin ; allantoin ; alpha-amyrin ; alpha-pinene ; alpha-spinasterol
; alpha-terpineol ; apigenin ;ascorbic-acid ; beta-
amyrin ; beta-damascenone ; beta-sitosterol ; caffeic-
acid ; carvacrol ; chlorogenic-acid ; cinnamic-acid ;
copper ; epicatechin ; eugenol ; gallic-acid ; hyperoside ; isoquercitrin ; kaempferitrin ; kaempferol ;
limonene ; linalool ; linoleic-acid ; lupeol ; magnesium ; menthol ; methyl-salicylate ; myricetin ; naringenin ; neo-chlorogenic-acid ; oleic-acid ; opcs ;
quercetin ; quercetin-3-o-beta-d-glucoside ; quercitrin
; rutin ; salicylates ; salicylic-acid ; stigmasterol ; thymol ; umbelliferone ; vitexin
Antiischemic: (-)-epigallocatechin-3-o-gallate ; epigallo-
catechin-3-o-gallate ; hyperoside ; tetramethyl-
pyrazine
Antioxidant: (+)-catechin ; (+)-gallocatechin ; (-)-epicat-
echin ; (-)-epicatechin-3-o-gallate ; (-)-epigallocatechin
; (-)-epigallocatechin-3-o-gallate ; (-)-epigallocatechin-
gallate ; 4-terpineol ; alanine ; allantoin ; apigenin ;
ascorbic-acid ; beta-carotene ; beta-sitosterol ; caffeic-
acid ; caffeine ; campesterol ; carvacrol ; chlorogenic-
acid ; chlorophyll ; cysteine ; epicatechin ;
epicatechin-3-o-gallate ; epicatechin-gallate ; epigallocatechin ; epigallocatechin-3-o-gallate ; eugenol ; gallic-acid ; histidine ; hyperoside ; isoquercitrin ;
isovitexin ; kaempferol ; lauric-acid ; lignin ; lupeol ;
lutein ; lycopene ; manganese ; methyl-salicylate ;
myrcene ; myricetin ; myristic-acid ; naringenin ; opcs
; palmitic-acid ; pedunculagin ; polyphenols ; pro-
cyanidin-b-2-3'-o-gallate ; procyanidin-b-2-3,3'-di-o-
gallate ; procyanidin-b-5-3,3'-di-o-gallate ; quercetin ;
quercitrin ; riboflavin ; rutin ; salicylic-acid ; stigmasterol ; tannic-acid ; tannin ; theaflavin ; thymol ;
vitexin
Antiplatelet: rutin
Antistress: apigenin ; ascorbic-acid ; beta-carotene ; calcium ; magnesium
Antistroke: magnesium ; potassium
Antithrombic: quercetin
Arteriodilator: tetramethyl-pyrazine ; theobromine ;
theophylline

Beta-Adrenergic Receptor Blocker: (+)-catechin ; (+)-gal-
locatechin ; (-)-epicatechin ; (-)-epigallocatechin ; (-)-
epigallocatechin-3-o-gallate ; ascorbic-acid ;
epigallocatechin ; pedunculagin ; procyanidin-b-2 ;
procyanidin-b-3 ; procyanidin-b-4
COX-2-Inhibitor: (+)-catechin ; apigenin ; beta-carotene
; caffeic-acid ; eugenol ; kaempferol ; lauric-acid ;
quercetin ; salicylic-acid
Calcium-Antagonist: ascorbic-acid ; caffeic-acid ;
eugenol ; hyperoside ; ligustrazine ; magnesium ;
menthol ; safrole ; tetramethyl-pyrazine
Cardioprotective: ascorbic-acid ; chlorogenic-acid ; copper ; fiber ; magnesium ; niacin ; potassium
Cardiotonic: (+)-catechin ; (-)-epicatechin ; benzyl-
acetate ; caffeine ; epicatechin ; guaiacol ; quercitrin ;
tetramethyl-pyrazine ; theobromine
Cyclooxygenase-Inhibitor: (+)-catechin ; (-)-epiafz-
elechin ; (-)-epigallocatechin-gallate ; apigenin ; carvacrol ; gallic-acid ; kaempferol ; polyphenols ;
quercetin ; salicylic-acid ; tannin ; thymol
Diuretic: 4-terpineol ; adenine ; apigenin ; arginine ;
ascorbic-acid ; asparagine ; caffeic-acid ; caffeine ;
calcium ; chlorogenic-acid ; fiber ; hyperoside ; isoquercitrin ; kaempferol ; kaempferol-3-rhamnogluco-
side ; magnesium ; myricetin ; potassium ; quercitrin ;
tetramethyl-pyrazine ; theobromine ; theophylline
Estrogenic: apigenin ; beta-sitosterol ; kaempferol ;
naringenin ; quercetin ; stigmasterol
Hypocholesterolemic: (-)-epicatechin ; (-)-epigallocate-
chin-gallate ; ascorbic-acid ; beta-ionone ; beta-sitosterol ; calcium ; campesterol ; copper ; epicatechin ;
fiber ; lignin ; linoleic-acid ; lycopene ; magnesium ; .
niacin ; nicotinic-acid ; oleic-acid ; phytosterols ; rutin
; stearic-acid ; stigmasterol ; theanine
Hypotensive: apigenin ; ascorbic-acid ; astragalin ; benzyl-acetate ; calcium ; fiber ; hyperoside ; isoquercitrin ; kaempferol ; lupeol ;magnesium ;
potassium ; quercitrin ; rutin ; tetramethyl-pyrazine ;
valeric-acid ; vitexin ; zinc
Myocardiotonic: adenine ; theobromine ; theophylline
Sedative: alpha-pinene ; alpha-terpineol ; angelic-acid ;
apigenin ; benzaldehyde ; benzyl-alcohol ; caffeic-acid
; citronellol ; eugenol ; farnesol ; geraniol ; limonene ;
linalool ; nerol ; niacin ; stigmasterol ; thymol ;
valeric-acid
Vasodilator: (-)-epicatechin ; adenine ; apigenin ; arginine ; ascorbic-acid ; caffeine ; calcium ; eugenol ;
fiber ; kaempferol ; magnesium ; myricetin ; niacin ;
potassium ; quercetin ; rutin ; tetramethyl-pyrazine ;
theobromine ; theophylline
Phytochemical Database, USDA - ARS - NGRL,
Beltsville Agricultural Research Center, Beltsville,
Maryland

A Suggested Book List
for Tea Lovers

Alexander, Meena, ed. *Indian Love Poems*. New York: Everyman's
   Library Pocket Poets, Alfred A. Knopf, 2005.

Allison, Robert J. *The Boston Tea Party*. Beverly, MA.:
   Commonwealth Editions, 2007.

Avery, Elllis. *The Teahouse Fire*. London: Riverhead Books, 2006.

Bard, Sharon and Birgit Nielsen. *Steeped in the World of Tea*.
   Northampton, MA.: Interlink Books, 2005.

Blofeld, John. *The Chinese Art of Tea*. London: George Allen &
   Unwin, 1985.

———, trans. and ed. *I Ching: The Book of Change*. New York:
   Penquin Books, 1965.

Boldt, Laurence G. *Zen Soup: Tasty Morsels of Wisdom from Great
   Minds East & West*. New York: Penquin Books, 1997.

Brooks, Svevo. *The Art of Good Living*.

Carroll, Michael. *From a Persian Tea House: Travels in Old Iran*.
   London & New York: Taurus Parks Paperbacks, 1960.

Chamney, Monfort. *The Story of the Tea Leaf*. Calcutta: The New
   India Press, NA.

Chaves, Jonathan, trans. and intro. *Pilgrim of the Clouds: Poems and
   Essays by Yuan Hung-Tao and His Brothers*. Buffalo, N.Y.: White
   Pine Press, 2005.

Cheung, Theresa. *Tea Bliss: Infuse Your Life with Health, Wisdom,
   and Contentment*. San Francisco: Conari Press, 2007.

Chow, Kit and Ione Kramer. *All the Tea in China*. San Francisco: China Books and Periodicals, Inc., 1990.

Chuen, Lam Kan. *The Way of Tea*. Hauppauge, NY: Barron's Educational Series, 1968.

Chuen, Master Lam Kam, with Lam Kai Sin and Lam Tin Yu. *The Way of Tea: The Sublime Art of Oriental Tea Drinking*. Hauppauge, NY: Barron's Educational Series, 2002.

Cleary, Thomas, trans. *The Essential Confucius: The Heart of Confucius' Teachings in Authentic I Ching Order*. San Francisco: Harper San Francisco, 1992.

Conder, Josiah. *Landscaping Gardening in Japan*. Tokyo: Kodansha International, 2002.

Confucius, trans. Thomas Cleary. *The Essential Confucius: The Heart of Confucius' Teachings in Authentic I Ching Order*. San Francisco: Harper SanFrancisco, 1992.

Cousineau, Phil. *The Art of Pilgrimage: A Seeker's Guide to Making Travel Sacred*. Berkeley, CA.: Conari Press, 1998.

Dexter, Pearl. *Tea Poetry*. Scotland, CT.: Olde English Tea Company, 2003.

Dougill, John. *Kyoto: Cultural History*. New York: Oxford Press, 2006.

Dusinberre, Deke. *The Book of Tea (originally published as Le Livre du Thé)*. Paris: Éditions Flamarion, 2005.

Exley, Helen. *Time for Tea*. XX, UK: Exley Publications, 1999.

Faulkner, Rupert, ed. *Tea: East & West*. New York: Harry N. Abrams, 2003.

Forrest, Denys S.

Fortune, Robert.

Friedman, Nancy. *The Book of Tea and Herbs*. Santa Rosa, CA: The Cole Group, 1993.

Gardella, Robert. *Harvesting Mountains: Fujian and the China Tea Trade, 1757–1937*. Berkeley, CA: University of California Press, 1994.

Gautier, Lydia with Jean-Francois Mallet (photographer). *Tea: Aromas and Flavors Around the World*. San Francisco: Chronicle

Books, 2007. Originally published as Le Thé: Aromes & Saveurs du Monde. Geneva: Aubanel and Éditions Minerva, 2005.

Gilbert, Jack. *The Paris Review Interviews,* vol 1. Philip Gourevitch, intro. London: Canongate, 2007.

———. *Refusing Heaven.* New York: Random House, 2004.

Guth, Christine M.C.E. *Art, Tea, and Industry.* Princeton, NJ: Princeton University Press, 1993.

Hammitzsch, Horst. *Zen in the Art of Tea Ceremony.* New York: St. Martin's Press, 1980.

Hohenegger, Beatrice. *Liquid Jade: The Story of Tea from East to West.* New York: Saint Martin's Press, 2006.

Hudson, Charles M. *Black Drink: A Native American Tea.* Athens, GA: The University of Georgia Press, 1979.

Huxley, Aldous. *The Perennial Philosophy.* New York: Harper & Row, 1944.

Huxley, Gervais. *Talking of Tea: Here is the Whole Fascinating Story of Tea.* Ivyland, PA: John Wagner & Sons, 1956.

Israel, Andrea. *Taking Tea.* New York: Grove Press, 2000.

Jacobs, Els M. *In Pursuit of Pepper and Tea: The Story of the Dutch East India Company.* Amsterdam: Netherlands Maritime Museum, 1991.

Kerouac, Jack. *The Book of Haikus.* New York: Penquin Books, 2003.

Kinchin, Perilla. *Taking Tea with Macintosh.* Rohnert Park, CA.: Pomegranate Communications, Inc., 1998.

King, Bruce. *Modern Indian Poetry in English.* Revised edition. New Delhi, India: Oxford University Press, 2004.

Knight, Elizabeth. *Celtic Teas with Friends: Traditions from Cornwall, Ireland, Scotland & Wales.* Perryville, KY.: Benjamin Press: 2008.

Maitland, Derek. *5000 Years of Tea: A Pictorial Companion.* New York: Gallery Books, 1982.

Martin, Laura C. *Tea: The Drink that Changed the World.* Rutland, VT: Tuttle, 2007.

Mascaro, Juan, ed. and trans. *The Dhammapada: the Buddha's Teachings.* New York: Penquin Classics, 1973.

McCann, Ruthanne Lum. *Chinese Proverbs*. San Francisco: Chronicle Books, 1991.

Merton, Thomas. *The Way of Chuang Tzu*. New York: New Directions, 1965.

Mortenson, Gregg with David Oliver Relin. *Three Cups of Tea: One Man's Mission to Fight Terrorism and Build Nations . . . One School at a Time*. New York: Viking Books, 2007.

Moxham, Roy. *Tea: Addiction, Exploitation and Empire*. New York: Carroll & Graf, 2003.

Mrabet, Mohammed. *M'Hashish*. Taped and translated from the Moghrebi by Paul Bowles. San Francisco: City Lights Books, 1969.

Murphy, Frank H. *The Spirit of Tea*. Santa Fe: Sherman Asher, 2008.

Okakura, Kakuzo. *The Book of Tea*. Rutland, VT. and Tokyo: Charles E. Tuttle Company, 1956.

Oz, Amos. *How to Cure a Fanatic*. Princeton, N. J.: Princeton University Press, 2006.

Paul, Jaiwant E. *The Story of Tea*. New Delhi: The Lotus Collection, Roli Books, 2001.

Paul, Varley and Isao Kumakura, eds. *History of Chanoy: Essays on Tea in Japan*. Honolulu: University of Hawai, 1980.

Perry, Sarah. *The New Book*. San Francisco: Chronicle Books, 2001.

Pratt, James Norwood. *New Tea Lover's Treasury: The Classic True Story of Tea*. Expanded and updated. San Francisco: Tea Society Press, 1999.

———. *Tea Dictionary: Preliminary Edition*. Los Angeles and San Francisco: Devan Shah and Ravi Sutodiya for the Tea Society Publishers, 2005.

Pruess, Joanna. *Eat Tea*. Guildford, CT: Lyons Press, 2001.

Pussel, Ryofu. *Tea and Buddhism*. Xlibris, 2005.

Raji, Noufissa Kessar. *L'Art du Thé au Moroc*. Paris: ACR Édition Internationale, 2003.

Rawson, Philip and Laszlo Legeza. *Tao: The Chinese Philosophy of Time and Change*. New York: Thames and Hudson, 1973.

Rep, Paul. Compiled by. *Zen Flesh, Zen Bones: A Collection of Zen & Pre-Zen Writings*. New York: Anchor Books, 1989.

Repplier, Agnes. *To Think of Tea!* London: Jonathan Cape, 1933.

Richardson, Bruce. *The Great Tea Rooms of America.* Perryville, KY: Benjamin Press, 2002.

Rubin, Ron and Stuart Avery Gold. *Tea Chings: The Tea and Herb Companion: Appreciating the Varietals and Virtues of Fine Tea and Herbs.* New York: New Market Press, 2002.

Sauer, Jennifer. Foreword by James Norwood Pratt. *The Way to Tea: Your Adventure Guide to San Francisco Tea Culture.* San Rafael, CA: Earth Aware Editions, 2007.

Schapira, Joel, David and Karl. *The Book of Coffee & Tea: A Guide to the Appreciation of Fine Coffees, Teas, and Herbal Beverages.* New York: St. Martin's Press, 1975.

Schivelbusch, Wolfgang. *Tastes of Paradise: A Social History of Spices, Stimulants, and Intoxicants.* David Jacobson, trans. New York: Random House, 1992.

Scott, J. M. *The Great Tea Adventure.* New York: E. P. Dutton, 1965.

Sen, Shoshitsu. *Tea Life, Tea Mind.* Tokyo and New York: Weatherhill, 1979.

Soshitsu, Sen. *The Spirit of Tea.* Kyoto: Tankosha, 2002.

Standage, Tom. *A History of the World in 6 Glasses.* New York: Atlantic Books, 2007.

Suzuki, D. T. *Zen and Japanese Culture.* Princeton, NJ: Princeton University Press, 1959.

Symington, John. *In a Bengal Jungle.* Chapel Hill, NC: University of North Carolina Press, 1935.

Tagore, Rabindranath. *Fireflies.* New York: Collier Books, 1975.

Theodore, William and Donald Keene, eds. *Sources of Japanese Tradition: Earliest Times to 1600.* George Tanabe and Paul Varley, eds. New York: Columbia University Press, ND, sec.ed., vol 1.

Tompkins, Peter and Christopher Bird. *The Secret Life of Plants.* New York: Harper & Row, 1973.

Tong, Liu. *Chinese Tea.* Trans. by Yue Liwen. Cultural Chinese Series. Taipei: Taiwan: Chinese International Press, 2005.

Twining, Stephen H. *The House of Twining: 1706–1956.* London: R. Twining, 1956.

Ukers, William H. *All About Tea, vols. 1 and 2*. Rochester, NJ: Olde Ridge Bookbindery and Hyperion Press Reprint, 1999.

Vitell, Bettina. *The World in a Bowl of Tea: Healthy, Seasonal Foods Inspired by the Japanese Way of Tea*. New York: Harper Collins, 1997.

Waddell, Norman. English translation and biography by. *The Old Tea Seller: Life and Zen Poetry in 18th Century Kyoto Baiso*. Berkeley, CA.: Counterpoint Press, 2008.

Waley, Arthur. Translated from the Chinese. *The Book of Songs: The Ancient Chinese Classic of Poetry*. New York: Grove Press, 1937.

———. *Translations from the Chinese*. New York: Alfred A. Knopf, 1919.

Wang, Ling. *Tea & Chinese Culture*. South San Francisco: Long River Press, 2005.

Woodruff, Paul. *Reverence: A Forgotten Virtue*. Oxford: Oxford University Press, 2001.

Ying-Chang, Li. *Lao-Tzu's Treatise on the Response of the Tao*. Translated with an Introduction by Eva Wong. New York: Harper Collins, 1992.

Yu Lu, trans. and ed. Francis Rose Carpenter, intro. *The Classic of Tea*. Hopewell, NJ: Ecco Press, 1974.

The Order of the Teaspoon

Amos Oz

"I believe that if one person is watching a huge calamity—let's say a conflagration—there are always three principal options. Option 1: Run away as fast as you can, and let those who cannot run burn. Option 2: Write a very angry letter to the editor of your local paper demanding that the responsible people be removed from office in disgrace. Or for that matter, launch a demonstration. Option 3: Bring a bucket of water and throw it on the fire, and if you don't have a bucket bring a glass, and if you don't have a glass use a teaspoon—everyone has a teaspoon. And yes I know, a teaspoon is little, and the fire is huge, but there are millions of us, and everyone has a teaspoon. Now I would like to establish the Order of the Teaspoon. People who share my attitude—not the runaway attitude, or the letter attitude, but the teaspoon attitude—I would like them to walk around wearing a little teaspoon on the lapel of their jackets, so that we know we are in the same movement, in the same brotherhood, in the same order, the Order of the Teaspoon. This is my philosophy in a nutshell—or in a teaspoon, if you will."

—Amos Oz, from "The Order of the Teaspoon,"
in *How to Cure a Fanatic,* 2002

The Meaning of Tea on DVD

Director Scott Chamberlin Hoyt travels through India, Japan, Taiwan, Morocco, England, France, Ireland, and even Tea, South Dakota. Unveiling tea's mysterious appeal, the film considers the question of whether there is any inherent "meaning" to be found in tea, particularly in an amped-up, high-tech era increasingly dominated by mass-marketing and fast food. The DVD offers Special Features including a director interview on the making of the film. Experience the Japanese Tea Ceremony; enjoy additional interviews with "Tea People"; meet the "Tea Contrarian"; and see an alternate opening and ending to the film. By visiting places where tea is still revered and by investigating its role in these societies, the film suggests the profoundly positive role tea may play in the renewal of our world. 74 minutes with 45 minutes of Special Features. Available in Multi-Language Edition.

Music of Tea CD

Original world music inspired and played by the instruments of India, China, Japan, Morocco, and Europe, as well as the American folk tradition. This collection formed the original soundtrack by Joel Douek and Eric Czar for the documentary film *The Meaning of Tea* directed by Scott Chamberlin Hoyt. Besides sixteen soothing instrumentals with hints of natural sounds, this CD offers two additional bonus tracks: Marco Polo by Loreena McKennitt on CD, as well as an original song, "Tea, SD—Living Easy" with lyrics by Danna Rosenthal and sung by Hillary Fortin. 18 Tracks with 51 minutes of music.

Making of Tea

A short silent film that captures the art and beauty of making a "white filament" Oolong tea called Oriental Beauty. 11 minutes with original tea music.

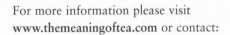

For more information please visit
www.themeaningoftea.com or contact:

TEA DRAGON FILMS
70 A Greenwich Avenue
New York, NY 10011
(212) 691-8899
info@teadragonfilms.com

Acknowledgments

To the entire crew who worked on the documentary film from which this book is derived. To Gordon Arkenberg again and again, for shooting the film in 16mm and video, which also required charming the gatekeepers in many airports throughout the world to yield to the imperative of making a film about tea! To Keir Moreano, who as producer and editor dedicated a good year of his life to making this film, thereby helping to establish SCH as a filmmaker. To Michaela McKee, who as producer, uncovered the ways and means to get us to where we needed to be in many far away places: to capture those tea-time moments that appear in the film and in this companion book.

To Phil Cousineau, son of Stan, grandson of Charlemagne, who encouraged me to make my first feature length film, *The Meaning of Tea*, and who has worked unceasingly to enable everyone on the team to, "break on through to the other side" of this project. To Jen Ahlstrom, who appeared suddenly from behind her computer one day to completely re-organize the way this book almost was, and a whole lot more too. To Julia Kao, who virtually rescued this book and worked with Emily Wang and Gordon Arkenberg with the photographs that appear here. To Deborah Dutton, who managed to bring the book's design—in a very easygoing, professional manner—to a much higher level of art. Annette Compton, who helped this project in the early stages with typesetting and layout/design. Kathryn Kerr, who added a touch of very fine art to the book's design. Ever grateful to Patricia Brennan, who has supported this project with thoughtfulness and the keenest of insight.

To all who were so very generous with their support, for their knowledge of the world's finest teas and where to find them: James Norwood Pratt, Roy Fong, Mei-Guey Jan, Mridul Tiwari, Sunil Joshi, J.P. Gurung, Lin Tse-Pei, and, to name but just a few more, Deborah Koons Garcia, Mark Blumenthal, Jim Duke, Pamela Yee, Rosemary Gladstar, Annie McCleary, Paul Shu, Pearl Dexter, Michelle Brown, Kim Barnes, Nicky Perry, John Eastman, LuLu McAllister, and Jan Gronvold.

And a heartfelt thanks to E. Razzaghi for his magnificent poem entitled "The Meaning of Tea"; and to his son, my dear friend Fred Razzaghi, who translated the poem into English.

Long ago, Ch'an master Yang-chi spent a morning meditating in the temple with his fellow monks. When he stood up to deliver a formal lecture on the nature of enlighten-ment, he paused—and suddenly burst out laughing: "Ha-ha-ha! What are you look-ing at me for? Ha-ha-ha! Turn around and walk to the back of the hall! Ha-ha-ha! Drink some tea!"

—P. C.